MW01256195

WANING CRESCENT

WANING CRESCENT

The Rise and Fall of Global Islam

FAISAL DEVJI

Yale

UNIVERSITY

PRESS

New Haven and London

Published with assistance from the Louis Stern Memorial Fund.

Copyright © 2025 by Faisal Devji.
All rights reserved.
This book may not be reproduced, in whole or in part, including
illustrations, in any form (beyond that copying permitted by Sections
107 and 108 of the U.S. Copyright Law and except by reviewers for
the public press), without written permission from the publishers.

Yale University Press books may be purchased in quantity for
educational, business, or promotional use. For information, please
e-mail sales.press@yale.edu (U.S. office) or sales@yaleup.co.uk
(U.K. office).

Set in Janson type by IDS Infotech, Ltd.
Printed in the United States of America.

Library of Congress Control Number: 2024947882
ISBN 978-0-300-27663-3 (hardcover)

A catalogue record for this book is available from the British
Library.

Authorized Representative in the EU: Easy Access System
Europe, Mustamäe tee 50, 10621 Tallinn, Estonia,
gpsr.requests@easproject.com

10 9 8 7 6 5 4 3 2 1

In memory of my mother

Contents

INTRODUCTION   1

1.   The Proper Name   15

2.   A Prophet Disarmed   50

3.   The Idols Return   87

4.   Women on the Verge   117

5.   Half in Love   146

6.   Hollow Men   180

CONCLUSION   219

Notes   235
Acknowledgments   253
Index   255

Introduction

A COUPLET BY THE eighteenth-century poet Mir of Delhi reads, "Why do you ask Mir about his religion and school? He's daubed saffron on his forehead and is sitting in a temple having long abandoned Islam."[1] The lines are from one of Mir's most popular poems, which continues to be sung, recited, and recorded in both India and Pakistan. Although his words invoke Hindu imagery, there is nothing peculiarly Indian, let alone syncretic, about them. Similar verses using Zoroastrian or Christian images could have been written in the Safavid and Ottoman empires as much as in the Mughal one in which Mir lived. In all cases they would have been understood as forsaking the narrow dimensions of ritual worship for a philosophical universality that held such rites to be equally true or false. This is still the way Mir's lines are appreciated today by both observant Muslims and uncaring ones. None has ever thought of Mir as anything but a coreligionist, whether in his personal life or in his poetic persona.

By far the most popular genre of writing through Muslim history, poetry is also one of the few traditions in which archaic terms still make sense to modern readers. "Islam" was a rare word with a largely negative meaning in the poetic canon. That is because in Mir's time it had not yet become the only or even the most important name by which Muslims could be identified. While "Islam" did not possess a singular meaning in Mir's day, his verse describing Islam as a set of

I

ritual practices comparable to marking one's forehead and sitting in a
temple would have been immediately understood by his contemporaries, as would the idea of abandoning such rituals for some higher
wisdom. "Islam," moreover, was not a synonym for the religion (*din*)
or school (*mazhab*) also mentioned in Mir's couplet; substituting one
for another of these terms would be an impoverished reading of it.[2]
"Islam" served instead as the third and final example in Mir's list of
pious practices and simply named the most specific form they took in
his verse.

Rather than defining the totality of Muslim beliefs and practices,
as the word "Islam" generally does today, the word in Mir's poem describes their most ritualistic details. And yet these particularities were
not folded into the apparently more capacious categories of "school"
or "religion." Each of these terms was instead related to but distinct
from the others. The relations between them were evident not only
in poetry but in theology as well, with the word "religion" traditionally taking pride of place in the titles of treatises while "Islam" put in
an infrequent appearance inside them.[3] Today's Muslim, moreover,
might also once have been called "faithful" (*mumin*), "religious" (*din-
dar*), or a "unitarian" (*muwwahid*). How, then, did "Islam" end up
subordinating such alternative identifications, since it now contains
these erstwhile peers as particularities? The word's ascent in modern
times has made Islam and so Muslims into new kinds of subjects
whose career and contradictions I explore in this book.

Islam emerged as a subject of this kind only in the latter half of
the nineteenth century. A poet living some seventy years after Mir's
passing, in what had by then become colonial Delhi, once again
brought together religion and Islam in a verse about Islam's repudiation. But whereas Mir's abandonment was personal and did not
imply any threat to Islam itself, his successor was anguished by the
possibility of its decline and the threat this posed to the collective
life of Muslims. "Neither religion nor Islam was left; only the
name of Islam was left."[4] The lines are from Hali's epic *Madd-o
Jazr-e Islam* (The Flow and Ebb of Islam). As in Mir's couplet,
here, too, "Islam" and "religion" were distinguished one from the
other but with their roles reversed. Islam now represented a
broader idea than religion, which it had also come to include
within itself. This all-encompassing understanding of Islam made

it into something that exceeded its traditional definitions, whether as a theological idea, conception of law, or set of ritual practices.

Mir's couplet was part of a lyric, or *ghazal*, a form dedicated to love and philosophy with a history going back centuries. Hali's lines belonged to a genre of narrative and often elegiac poetry, the *musaddas*, with a similar pedigree, but one that had not previously included Islam as a subject. Whereas Islam, furthermore, had served as an occasional and fragmentary reference for Mir, underlining its relative unimportance for his work, it constituted the only subject of Hali's poem, as indeed his career as a writer. Yet, like Mir's poem before him, Hali's was not a devotional or religious work either, with its focus on a narrative of Islam's decline being in addition a modern innovation. Whereas Mir had dealt with Islam philosophically, however, Hali did so historically by personifying it as an actor in the poem, published in 1879, that became the century's most popular Urdu work. I describe in this book how the emergence of Islam as a protagonist in history has altered the understanding and experience of Muslim life into our own day.

Unlike Mir's use of "Islam" to describe a set of ritual practices that could be repudiated by Muslims, for Hali it had become the proper name of an actor in its own right. And it is this vision of Islam that, while not without precedent, has come to define and even dominate its modern history. This was a common nineteenth-century development, with Hegel being perhaps the most sophisticated thinker to turn Christianity as much as Islam into protagonists in his philosophy of history. But we shall see that the causes and consequences of such a development differed from one case to another, with Islam becoming more of an agent for Muslims than Christianity was for its adherents. Islam assumed subjectivity not as a person in some metaphorical sense, but rather as a structure or system that acts in the world in the way that civilizations in the nineteenth century and ideologies in the twentieth were imagined to act. As a new kind of subject in the story of decline that Hali sketched, moreover, Islam for the first time faced the possibility of its own end in an historical rather than a metaphysical way. And the anxiety of such an ending marks its whole career. To be a Muslim was to live in the shadow of Islam as the true subject of history, while trying to prevent its demise in projects of reform and revival that put its agency in doubt. It remains a paradoxical figure with which Muslims enjoy a contradictory relationship.

Making History

It has long been known that the word "Islam" and its various grammatical derivatives appear infrequently in the Qur'an and the Muslim texts that followed it for centuries afterward. Far more popular were terms like "religion," which could be used for Jews and Christians in addition to Muslims.[5] Like "school" and "religion," the word "Islam," too, possesses a rich and varied history. But it only becomes a key word and begins to proliferate in Muslim texts from the middle of the nineteenth century. And it does so as a proper name rather than adhering to its grammatical status as a verbal noun. This means that "Islam" was now understood as a subject endowed with volition and no longer described the practice of Muslim devotion its literal meaning suggested, to say nothing about the variety of other meanings it might also have come to possess. From doing things like defining the action of Muslims, in other words, "Islam" became an actor in its own right and even in their place.

As an agent of history Islam is defined by the totality of Muslim beliefs and practices. But this means that it has become not just an historical but also a sociological rather than theological subject. For traditional conceptions of religion have been minoritized within Islam's expansive new form, one that now regularly includes economics and politics as much as the arts and sciences. "Islam" is in this sense a far less religious term than "Christianity." Witness commonplace categories like "Islamic art," which, unlike "Christian art," refers not to objects or representations of devotion but to any kind of artifact produced within the penumbra of Islam seen as a civilization. This is even truer of related categories like "Islamic science." This profane if not secular understanding of Islam was so pervasive that Marshall Hodgson, perhaps its most eminent American scholar in the middle of the last century, felt the need to coin the still-influential term "Islamicate" to describe it.[6]

Modeled on the aesthetic category of the Italianate, the word "Islamicate" was meant to describe the nonreligious and even non-

Muslim aspects of a civilization. But by distinguishing it from Islam, this neologism also worked to preserve the latter as the name of a religion. Lost in the process was Hodgson's glimmering recognition that for modern Muslims it had become a different kind of subject. How and why did such a shift occur? I argue that Islam became a subject by displacing traditionally religious and political forms of authority in the age of Europe's world-spanning empires. That new subjectivity also made Islam into an historical agent and not a metaphysical one like God. And it came to be imagined as an actor on the world's stage at the height of European colonialism, whose power could now be planned and projected globally. On this model Islam, too, was able act in its own name on a global scale, and to possess ideals, interests, and even a spirit, as we shall see.

It is only from the nineteenth century that statements like "Islam wants, says, or does such-and-such" have become conceivable and indeed commonplace. The originality of this development was tardily recognized by the middle of the twentieth century, with Hodgson, for example, who was a professor at the University of Chicago, writing, "Rather than a personal posture of faith or as loyalty to a historical community, it [Islam] now was thought of as a complete pattern of ideal life, subsisting in itself apart from the community which might embody it."[7] While Hodgson recognized that such an understanding of Islam had been separated from the Muslim community and its practices, however, he did not ask about the kind of relationship these figures now enjoyed with each other. For him, Islam in its modern incarnation was little more than a "blueprint for a social order which could be set off against capitalism or communism as rival social orders."[8] While approving of Islam's nineteenth-century definition as a civilization, in other words, he was uncomfortable with its twentieth-century transformation into an ideology.

Hodgson, like others who noted Islam's novelty, rarely dwelled on its role as an actor in history, treating it instead as a purely textual phenomenon akin to a doctrine.[9] And in this way he assimilated it to a religious as much as a political form of enunciation, comparable to a dogma, constitution, manifesto, or indeed blueprint, rather than looking at the varied ways in which Islam acted in the world through its followers. Lost to view were the formidable consequences of this new understanding of Islam. This was perhaps due to the fact that Muslims never conceived of Islam acting in history as a legal or artificial person like a church, state, or corporation. Instead, it retained for them the impersonal agency of a civilization, and later of an ideological system like communism. But Islam could also be seen as an abstract and supposedly self-propelling structure like capitalism. Its emergence was therefore a new but not unfamiliar development, with parallels in other traditions.

Christianity and Islam are the only religions whose names have not been given to them by modern scholarship. Yet they, too, do not become popular in the textual record until quite recently. The Oxford English Dictionary dates the emergence of "Christianity" as a noun to around 1400 and "Islam" to 1625, each term referring as much to a community of believers as to their beliefs and practices. But these words occurred very infrequently until the nineteenth century, when they came to adopt their modern forms as proper names. Around the middle of the century, "Christianity" was used 81 times per million words, whereas "Islam" made only 1.4 appearances. But the latter's growth was much faster starting around midcentury and coinciding with the expansion of Britain's empire. By 2010 it appeared 26 times in every million words, as opposed to 28 times for "Christianity," the frequency of whose appearance has seen a steady decline since its high point in 1840. Both are now among the five thousand most used words in the English language.

Although we don't have a comparable Arabic database to search for the frequency of such terms over time, there is one whose corpus is made up of more than two billion words from machine-readable texts.[10] It shows us that the absolute and relative frequency of the words "Islam," "religion," and "school" over fourteen hundred years can be plotted as a gradual upward trajectory for the first two, with the third remaining low throughout. Around the thirteenth century, "religion," which had always been the most frequent in its textual appearance, suddenly pulls away from the others in a spectacular rise and comes down again only in the sixteenth century. But it still remains the most commonly used of the three terms. "Islam" joins "religion" in a steep upward climb only from the nineteenth century. What can this evidence tell us? That "Islam" has historically been overshadowed by "religion" while claiming more and more ground for itself in modern times.

As an historical subject formed out of the sociology of Muslim beliefs and practices, Islam may be modeled on a secular understanding of Christianity. Yet it was rarely understood as Christianity's equivalent even when the latter was taken to be Islam's rival. Hali's epic *The Flow and Ebb of Islam* might have borrowed its maritime metaphor from Matthew Arnold's celebrated poem of 1867 "Dover Beach," about the "melancholy, long, withdrawing roar" of the sea of Christian faith. But it was the West's modernity and not its faith that concerned him. Instead of comparing Islam to any faith, he placed it in a context where religion had become irrelevant. Its relations with civilizations and ideologies tells us that Islam's real interlocutor was modernity, or what people commonly called modern civilization in Hali's day. Christianity may have had a founding part in the making of modern civilization but no longer a dominant one. In this way Islam belongs not to the world of religions at all but to that of social and political thought more generally.

Despite its striking originality, this conceptual as much as existential development in the role and meaning of modern Islam has received scant attention from scholars, apart from the kinds of disparaging statements we have seen Hodgson make. This is probably because it was so rarely made a subject of debate by Muslims themselves.[11] That such a novel vision of Islam was so quickly naturalized by Muslims both globally and across sectarian and other divides is curious. It suggests that the liberals or modernists, as we might call them, who pioneered this global understanding of Islam's historical agency have been far more influential intellectually than they ever were religiously or politically. It was likely their inability to own this idea of Islam that allowed it to be so easily appropriated by others almost without discussion. While different groups of Muslims made differing uses of Islam's new subjectivity, however, its status as an historical actor ended up defining them all as participants in a new kind of enterprise.

Its unprecedented role as an agent of history made Islam into a self-consciously global figure for the first time and quite apart from the age-old process of its geographical expansion. For to understand globalization in terms of territorial mobility and expansiveness alone is to adopt the rhetoric of colonial adventurism.[12] More important was the development of a global imagination even in the absence of such expansion. It was Islam understood as an actor in human history and not just as a demographic or geograph-ical fact that made it global. But as a consequence of turning into an historical actor, Islam lost its theological character to become mortal. It was now a potential victim of the very history in which it acted and over which it sought dominion. There was no longer the need of an apocalypse to imagine Islam's end. Understanding Islam in temporal terms was crucial to its emergence as a subject, yet one whose career posed a problem because it was neither human nor divine.

Because of its ambiguous status, it is difficult to describe Islam as being primarily religious or political in character. For in liberal thought these terms are understood spatially, with the realm of each demarcated by a secular state. But Islam was conceived tem-porally as an actor in human history. It is routinely imagined as containing and so transcending such terms rather than being de-fined by them, thus taking on the mediating role of the secular state. Muslims and the scholars who study them also speak about "religion in Islam" or "politics in Islam," just as we might speak of both in Western civilization. In the past religion (*din*) had been ste-reotypically contrasted with the world (*dunya*) as well as the state (*dawla*), just as the sacred law (*sharia*) was distinguished from its royal counterpart (*qanun*) as well as from the path of mysticism (*tariqa*). But such contrasting terms were not reconciled in some higher unity. And Islam had never been among these pairings but was contrasted instead with terms like "belief" (*iman*) precisely as a set of ritual practices. Yet it came to subsume them all and cannot therefore be understood in religious or political terms.

Islam even lacks theology as a mode of thinking about divine authority or justifying arguments in its name. God has come in-stead to illustrate or supplement rather than to define such argu-ments. One historian has even noted that while "God" appears in the Qur'an more than two thousand times as frequently as "Islam," "in a good deal of modern Muslim writing this ratio is perhaps, roughly, reversed."[13] Because it did not resort to divine authority, for example, Hali's epic was not theological despite his own reli-gious belief. No longer tied to any single polity or jurisdiction where the sacred law operated, Islam in the age of imperialism also became an unpredictable agent. For it had ceased to represent the divine authority meant to be spread by kings or mystics and protected by clerics.[14] Understood as an ideology or civilization, it enjoyed an autonomous existence even when claimed by individuals, parties, and states. Making Islam into a subject of this kind entailed momentous consequences. They include subordinating the theological role played by God and Muhammad to Islam's historical one; robbing Muslim political thought of its inherited vocabulary by replacing the agency of rulers with that of Islam; and turning Muslims from individuals with their own virtues and vices into good or bad representatives of Islam as the true subject of their history.

The emergence of Islam as an actor in history, in other words, transformed Muslim religion, politics, and notions of selfhood. It is not that Islam directly caused these transformations, however, since the reverse is more likely to be true, with them having produced it instead. Whatever their causes, after all, the rise of global subjects like Islam requires the diminution and appropriation of all prior forms of agency. Capitalism as an equally global subject that is also said to act, want, and need, for example, turns all other agents into its producers or consumers even as they literally bring it into existence. Islam, therefore, was not the cause of any transformation but rather its product. Its arrival on the stage of global history signaled the limits of religion as much as of politics and hollowed out the very Muslims who brought it into being. But this idea contradicts the conventional view of Islam defined by a distinctive, even excessive, relationship between religion and politics in Muslim tradition.

As familiar as it is false, the idea of such a relationship between religion and politics in Islam dates from the advent of the modern state in seventeenth-century Europe. The Ottoman, Safavid, and Mughal empires came at the time to represent mirrors in which Christian thinkers could see reflected the past, present, or future of their debates about politics and its relationship with religion.[15] It took two centuries and colonial rule for Muslims to start thinking about Islam in this way, but only to reverse the terms of its relationship with politics and see their own anxieties reflected in a European mirror. Much of modern Muslim thought has therefore been dedicated to showing how Islam, supposedly unlike the West, does not bifurcate religion and politics but maintains a salutary relationship between them. Rather than constituting a repudiation of secularism, which played only a minor role in such debates about Islam, this narrative sought to displace both religion and politics from having any defining role in Muslim life. Instead, it was Islam as an historical actor that was brought to the fore, the question it posed being how to conceptualize agency at a global level.

Two versions exist today of the alleged relationship between religion and politics in Islam. The first is a journalistic narrative about the return of religion and crisis of secularism in modern times. It begins with the end of decolonization in the 1970s and seeks to explain why newly independent countries have not followed the route marked out by modernization theory to become liberal democracies like so many of their former colonizers. With the Iranian Revolution at the end of the decade, this question came to be asked of Islam specifically, whether in the societies it dominated or among Muslim immigrants in Europe. The second narrative is an academic one about political theology or the translation of metaphysical categories like sovereignty into the modern state. Established between the two world wars, it was revived at the end of the Cold War to replace a history of revolution represented by the Soviet Union with one of historical continuity. Against these views I argue that Islam illustrates the limits of religion as much as of politics in the global arena.

Islam emerged as an autonomous subject in the nineteenth century because of the marginalization of Muslim power, profane as much as sacred, in the face of Europe's imperial expansion. The princes, preachers, and other authorities who had once governed Muslim societies now had to compete with one another and with newer rivals to represent an Islam suddenly beyond their reach and newly conceptualized as an historical actor by believers and unbelievers alike. The new claimants in this competition numbered not only colonial states with the modern forms of knowledge they promoted, but also Western-educated Muslim elites and the masses they sought to lead. But the more open Islam became to such claims with the decline of Muslim political power, the less it could be possessed by any single group or state. Freed from ownership within a capitalist marketplace of ideas, Islam became not only an agent in its own right, but a global one taking the history of humanity as its field of action.

Rather than the increasing power of its adherents, then, Islam's globalization represents their weakness. Its personification as much as expansion into an agent of history suggests both their marginalization and their inability to control this new idea and experience of Islam, one whose agency confiscated that of Muslims themselves to the extent of rendering it illegitimate. And the attempt to shape a singular Islam globally has only resulted in a thin and brittle Muslim subject divorced from its more complex past.[16] This is a predicament that faces all those who struggle with defining human action at the inhuman scale of the globe. But it is addressed by Muslims by putting religion and politics into question along with any conventional relationship between them. And it is the impossible effort to reconstitute such categories at a global level that I argue has today brought Islam itself to a breaking point. The story of modern Islam is not about joining religion to politics but instead demonstrates the inability of Muslims to do so.[17]

Changing the Subject

Understood as an actor in human history, Islam repeats God's role while stripping it of theological meaning since Islam is not itself divine. Like any historical subject, Islam is capable of being defeated, which is what makes its defense so crucial for modern Muslims. God requires no such defense. But what kind of relationship can Muslims have with an Islam indifferent to theology? In my first chapter I describe how Islam stands in for the absent political subjectivity of Muslims individually and collectively. But if it has become a global actor in place of the Muslim community, how might Islam encompass the role of figures like Muhammad? My second chapter looks at controversies about insults to the Prophet, starting in India during the middle of the nineteenth century and becoming global at the end of the Cold War. I explore how such controversies emerge from the stripping away of Muhammad's religious as much as political character such that he becomes vulnerable to insult as an ordinary person. The passions aroused among Muslims by insults to a prophet so much like themselves take the place of his vanishing religio-political role as it is subordinated to Islam.

By doubling and so displacing God's theological agency with its historical one, Islam takes as its opponents equally redoubled forms of idolatry as if to disavow its own assumption of divine status. God's absence from the arena of Islam's historical action, in other words, leads to the unprecedented proliferation of idols in Muslim political debate. Islamist thinkers like the Pakistani Abul Ala Maududi and the Egyptian Sayyid Qutb, for instance, described their present as a return to pre-Islamic paganism. Its idolatry no longer refers to actual objects of worship, but rather to political forms such as monarchy, nationalism, or communism, all abstract agents much like Islam and so its rivals. My third chapter examines the consequences of repudiating such idolatrous forms of political authority as so many Muslim thinkers have done. Condemning political and religious forms of authority as idolatrous, however, places believers in an unmediated relationship with God. And this results in the possibility that they may encroach upon God's sovereignty by claiming independent agency for themselves.

This is why one of the crucial themes of twentieth-century Islamic thought has to do with the effort to displace and even expel sovereignty into the keeping of God and so effectively make Muslims into antipolitical subjects in some sense. This contradictory project often ends by emptying out all agency from the virtuous Muslim individual, who thus becomes a curiously opaque figure. My fourth chapter therefore deals with the gender of Islam's antipolitical subject, making the case that women have replaced men as generic Muslims in allowing Islam to speak through them in a privileged way as the most common and visible symbols of individual piety. This happens not by stressing some inner or biological difference between the sexes, but instead by repudiating a biopolitical identity of this kind for one made up of external or sartorial appearances. It is as superficial, empty, and finally unknowable figures lacking sovereignty that women become Islam's ideal representatives.

My fifth chapter is about the relationship between Islam and the West, which I see as one of anxious intimacy and identification rather than difference. This is because Islam as an ungrounded global subject cannot be owned but forever escapes the grasp of those who claim it. The West enters into a relationship with Islam not through hostility so much as by its alleged theft of Muslim virtues to replace Muhammad's followers as God's favored community. Islam therefore needs to be recovered from the West as an alter ego. The relationship between the two is understood as intensely familiar and even fraternal, which explains the intensity of the violence that occasionally mars it. And my final chapter focuses on violence by attending to the consequences of imputing such a negative character to Muslim subjectivity. In it I track a shift from the posthumous subject of martyrdom in the videotapes of Al-Qaeda's suicide bombers to a virtual selfhood defined by pleasure in the brutal spectacles filmed by the Islamic State (ISIS). In both, the ideal Muslim must vanish.

I take as the object of my analysis debates about Islam within three self-consciously global movements. The first is liberalism, or Islamic modernism as it is often known, which flourished in the heyday of European imperialism from the middle of the nineteenth century to the end of the Second World War and the process of decolonization that followed it. The second is fundamentalism, or Islamism as it is now called, which dominated Cold War discussions about ideological states and survived into the 1990s. And the third is a hyperindividualized form or militancy, whose brief but spectacular moment came in the first decade of the twenty-first century. It was linked to the triumph of neoliberalism following the Soviet collapse and, with it, the decline of all utopias defined by popular revolutions and ideological states. These movements, which both emerge from and comment upon larger events outside the Muslim fold, describe the career of Islam as a global actor and the limitations of such agency more generally.

Responsible for making Islam into a global subject, these three movements I focus on are all in crisis today. Modernism is confined to Westernized elites, having been instrumentalized by military dictators for much of the twentieth century. Islamism was pushed in a more liberal direction by the rise of militancy early in the twenty-first century and subsequently crushed by new kinds of dictatorial regimes in places like Egypt and Tunisia. And militancy itself appears to have been a transient phenomenon that came and went in a decade. But instead of new alternatives there seem only to be efforts at recycling this history. Saudi Arabia has embarked upon an experiment in authoritarian secularism of the kind last seen in Turkey and Iran early in the last century. The Taliban has returned to power in Afghanistan but is torn between instituting a nation-state and an Islamic emirate. And a neotraditionalism seeking to recover Islam as it was before modernism, Islamism, and militancy wins allegedly apolitical converts in Europe and North America.[18]

While little of intellectual let alone political worth can be expected from such recycling projects, the dead end they have reached offers us a sign that the reign of Islam as a global subject might be approaching its end. What will Muslim life look like after Islam? Should we expect a new theology or politics from it? The future is not clear, but we can always read its auguries, from the Arab uprisings of 2010 to the Muslim protests in India of 2020, and from the Green Movement of 2009 to the women's uprising in Iran of 2022, none of which has opted for any of the global movements mentioned above. Islam is no longer a subject in these or other events, from the Gezi Park protests of 2013 in Turkey to the mass mobilizations that led to the fall of Bangladesh's government in 2024. Their participants have neither championed religion nor for the most part repudiated it, while their politics remain experimental and unanchored in any received model. Something new is afoot, and in my conclusion I explore a few of its possibilities, both for Muslim societies and for what they tell us about other ways in which we all understand and inhabit the world.

Apart from God in the theological imagination, any historical protagonist attributed with life must also meet with its death. The enlivening of Islam as a subject in history, therefore, was inevitably linked to forebodings about its ending. It was not simply the fact that Muslims in many parts of the world had fallen under colonial rule that gave rise to such fears, but the emergence of Islam itself as an agent. And so it may be that Islam's career as a subject has today reached its end in a kind of self-fulfilling prophecy. Its role as an actor in history nevertheless continues to pose instructive questions about how agency and authority can exist in a global arena. But if the rise and fall of global Islam tells us anything, it is that such questions are no longer to be understood in conventionally religious or political terms. Its fate serves instead as a testament to the failure of such categories in grasping the globe.

CHAPTER ONE

The Proper Name

A T THE HEIGHT OF Europe's imperial expansion in the late nineteenth century, a sometime British diplomat, Arabist, and horse-breeder named Wilfrid Scawen Blunt published perhaps the first truly global account of modern Islam. A friend and advisor of Lord Randolph Churchill's who subsequently went on to advise Lord Randolph's more famous son Winston, Blunt was nevertheless one of the great critics of imperialism in his time.[1] His book, called *The Future of Islam*, initially took the form of two essays in the *Fortnightly Review* of 1881 to appear as a single volume the year after. Before turning to his argument, let us consider Blunt's very unusual title for the period in which he wrote. It is not just that he used "Islam" rather than the more commonplace term of the time, "Mohammedanism," as being a more authentic one, but by attributing a future to Islam, he also made it into a changing historical subject rather than understanding it as a set of unchanging doctrines.

Yet Blunt continued to use the terms "Mohammedan" and "Mohammedanism" in his book, where they named those faithful precisely to a set of unchanging beliefs and practices that could familiarly be described as a religion in the modern, Christian sense of the term. "Islam," on the other hand, he used in referring to a new and more expansive entity, a kind of historical structure in which religion was subordinated to varying sociological factors like demography, cartography, and the profane kind of politics they made possible. This is why his book opens with a census of pilgrims in Mecca and goes on to estimate the numbers of Muslims in different parts of the world. This suggested to Blunt that Islam's greatest redoubts, as well as the places where Mohammedanism continued to augment its numbers, were located in India, the Malay Archipelago, and tropical Africa. It was in these places, mostly under colonial rule, that he thought Islam had a future.

But this also meant that Islam was more closely tied up with Britain and Holland, at least in demographic and cartographic terms, than with any other power, including the Ottomans who claimed the caliphate. The fact that Britain possessed more Muslim subjects than the latter even became something of a fixation for its proconsuls and prime ministers, who routinely described their empire as the "world's greatest Mohammedan power." By displacing the ritual legitimacy of the Ottomans with a demographic one, they demonstrated the importance of sociological thinking in the modern understanding of Islam. Even more important was the fact that Islam's global dispersal was comparable only to that of the British Empire in its discontinuous and difficult-to-defend geography. It could not, therefore, be aligned with the geographically contiguous empires of the past in which the Ottomans, like the Habsburgs and Romanovs, belonged.

Strangely, Blunt did not compare Islam's discontinuous dispersal to that of Christianity. Perhaps he understood the latter as a purely religious reality, or one that had been dissolved into European empires if not the idea of the West. Indeed, it was the West or its modern civilization rather than Christianity that was Islam's rival. He writes that "Islam, if she relies only on the sword, must in the end perish by it, for her forces, vast as they are, are without physical cohesion, being scattered widely over the surface of three continents and divided by insuperable accidents of seas and deserts; and the enemy she would have to face is intelligent as well as strong, and would not let her rest."[2] It was, in other words, Islam's very magnitude that rendered it politically ineffective, just as Christianity had no political presence without European imperialism. The problem facing Islam as a largely colonized figure was therefore how to maintain or recover its role as a subject and not remain merely the object of history.

Comparable though it geographically was to the British Empire, then, Islam as a global entity possessed only the potential for action because it was ungoverned by any authority like a church or state. Whatever possibility the Ottomans or any other Muslim power had of claiming such an authority, for Blunt it was Islam's lack of juridical sovereignty that caused more concern. For only such power to decide the future could turn Islam into a self-conscious subject able to remake itself into an agent of history. He comments: "What they want is a *legal authority to change.* Now, no such authority exists, either in the Ottoman Sultan, or in the Sherif, or in any Sheykh el Islam, Mufti, or body of Ulema in the world. . . . There is not even one universally recognized tribunal to which all Moslems may refer their doubts about the law's proper reading, and have their disputes resolved."[3]

In order for Islam to fulfill its potential and turn from a possible or rather accidental and unthinking subject into a properly historical and so political one, it needed to enter into a partnership with Britain as a power with which Muslims were already closely entwined and whose dispersed geography they shared. But this was to be a reciprocal partnership, since "it would seem . . . difficult for England to ally herself, in dealing with Islam, with what may be called the Crusading States of Europe. Her position is absolutely distinct from that of any of them, and her interests find no parallel among Christian nations, except perhaps the Dutch. For good as for evil, she has admitted a vast body of Mohammedans into her social community, and contracted engagements from which she can hardly recede towards others among them, so that it is impossible she should really work in active antagonism to them."[4]

Britain should therefore accept the novel and non-European part that its empire compelled it to play by working with Islam in the cause of civilization around the world. One way of doing so would be to create a global Muslim authority by replacing the Ottoman caliph with an authentically Arab one, perhaps drawn from the Prophet's own tribe and situated in Mecca, within a peninsula linked to India and capable of being defended by the Royal Navy: "Since we are imagining many things we may imagine this one too—that our Caliph of the Koreysh, chosen by the faithful and installed at Mecca, should invite the Ulema of every land to a council at the time of the pilgrimage, and there, appointing a new Mujtahed, should propound to them certain modifications of the Sheriat, as things necessary to the welfare of Islam, and deducible from tradition. No point of doctrine need in any way be touched, only the law."[5]

The one thing that stood in the way of this highly speculative but remarkably prescient vision was the Ottoman Empire's claim to the caliphate, and Blunt devoted much of his book to criticizing it as reactionary and incompetent. But his real argument against the Ottomans was that their empire would be unable to survive the continuing European onslaught upon it, with the French and Spanish taking North Africa; the Austrians and Russians taking what was left of it in Eastern Europe, the Caucasus, and Central Asia; and the Germans and French competing with the British for the Middle East. With some changes in Blunt's cast of characters, this was exactly what happened in the run-up to the First World War and at its conclusion. Islam therefore had to be put in tutelage to Britain, at least temporarily, while its newly found authority could be only a spiritual not a political one.

The Jaws of Defeat

Wildly imaginative as it was, Blunt's understanding of Islam's future came to enjoy the support of a significant number of Muslims long after he had repudiated it and lost faith in Britain's good intentions. His book was translated into Urdu by one of India's most famous poets, Akbar Illahabadi, in 1886 and reprinted there as late as 1951.[6] His translation demonstrated that Blunt's ideas were more popular among Indian Muslims than the English author's own compatriots, though they had some purchase even for the latter. Crucial, for instance, was Blunt's effort to redraw the geography of what was coming to be called the Muslim world by making Arabia instead of Turkey central to it. This undid centuries of European thinking even before the Ottoman defeat in the First World War. As Blunt had envisaged, moreover, Arabia became important as a spiritual not political center. After the First World

War, similarly, there were a number of Muslim attempts to reinvent the caliphate as a kind of papacy to perform exactly the function Blunt had described.[7]

Blunt's definition of global Islam as being made up of Asian and African demography on the one hand and a global cartography defined by its symbolic center in Arabia on the other, provincialized doctrinal factors within sociological ones to make an inevitably profane subject of it. And in doing so, by putting Islam's future into question, he also made it vulnerable as an object to be manipulated by external forces and desires: "If she [Islam] would not be strangled by these influences she must use other arms than those of the flesh, and meet the intellectual invasion of her frontiers with a corresponding intelligence. Otherwise she has nothing to look forward to but a gradual decay, spiritual as well as political. Her law must become little by little a dead letter, her Caliphate an obsolete survival, and her creed a mere opinion. Islam as a living and controlling moral force in the world would then gradually cease."[8]

Blunt corresponded with prominent Muslim intellectuals around the world, and his book was unusually and explicitly addressed as much to them as to British politicians and leaders of opinion. The paranoia he voices about Islam's decline was therefore shared with many such thinkers, as was his prescription of its reformation. But this view of things had as its consequence the fact that as a global figure Islam was in a state of constant vacillation, torn between assuming its ordained role as a subject of history while at the same time running the risk of being reduced to an object in the hands of its enemies. Such an association of fear and longing describes the existential situation of all historical agents, a state that was heightened in the case of Islam since it had not even attained subjectivity yet. And how could it hope to do so when it was founded at the end of Muslim politics in the heart of Europe's empires?

Whether by defining Islam in sociological terms or placing it under colonial tutelage, Blunt's vision of Islam presumed its depoliticization, however relative and temporary this was meant to be. And this made it into even more of a target for conspiracies in Muslim perceptions, not excluding the most benign kind of relationship that he hoped to see develop between England and Islam. Instrumentality, in other words, came to characterize every possible

relationship between Islam and the West. And Islam could be politicized in this way precisely because Muslims had lost their own political authorities and so, political thought. But this was not simply
a matter of European powers using Islam for their own ends; instead it involved the most intimate exchanges of identity. Blunt's
most important example of this has to do with Pan-Islamism as an
Ottoman geopolitical strategy, which in an audacious move he argues originated with Napoleon's invasion of Egypt and apparent
conversion to Islam there.

The Ottoman caliphate, Blunt pointed out, had remained a dead
letter until the nineteenth century, lacking recognition from Muslims
in other parts of the world and confused in its own empire with the
more important figure of the sultanate. It was Napoleon who first
sought to turn Islam into a vehicle of his own global ambition by
making it, or rather Mohammedanism, into an independent variable
in politics. However exaggerated Blunt's telling of this tale, crucial
about it, and backed up by modern scholarship, is the fact that Napoleon was one of the earliest but by no means the only European political actor who tried to privilege Islam in this way by separating it
from profane Muslim power and so replace the latter. Blunt notes
that when Napoleon "publicly pronounced the Kelemat at Cairo,
and professed the faith of Islam, he intended to be its Head, arguing
rightly that what had been possible three centuries before to Selim
was possible also then to him."[9]

This modern way of thinking about religion, as a form of popular prejudice and social authority to be subordinated to the state's
political instrumentality, would already have been familiar to Napoleon and other European leaders from the period of absolutism
that followed the Wars of Religion. Its most famous example, indeed, was that of Henri IV, who converted to Catholicism in order
to rule over France and is credited with the laconic statement
"Paris is well worth a mass." One of the more recent accounts of
Napoleon's Egyptian conquest points out that the French general
was one of those responsible for establishing religion as the most
significant subject for any European understanding of the Middle
East.[10] This he did by focusing on the authority of the Prophet
rather than on that of the king and trying to delegitimize both the
Ottoman sultan and Egypt's Mamluk rulers in the process.

By asserting his friendship for Islam and spreading rumors about his own conversion to that religion, Napoleon dealt with it in a newly instrumental way as an autonomous object of knowledge in good Enlightenment fashion. But in repudiating the authority of Muslim kings and clerics, he went beyond the *raison d'état* of absolutist politics to prove himself a child of the revolution that had destroyed it. For stripped of its traditional authorities, Islam could be seen as a reflection of popular sentiment, however prejudiced. By ridding Muslims of their own ancien régime and appealing to them collectively, in other words, Napoleon, like all his successors in similar endeavors, could claim to represent them in a novel way. Rejecting the old Christian stereotype of Muhammad as an impostor, Napoleon, like the *philosophes* he read, saw the Prophet as representing a peculiarly modern form of political genius, one whose supposed appeal to the populace by way of religion he sought to emulate.

Islam therefore came to be thought of as an actor in history not in its own right but through the instrumentalization of others, beginning with Muhammad himself and followed by the caliphs who succeeded him. Its emergence as an agent, in other words, occurred simultaneously with its subjection. And in this way Islam was born as a subject in both senses of that word, its religious spirit lending coherence and integrity to the sociological dimensions of Muslim life that were the true objects of political instrumentality. And for this the Prophet provided the perfect model. No longer imagined in the Machiavellian terms that defined the instrumentality of absolutist politics, he came to be seen as a great mobilizer of collective identity, though perhaps naïve in believing in his own religion. His European admirers, however, could only think of following Muhammad's example in the language of instrumentality by focusing on Islam's sociological dimension.

Such views of Muhammad's popular appeal, shared by eighteenth-century British writers like Gibbon and nineteenth-century ones like Carlyle, ended up informing modern biographies of the Prophet by European and Muslim authors alike. These writers and their descendants located Islam's truth not in any theological or juridical category, such as the Muslim *ummah* (community) or the *dar al-Islam* (any jurisdiction where the sacred law operates), but in the sheer number and geography of its worldwide following. And this demographic as well as cartographic definition of Islam's truth was picked up by Muslim thinkers and activists as well. The celebrated nineteenth-century Muslim reformer Jamal al-Din Afghani, for example, was a friend of Blunt's and had been introduced by him to Randolph Churchill when the latter was in government.[11] Afghani criticized the French writer Ernest Renan's characterization of Islam as an enemy of science by referring precisely to its sociology only a year after Blunt's book was published.

Renan had delivered a lecture at the Sorbonne titled "Islam and Science," which was published in the *Journal des débats* on March 30, 1883. In it he argued that although all religions placed obstacles in the way of knowledge, this was particularly and ferociously true of Semitic as opposed to Aryan ones. In his response published in the journal on May 18, Afghani agreed with Renan's low estimation of religion in general but claimed that no single faith could be distinguished from the others as being exceptionally and irredeemably hostile to philosophy and science in the way Renan had suggested of Islam. Unlike the French thinker, who classified people by race and civilization, the Muslim reformer contended that all human beings possessed equal capacities. And this meant that Islam, which both had a history of cohabiting with science and was so much younger than Christianity, could also succeed in "breaking its bonds and marching resolutely in the path of civilization."[12]

Afghani said he was pleading "not the cause of the Muslim religion but that of several hundreds of millions of men who would thus be condemned to live in barbarism and ignorance."[13] He thus distinguished Islam as a civilization and so an historical agent from the Muslim religion on the one hand, while seeing it as part of a shared humanity understood as a sociological category in statistical terms on the other. In his own reply published the next day, Renan wrote praising Afghani while attributing his intelligence to his Aryan race, which supposedly had been little influenced by Islam as compared to its Semitic founders among the Arabs. These articles became immediately famous in many parts of the Muslim world, with Renan's initial lecture continuing to attract Muslim rebuttals into the next century. No debate better illustrates the intellectual

and political stakes of defining Islam in civilizational and sociological terms that linked it to the unity of the human race in a
nonracial way.

For many Europeans, too, Islam came to be seen as a model for
thinking about the globe as a potentially political arena. More than
a demographic or cartographic idea of truth, which is to say a nontheological and nonmetaphysical one, Islam therefore represented
for men like Napoleon a way of thinking about the new, world-
encompassing politics created by Anglo-French rivalry, which after
all occurred outside the bounds of traditional European categories
and institutions. And this epistemological as much as instrumental
manner of considering Islam has reemerged in our own day, as the
global arena coming to light after the Cold War allows Muslims
and others to define its still inchoate character. It has always been a
shared enterprise, bringing together, if unequally, Muslims and European or American scholars, politicians, and others in a joint project that constantly escapes the instrumental character attributed to
orientalism. If the West requires Islam for its globalization, in
other words, the latter needs it for the same reason.

On the one hand, of course, Napoleon's ideas, or at least Blunt's
understanding of them, betrayed the colonial fantasy of becoming a
god in the eyes of a subject population. But more consequential was
Blunt's focus on Islam as an independent political force, or rather
Mohammedanism turned into such a force by its submission to
European instrumentality. Islam, Blunt seems to suggest, was in this
way a creation of European desire because it was given more importance than Muslim power or political thought and indeed was
deployed against them both. This is why he claims that Napoleon's
plans, although they were reduced to a mere episode in the Battle
of the Nile, came to be taken up by Muhammad Ali, his Ottoman
successor as ruler of Egypt. And it was only after Ali's own failure
that the caliph took up the same task in Constantinople, which now
had Pan-Islamism as its name.

Fantastical as its sweeping account of Islam's modern history
may be, Blunt's book has the virtue of setting out at an early date a
number of the characteristics that would become essential for any
conception of Islam as a global subject. These include the importance of its sociological dimension, its repudiation of inherited

political institutions and authorities, and its intimate if reciprocally instrumental relations with the West. And yet, despite the worldly tenor of this vision, we have seen how Blunt's discussion of Pan-Islamism's origins in the Napoleonic Wars betrays his recognition that it was the European powers which insisted on foregrounding its religious aspect over the political one. While its antipolitical nature meant that Islam had to be a religious phenomenon in colonial societies, then, its instrumentalization made it a political one as well. This was to be its central contradiction.

Islam's Inheritance

Far from representing an obscure vision of Islam's global future, Blunt's understanding of it became a kind of shared fantasy among European and Muslim commentators. By the beginning of the twentieth century British claims to represent Islam worldwide by virtue of ruling more Muslims than the Ottomans did, and moreover permitting them more religious freedom than the latter, had come to constitute a kind of common sense among a number of Muslim thinkers. One of them was the Indian writer Muhammad Iqbal, who had a copy of Blunt's book in his library. He would go on to become the most famous Muslim philosopher and poet of the century and is today acclaimed as the spiritual founder of Pakistan. Educated at Cambridge and Munich in the first years of the twentieth century, and later knighted for his services to literature, Iqbal gave credence to such British claims so as to demand that its empire remain true to them. Britain, in other words, was called upon to transform itself into a truly "Mohammedan" power by representing its Muslim subjects in a more democratic way.

A long-standing concern with numbers and their peculiar form of truth, then, was translated into a specifically political claim by these Muslim thinkers. And while such claims to democratize the empire were common enough at the time, with Gandhi's being only the most well-known in the earlier part of his career, Iqbal's investment in a democratic empire was explicitly antinationalist in character. Partly because of India's great and sometimes violent diversity, but also because he considered nationalism to be the greatest source of violence in modern times, Iqbal saw in a democratic empire a vision of plurality that did not depend upon the domination of any racial, religious, or regional majority. While democratic, in other words, Iqbal's vision was politically amorphous because he thought in global and so human terms and understood Islam as providing both a precedent and a potential for the representation of the human race.

But the British Empire was crucial for the development of this understanding insofar as its vast demographic and cartographic expanse allowed it, more than any other power, to speak in the name of the species. Indeed, the German jurist and sometime Nazi Carl Schmitt would argue after the First World War that the empire's lack of territorial integrity compelled it to take the globe as its context and so the human race as its political and intellectual object.[14] And it was this rather than moralism or hypocrisy that made humanitarianism indispensable to British imperialism. The abolition of slavery, for example, was enforced globally by the Royal Navy's seizure of human cargo even in foreign vessels on the high seas in violation of international law. More recently, the historian Maeve Ryan has lent support to this argument by showing how British abolitionism created a "world system" for humanitarian governance.[15]

Before the First World War, therefore, Iqbal's antinationalism entailed adopting the British Empire as a model for the working out of democracy as a purely human destiny. So, in "Islam as a Moral and Political Idea," an essay published in the *Hindustan Review* in 1909, he wrote: "The membership of Islam as a community is not determined by birth, locality or naturalisation; it consists in the identity of belief. . . . Nationality with us is a pure idea; it has no geographical basis. But inasmuch as the average man demands a material centre of nationality, the Muslim looks for it in the holy town of Mecca, so that the basis of Muslim nationality combines the real and the ideal, the concrete and the abstract."[16]

This demographically vast but cartographically dispersed ideal, suggested Iqbal, could also be seen operating in the British Empire, "since it is one aspect of our own political ideal that is being slowly worked out in it. England, in fact, is doing one of our own great duties, which unfavourable circumstances did not permit us to perform. It is not the number of Muhammadans which it protects, but the spirit of the British Empire that makes it the greatest

Muhammadan Empire in the world."[17] For Iqbal, in other words, Islam, in its rejection of the "idolatry" of race and geography as forms of property, constituted nothing more than an example of a nonmaterial claim to universality, though like previous attempts made by the Greeks and Romans to create a world-state on this principle, the Arab conquests had also proved futile. Islam, then, served as both a promise and a warning to European imperialism and was not a political figure in its own right.

As Iqbal put it in his essay "Political Thought in Islam," published a year later also in the *Hindustan Review:* "The life of early Muslims was a life of conquest. The whole energy was devoted to political expansion which tends to concentrate political power in fewer hands; and thus serves as an unconscious handmaid of despotism. Democracy does not seem to be quite willing to get on with Empire—a lesson which the modern English Imperialists might well take to heart."[18] Nevertheless, he thought that such an ideal was still capable of realization, since "the life of modern political communities finds expression, to a great extent, in common institutions, Law and Government; and the various sociological circles, so to speak, are continually expanding to touch one another."[19] Not the political aims of states, then, but their sociological connections with one another made a common or shared outlook on life possible.

Before the First World War Iqbal thought that the British Empire might learn from the fate as much as destiny of Islam and convert itself into a democratic polity along spiritual lines. By its end he had become a stern critic of imperialism and now considered communism to be Islam's greatest rival as well as model in the establishment of a universal polity based upon a shared or ideological understanding of the world. His arguments against nationalism, too, had come to be couched in vaguely Marxist terms, with the nation-state, being itself a mythical form of collective ownership, seen as representing the apotheosis of private property in social life. But he thought that communism, by transferring all property to the state, actually made such property an even more oppressive presence in society, smuggling back into everyday life the very forms of alienation that it criticized in private ownership.

Iqbal maintained that territorial belonging, in the populist form it assumed with the nation-state, destroyed or at the very least enfeebled all ethical or idealistic imperatives in political life, making for an international regime of parochial and so continuously warring interests. Indeed, the establishment of the Soviet Union had as a consequence the collapse of European imperialism as a model or site for Islam. As should be clear from my summary of Iqbal's views, he worked, like Blunt, with the idea of Britain as the world's "greatest Mohammedan power" in order to conceptualize global agency as a necessarily shared enterprise. And he did so by emphasizing Islam's sociological as much as intellectual or ideological rather than properly theological dimension, the latter giving Britain's imperial project the philosophical not political foundation it required.

His vision, however, was both much grander and more radical than Blunt's since it did not depend on the continuing dominance of European imperialism and eventually shifted to a consideration of communism in the wake of the Russian Revolution and its making of a new form of global politics. The instrumentalist understanding of a partnership between the West and Islam may have receded from Muslim minds after the First World War, but it maintained a presence in European and later American political thought until the end of the Cold War. Indeed, its last great proponent was the US president Ronald Reagan, who put this narrative to work in the anti-Soviet jihad in Afghanistan. All the themes we have explored here, from Islam's potential role as a global actor instrumentalized by the West to its religious or nonpolitical character, were present in the Cold War's last great battle.

But this narrative had received perhaps its superlative treatment in John Buchan's 1916 book *Greenmantle*, one of the most popular novels to come out of the First World War. Buchan, who worked for Britain's War Propaganda Bureau and Intelligence Corps during the war and went on to hold high office as governor-general of Canada, based his plot on a series of facts intertwined with fictions. It dealt with the very real German efforts to mobilize Muslims within the British Empire on behalf of the jihad proclaimed in the name of the Ottoman caliph by their Turkish allies. The novel traces the adventures of a band of heroes across Europe to discover and unravel a German plot to make use of a prophetic figure called Greenmantle in rousing the Muslim world and particularly India against Britain. His name, of course, refers to Muhammad's famous green mantle, a relic last donned by Mullah Omar when the Taliban first took over Afghanistan.

The drama of the story has to do with the identification of its English heroes with Islam. And so, it is not incidental that one of these was modeled at least in part on the real-life hero T. E. Lawrence, who helped support the Arab Revolt against the Ottomans during the First World War. In this way he even seems to have fulfilled Blunt's vision of Islam's future, and so it is not surprising that he should have been a friend and admirer of both Blunt and Winston Churchill. What Buchan in effect does is to divide up the stereotypes about Islam, assigning the bad ones to Germany and the good ones to Britain. The Germans are routinely depicted as fanatical and effeminate at the same time. When the prophet is finally discovered, in the keeping of the novel's villainess, Hilda von Einem, he is described as "a dreamer and a poet, too—a genius if I can judge these things. . . . The West knows nothing of the true Oriental. It pictures him as lapped in colour and idleness and luxury and gorgeous dreams. But it is all wrong. The *Kaf* he yearns for is an austere thing. It is the austerity of the East that is its beauty and its terror. . . . The Turk and the Arab came out of big spaces, and they have the desire of them in their bones."[20]

Full of orientalist themes about the virtue and terror of Muslim austerity, linked in an enduring cliché to the ancestral desert and steppe of its believers, this passage also treats the prophet as a naïve plaything in the hands of sophisticated Europeans. And yet it is precisely this patronizing fantasy that calls for British identification, in a seduction that threatens to undo the carefully contrived hierarchy between East and West. After all, if instrumentality provided a full explanation of the West's relations with Islam, why was the fantasy of a partnership required? Greenmantle is contrasted with his German handler as "the prophet of this great simplicity. He speaks straight to the heart of Islam, and it's an honourable message. But for our sins it's been twisted into part of that damned German propaganda. His unworldliness has been used for a cunning political move, and his creed of space and simplicity for the furtherance of the last word in human degeneracy."[21]

Important about this equally orientalist passage is the inability of its various characters, whether English, German, or Muslim, to separate one from the other. And this includes its English narrator, who has nearly been seduced by Hilda von Einem's perverted vision of Germany's great "simplification," which nevertheless takes its strength from Greenmantle's virtuous and purely Islamic simplicity. So, it is not surprising when, at the end, this perfect Englishman goes on to take the place of the prophet, who has unexpectedly died before being able to accomplish his task, only to lead the defeated Turkish troops against rather than for Germany. As the novel's last sentences proclaim: "Then I knew that the prophecy had been true, and that their prophet had not failed them. The long looked-for revelation had come. Greenmantle had appeared at last to an awaiting people."[22]

The colonial fantasy of becoming a living god for natives is also in full evidence here, but perhaps more interesting is the Englishman's loss of himself within it. And this is crucial because from Napoleon's time until our own, global agency requires the kind of model and partnership that Islam has historically provided. While Blunt or Buchan after him might envision such a relationship in terms of Islam's need for or instrumentalization by the West, their books demonstrate the opposite in seeking the loyalty of Muslims to make a German or British claim to global supremacy imaginable. In some ways, Islam plays the role of Christianity, taking the place of this even more populous and dispersed religion that could not be mobilized by Western powers against each other in the same way. Islam, in other words, was understood both as a precedent for something like Britain's world empire and as a partner in the endeavor to establish it.

We shall see in subsequent chapters how Muslims took up these characteristics of Islam as a global subject and remade them in a variety of ways. But this is not to suggest they possessed a European origin, constituting instead the joint intellectual product of Christian and Muslim understandings of the colonial world and the global future it portended. For the rest of this chapter, however, I look at the way in which Islam was understood as a subject of history by an important Muslim thinker who was Blunt's contemporary. He was one of those who held on to Blunt's vision of a partnership between Britain and Islam long after the latter had abandoned it, something for which Blunt attacked him. But

I do not look at Syed Ameer Ali's vision of Britain's role in the revival of Islam or even his defense of the defeated Ottoman caliphate after the First World War. What interests me instead is his
conception of Islam as a kind of machine for producing agency at a
global level.

Deus ex Machina

The historian and jurist Syed Ameer Ali was likely the world's best-
known Muslim writer between the end of the nineteenth and the
middle of the twentieth century. Judge of the Calcutta High Court
and a celebrated authority on Islamic law, he was knighted and became the first non-European appointed to the privy council in
London. While there, he spoke in support of Muslim causes arising
from political developments in India, Persia, and the Ottoman Empire, dispensing advice to the British government as well as in the
pages of the *Times*. Ameer Ali's most popular book was *The Spirit of
Islam*, first published in 1890 by that name, with a briefer version
initially appearing in 1873 as the *Critical Examination of the Life and
Teaching of Mohammed*. It was the first global best seller on Islam,
going through many translations and editions to become a favorite
among Muslims worldwide. Ameer Ali thanks Iqbal, then a student
at Cambridge, for his help in putting together a revised edition of
the book in 1905–1906.

The Spirit of Islam was influential because it disregarded the
specialized audiences of technical fields like Islamic theology or law
to address a general reading public across religious and national
lines. Its argument particularly appealed to Muslims of all stripes
because it contested European understandings of their tradition
with all the weight of Western scholarship, showing Ameer Ali to
be the equal of his non-Muslim interlocutors. It went on, moreover,
to proclaim Islam's superiority over Christianity and other religions, with the book drawing upon a global history of comparisons.
Many of Ameer Ali's arguments defending Islamic beliefs and practices continue to be deployed by Muslims across the religious and
political spectrum to this day, perhaps because they were historical
rather than theological in nature and thus potentially available for
the use of all sects and schools.

Yet Ameer Ali had by no means adopted the academic's agnostic style in expounding his argument, and in the preface to the book's 1922 edition, he wrote that it "may be of help to wanderers in quest of a constructive faith to steady the human mind after the strain of the recent cataclysm [the First World War]; it is also hoped that to those who follow the Faith of Islam it may be of assistance in the understanding and exposition of the foundations of their conviction."[23] *The Spirit of Islam*, in other words, sought to provoke faith in non-Muslims shaken by the First World War while justifying that faith on profane grounds for believers, and in doing so it pioneered an understanding of Islam divorced from metaphysics even among its most traditional followers. As a result of such approaches, I suggest, Islam today can be understood only as a nontheological category insofar as it has become a general object of knowledge.

Islam emerges in modern times as a category that is increasingly denuded of theological status by Muslims themselves, including even the most orthodox. This process is linked to its novel transformation into a proper name. Ameer Ali, for instance, begins his chapter "The Ideal of Islam" with the following sentences: "The religion of Jesus bears the name of Christianity, derived from his designation of Christ; that of Moses and of Buddha are known by the respective names of their teachers. The religion of Mohammed alone has a distinctive appellation. It is Islam."[24] Such an argument entails significant theological as much as political implications, for its effort to objectify Islam as an autonomous reality effectively secularizes it while at the same time diminishing its founding figures.

Coming as it does after more than a hundred pages of panegyric about the Prophet's person and mission, Ameer Ali's statement separating Muhammad from Islam makes visible a tension in his argument. It is precisely because the Prophet must be distanced from the divine or semidivine status which characterizes the founders of other religions that he requires so much praise and, as we shall see in the next chapter, increasingly ardent defense from insult or injury. This paradoxical situation nicely describes the problem posed by what I am calling Islam's loss of theology. At the very moment when Muslims insisted upon being distinguished from other communities by repudiating names such as "Mohammedan" and "Mohammedanism," they turned the Prophet into a model of human rather than divine perfection and so made him vulnerable to attack in new ways.

But the emergence of Islam as a proper name has to do with far more than Muhammad's changing role in Muslim devotion. In a famous essay on the subject, which I referred to in the Introduction, the historian of religion Wilfred Cantwell Smith argued that Islam only shed its grammatical status as a verbal noun denoting a believer's action or practice of some kind starting in the middle of the nineteenth century.[25] Of rare occurrence in the Qur'an and Muslim texts from premodern times, the term "Islam" suddenly began proliferating in Muslim usage as a proper name, and therefore an identity, whereas it had once described the individual or collective life of the faithful in ritual and juridical terms. Smith points out that such a usage often precluded any theological understanding of the word, for example in hitherto contradictory locutions like "heresy in Islam" where the name referred primarily to a sociological and historical reality.

Ameer Ali was aware of Islam's verbal dimension as a grammatical category, writing that "*Salam* (*salama*), in its primary sense, means, to be tranquil, at rest, to have done one's duty, to have paid up, *to be at perfect peace;* in its secondary sense, to surrender oneself to Him with whom peace is made. The noun derived from it means peace, greeting, safety, salvation. The word does not imply, as is commonly supposed, absolute submission to God's will, but means, on the contrary, *striving after righteousness.*"[26] While his definition is meant to criticize European ideas about Islam's apparently despotic demand for pure obedience, Ameer Ali does not elaborate upon his own suggestion that it might be understood as describing a foundational political relationship: that of making peace with God. Instead, he distances God from Islam in the same way as he had Muhammad, so as to render it an autonomous reality.

To do this, Ameer Ali doubles down on Islam as the proper name of an objective reality, one conceptualized in modern scientistic or rather positivist terms. And as we have seen, he explicitly contrasts this understanding of Islam to the way in which other religions are defined by their founders. In doing so he is not simply objecting to the divinization of such figures, but also to religion as a practice of fidelity to a founder and even to God rather than comprising a reality in its own right. Excluded from the definition of Islam, in other words, is any idea that it might refer chiefly to a relationship either between founder and follower or, and as a consequence, among believers themselves. By ending his explication of its name with the phrase "striving after righteousness," Ameer Ali's preference for abstract effort excludes both a theological and a political relationship from the definition of Islam.

While he may have dismissed Hinduism as a European name given to a disparate and disunited tradition, Ameer Ali's definition of Islam as a proper name is nevertheless comparable to it more than to any other religion. Hinduism, too, after all, was not named after a founder, and unlike monotheistic religions had no founder at all, as its apologists were beginning to point out in Ameer Ali's own day. As a pure and so miraculous product of history, it, too, was the proper name for an objective reality that was coming to be understood as the property of its adherents. The primary relationship Hindus and Muslims increasingly had with their religions, then, was one defined by ownership. And it was this relationship mediated by colonial capitalism that allows us to make sense of the disputes between them, which often entailed conflicts over the ownership of temples and mosques or the control of streets and neighborhoods.[27]

But more than either physical property or identity understood as a form of ownership, this new relationship of believers with their religion considered as an objective reality, the proper name of an historical agent, involved thinking about that religion in sociological terms. Just as this new agent could be represented in Hinduism by caste, so, too, might it be represented in Islam by the law, about which Ameer Ali was the greatest authority of his generation. Caste and law constituted the primary manifestations of Hinduism and Islam in colonial India, defining their followers' lives more effectively than any other aspect of their beliefs. And while it was possible to work for the reform of both, these social structures remained foundational for any conception of religion, much like churches did for Christianity. And they did so because these religions had formally been separated from the political realm to become primarily social realities.

If Hinduism and Islam are comparable in the way I am claiming, it is because they represent colonized versions of religion that have been deprived of political meaning and reduced to their social structures. *The Spirit of Islam*, for instance, contains chapters called "The Political Spirit of Islam" and "The Political Divisions and Schisms of Islam," but their details are treated as being extraneous to the principles of equality and justice that Ameer Ali sees enunciated most perfectly in scripture and law. And these principles, enshrined in a social structure understood as being impervious to royal authority down the ages, dissociate Islam from politics in the same way that caste separated from kingship does for modern Hinduism.[28] In both cases a preexisting social structure is meant to limit politics, a way of thinking with a long afterlife among Muslims far removed from Ameer Ali's liberal views. Both religions, in other words, owe their autonomy and even names to the expulsion of politics as much as of theology.

All of this suggests that colonial societies were the first secular ones. Unlike the established churches of Europe or the shared beliefs that allowed American politicians to invoke God even as they separated church from state, colonial societies in Asia and parts of Africa were marked by fundamental religious differences between rulers and subjects. This meant that theological categories were either very rarely used by imperial states or deployed in purely secular ways. Subject religions, for their part, were deprived of playing any substantive role in these states. In this sense Islam like Hinduism had become secularized in European empires far more genuinely than Christianity in their metropoles. The British sovereign, after all, was Defender of the Faith at home but possessed no religious status in India, which in this way became a secular country before the United Kingdom.

Colonial societies like India can even be described as primarily secular in character since freedom of conscience was the most fundamental right their subjects enjoyed. It is not accidental that the queen's proclamation of 1858, for example, which announced the crown's sovereignty over India in the aftermath of the mutiny that had swept away the East India Company, would define Victoria's new subjects in religious terms and guarantee their liberty of conscience over all other rights. Freeing Islam from political authority, however, allowed for its luxuriant spread in the colonies. Alexis de Tocqueville, the last of the eighteenth century's *philosophes*, famously

attributed the religious revivalism of the United States to its secularism. So, too, did the disappearance of royal authority over Islamic
practice enable the expansion of clerical and other forms of religion
in colonial societies, where they took the form of individual and
collective property in very modern ways.

Yet this new conception of Islam could not be owned by any
one group or authority, struggle as each might against the others to
do so. In earlier times, kings, clerics, and mystics had fought over
specific practices and beliefs, each part of some tradition or institution with its lineage of texts and authorities. Now it was Islam itself
as a proper name, one that turned Muslims, their monuments, and
their practices into forms of property, that became the object of a
much wider struggle. But in the absence of political authority and
theological meaning, Islam could not be owned by anyone and
even rose up against its claimants as an authoritative subject in its
own right. For Tocqueville, Christianity's loss of political authority
in secular America led to its simultaneous growth and fragmentation. In places like secular India, Islam as a phantasm of collective
ownership came to occupy the place of both subject and object in
Muslim thought.

Islam has come to be imagined as an historical actor among
people and in languages spread around the world. Since the latter
half of the nineteenth century, it has been able to desire, will, and
act in moral as much as political terms. In his preface to *The Spirit
of Islam*, Ameer Ali says of Islam that the "impulse it gave to the intellectual development of the human race is generally recognized.
But its great work in the uplifting of humanity is either ignored or
not appreciated; nor are its rationale, its ideals and its aspirations
properly understood."[29] It is clear that Islam has been made into an
historical actor here, complete with ideals and aspirations—and
that its ambition is nothing less than to improve the moral, material, and intellectual lot of humanity. How could such an unprecedented understanding of Islam, as an agent of history, receive so
little attention while being so quickly normalized by Muslims?

Islam emerged as an historical subject to occupy a new global
arena. But it did not do so through the familiar expansion of Muslim populations, institutions, and ideas across the world. Such patterns of movement and dispersal were instead appropriated and

given new meaning by Islam's remaking into an agent of history. Its subjectivation, however, made its relationship with these institutions and populations into a problem. For despite the fitful history of Pan-Islamism, also a product of the nineteenth century and represented today by moribund institutions like the Organization of Islamic Cooperation, the Muslim community itself has rarely been imagined as an historical actor. Is Islam, then, its vanguard, projection into the future, or even an obstacle to the community's emergence as a global subject? This question, I contend in Chapter 3, frames all modern debates about Islam's politics.

Unlike Hobbes's Leviathan or other, premodern figures of the body politic, furthermore, Islam has never been seen by Muslims as an artificial or juridical person. Nor, therefore, does it contain or represent them as a church, state, or company might its congregants, citizens, or shareholders. And though Islam may constitute the orthodox ideal Muslims are meant to follow, this does not account for its historical role as a subject. Instead, it is defined by a distinctly modern understanding of abstract agency, the kind exemplified by economic or political ideologies like capitalism and communism. And Muslims, starting early in the twentieth century, did sometimes compare their sacred to such secular abstractions. More than making metaphorical persons, however, their attribution of life to these abstractions referred to the new kind of functionality that belonged to systems.

Like a machine in its capacity to act without personhood, the functioning of Islam as a system put the agency of both human and divine persons into question. How could Islam's functionality, for instance, be related to the very different kind of action exercised by God and his prophet? This question, I hope to show, frames all modern debates about Islam's theology. In this way Islam also bears comparison to the economy as the archetypical system governing modern societies, one whose "invisible hand" appropriates a theological figure while making its original referent impossible. Unlike the Enlightenment vision of God as a clockmaker whose creation ran itself as a perpetual motion machine, the kind of system named by Islam did not just tell the time but made it as history. Like communism or capitalism, it was envisaged as an industrial machine meant to produce the future as a utopia fit for the globe.

One of the most common terms used to describe Islam as a system is *nizam*, earlier meaning order, arrangement, or governance. Not to be found in the Qur'an, the term was familiar as a title, for instance that of the famous medieval vizier Nizam al-Mulk, Governor of the Realm, or of the premier Indian prince in colonial times, the Nizam of Hyderabad. While it might still be a personal name in parts of Asia, the term has now come to signify a modern system. And this means that it no longer refers to an old-fashioned idea of governance, often visualized in some version of Aristotle's circle of virtue or as a tree representing the hierarchical relations between different kinds of authorities, with some identified as its roots and others as its branches. Unlike these models, in which movement was possible only step by step and along defined paths, modern systems are understood as producing change through the simultaneous working of their interacting parts as a single whole.

Let us return to Ameer Ali's book by way of illustration. He writes that the "principal bases on which the Islamic system is founded are (1) a belief in the unity, immateriality, power, mercy, and supreme love of the Creator; (2) charity and brotherhood among mankind; (3) subjugation of the passions; (4) the outpouring of a grateful heart to the Giver of all good; and (5) accountability for human action in another existence."[30] They are five in number, like the traditional pillars of Islam comprising the profession of faith, prayer, almsgiving, fasting, and pilgrimage. But unlike the latter these bases are general principles shorn of any ritual element. Their interaction produces a society whose achievements Ameer Ali discusses in chapters on "the church militant," "the status of women," "bondage," "political divisions," "the literary and scientific spirit," "the rationalistic and philosophical spirit," and "the idealistic and mystical spirit" of Islam. Here, too, theological categories are absent since Islam has been rendered into a global figure not just for Ameer Ali but all other ways of thinking about it as a system.

While other authors might invoke different principles to describe Islam, important about them all is the effort to encompass as many realms of human life under that name as possible. Whatever their motives, in other words, those who thought about Islam as a subject and system were compelled to include materials within it that broke through the carapace of scripture and law. The very quest for totality, then, divested Islam of its metaphysical character, even as Muslims sought to appropriate new fields for it in adjectival forms ranging from "Islamic architecture" to "Islamic economics." It was in this civilizational context that "Islamic politics," too, was placed, which meant there was nothing very special about it. Often deployed by non-Muslim minorities as much as by European scholars and modernizing Muslims, civilization was a category meant to encompass and secularize theological ideas into a generic or national tradition available to all.

But it was appropriated in turn by Muslims to be made into Islam's content beyond the reach of any traditional authority, since civilization was too capacious to be owned by any one of those authorities. And this made Islam into a far more robust or autonomous historical actor whose profane rather than theological content came to constitute its claim to universality. This is why it was contrasted not to a religion like Christianity, but rather to Western and indeed modern civilization. Islam's functioning as a subject is best described by the title of Ameer Ali's book. His reference to "spirit" has little to do with the distinction of letter and spirit in the Gospels, which in traditionally Muslim terms could be understood as one between the exoteric and esoteric dimensions of law or scripture. To ascribe a spirit to Islam, Ameer Ali needed to have at least a passing acquaintance with works like Montesquieu's *Spirit of the Laws* or Hegel's *Phenomenology of Spirit*, in which "spirit" serves to describe the action, product, or character of a system.

"Spirit" is the pseudo-theological name for abstract agency conceived as the functioning of a machine. It cannot be envisioned as a whole but identified only in the working of a system's parts. This is why Ameer Ali turns to specific issues like the status of women or slavery to see within them the functioning of Islam as a system. Thus, the rules governing marriage, divorce, and alimony suggest to him that the spirit of Islam demands equality between men and women. Or that scriptural passages recognizing the legal personhood and rights of slaves while at the same time recommending their manumission reveal Islam's egalitarian spirit. These may seem like disingenuous and certainly apologetic arguments, though their method holds true for all disquisitions on "spirit" as representing the quintessence of the whole in its parts. But who is to operate this system and how? The answer provided by all the texts to which Ameer Ali's book referred, even if only by inference, is that systems can only run themselves.

Humanity's Empire

Muslims looked with suspicion upon the forms and institutions that might govern or represent Islam, from the political party to the free market. This is because it emerged to contest the legitimacy of human institutions, from traditional kingship to the modern state. The former was understood as decadent because it had failed to prevent the European colonization of Muslim societies, while the latter was tainted by its association with the West. The problem facing Islam, then, was how it might possess a political life beyond the authorities that could mediate it only in conventional ways. These included figures with old pedigrees, like scholars, saints, and sultans, as well as the new claims of Western-educated bureaucrats, politicians, and military leaders. The emergence of Islam as a global category made for an endless competition between these rivals. For there exists no institutional way in which Islam can be either represented or governed.

Islam's global character was defined by its propulsive force, as a system whose interlocking parts functioned to create the future. And the role of Muslims was both to fuel this system by their actions and to submit to being remade by it. Islam, in other words, might require Muslim identification, but it did not entail Muslim representation. Its ambitions were in any case wider than the Muslim community itself, being understood as a machine for the social and so also political assertion of humanity as a whole. We have already seen how Ameer Ali is so insistent about Islam's role in the uplift of the human race, and indeed it was Islam's supposed mission to the entire species that came to define its universality among Muslim thinkers, who condemned the West for dividing humanity into racial and political hierarchies. In this way they took up European rather than any peculiarly Islamic ideas of universality and claimed to fulfill them.

This was why so many Muslim writers including Ameer Ali gloried in a little phrase from the Qur'an that described Muhammad as a "mercy to all mankind." Except that in its literal translation, this phrase means a "mercy to the worlds" (*rahmatul lil-alamin*). Its routine redefinition starting in the nineteenth century, then, illustrates how older cosmologies that contain a plurality of worlds, such as those that angels or genies may inhabit, have been replaced by a singular vision of the globe in which humanity as a sociological or rather numerical figure plays its solitary role as the only true subject and object of history. The world, by contrast, continues in many ways to remain a metaphysical category referring to another or other worlds, as in the originally religious but now also profane use of words like "worldly" and "otherworldly," to say nothing of this world and the next. The Earth, for its part, derives its meaning from the solar system of which it is a planet, though it may also partake of the world's metaphysical character in phrases like "earthly existence."

Both words are also used as synonyms of "globe," though they don't cover all of its meanings even colloquially. Unique about the globe is the fact that it appears to have no context and is instead entirely self-referential in its popular and scholarly usages. Global issues such as climate change cannot be spoken about in galactic or otherworldly terms. The globe therefore has the paradoxical role of naming vast spaces and populations while at the same time emphasizing their finitude. And this contradictory pairing of large and small is precisely what the archaeology of global issues so well illustrates, from worries about a nuclear holocaust during the Cold War to global warming in our own times, by way of fears about overpopulation in the era of decolonization. On the one hand we call "global" any phenomenon too large to master in a conventional way, and on the other we use the word to describe a shrinking habitat that makes escape impossible.

In keeping with its self-referential character or lack of context, the globe possesses a single true subject that is also its object. Whether it is the mutually assured destruction of the atomic age or climate change, humanity as a subject, rather than the human race as a species, represents the simultaneous agent and victim of all such global phenomena. An asteroid hitting the Earth belongs in another context altogether, constituting a planetary rather than a global possibility, one that makes of humanity one species among others at risk. At first glance, of course, it seems odd to pair a self-referential and finite view of the globe with a religion for which transcendence of various kinds, including a deity, paradise, and angels, is so crucial.

But as we see very frequently in the present book, Islam's globalization, whether in its liberal, conservative, or even militant form, is
premised upon the attenuation of such transcendence.

It is in this context bereft of theological meaning that Islam has
come to find its place as an actor or operating system, one whose
task it is to turn the human race from an object of global history
into a subject. The circular process this involves, starting from and
returning to humanity, serves as a good illustration of the globe's
introverted or self-referential form, which in addition to being suf-
focatingly narrow is closed to any possibility of transcendence.
That is why contemporary Islam is marked not by transcendence
so much as the effort of believers to take responsibility for Muslims as a global community or *ummah*, one that is in addition seen
to represent the human race as its vanguard. Unlike other systems
such as liberalism or democracy that also served as historical actors
on a global stage, Islam was conceptualized not as a mode of government so much as a social medium for the species. Dispersed as
they were across races, languages, and continents, after all, Muslims could not be placed within any single political framework, and
so the *ummah* represented humanity itself in miniature.

Like other colonized intellectuals, Muslim thinkers during this
period sought to both engage with and contest European ideas of
universality, manifested and justified as they were by the West's
unprecedented power over large parts of the world. And Muslims
frequently did so by claiming to represent these ideals better than
the British or French, who either were urged to fulfill their self-
proclaimed missions of civilization and freedom in the colonies or
were dismissed by arguing that Islam was more capable of such
universality. The resonance of these apologetics continues to be
heard in contemporary Muslim, and indeed Asian and African, polemics more generally, which still take as their theme the alleged
hypocrisy of European and now American claims to embody universal values. The two great categories that such thinkers struggled
with were race and civilization, each of which had significant legal
implications within European empires and even outside them, as
illustrated by the "standard of civilization" that was required for
non-European powers to be treated as equals and included within
the bounds of international law.[31]

While race was routinely if often rather disingenuously rejected by Muslim thinkers, who sought to argue that Islam was not discriminatory along these lines, civilization was a category they tended to engage with more intimately, by saying that Islamic history represented it more perfectly than Christian Europe. The word "civilization" had not yet been used as a plural in referring to parallel and comparable histories. It was still understood as a singular figure at whose apex stood European modernity freed of all cultural and territorial particularity. By civilization, then, Muslim like European thinkers meant what we would call modernity, whose universality was therefore often described by the term "modern civilization" in the nineteenth and early twentieth centuries. And it was this kind of universality that Islam was held to represent because it supposedly repudiated the hierarchies of race and civilization (to which was added class in the twentieth century) and staked its claim on humanity as a whole.

The alleged equality that Islam made possible among its believers across racial, cultural, and political lines, therefore, not only gave the lie to European ideas of universality in the eyes of men like Ameer Ali, but also provided them with a kind of supra-political unity that might give rise to states but could never be defined by them. Islam's universality was, after all, made evident in science and philosophy as well as art and literature, all seen as parts of a common human inheritance. This universality, in other words, was neither political nor theological but fundamentally social or, to use the favored nineteenth-century term, civilizational in nature.[32] And it was at this level that Islam could be understood as a global actor, one whose appeal rose above all political specificities because it was directed at humanity as a whole. But this, of course, also meant that it could never be grasped by any Muslim authority or enterprise and always escaped to put their legitimacy into question.

Humanity, of course, is the ultimate, indeed, sole global subject, and so it is only natural for Islam to be linked with it as the vehicle of an expansive and ambitious world community. No claim to global stature or agency is possible in the absence of such an identification with the species. Yet, the model for such claims to work for and in the name of humanity was likely colonialism, which in the absence of representative government justified its rule by the logic of humanitarianism. The human race, in other words, could be recognized and addressed only from the outside, by unilateral if also dutiful acts that were premised upon its lack of agency and representation. Muslims keen to foreground Islam as the true instrument and identity of the species were well aware of this imperial model, which as I have argued they sought to dismiss as being insufficiently universal by reason of its reliance on racial and civilizational hierarchies as compared with Islam.

The British Empire claimed to speak universally by reason of its global expanse, which we have seen allowed it to enforce self-declared duties like the abolition of slavery even in international waters by the capture of foreign vessels. It also did so unilaterally and ostensibly by foregoing politics for morality. This way of practicing humanitarianism, in the name of people who were not themselves involved in deciding its terms, was eventually made into the defining characteristic of international and global institutions. From the League of Nations to the United Nations, claims to universality have always been made in the absence of political representation and as a moral duty. Such claims, of course, are routinely seen as hypocritical, with critics pointing to the particular motives and benefits that often underlie them. And this is possible to do because the human race has in modern times become a paradoxical figure.

On the one hand, the species has assumed an empirical reality in our ability to count its numbers, map its extent, and alter its behavior by deliberate policy in practices like mass immunization and population control. But on the other, it has no political reality and cannot represent itself. This is why humanity also tends to assume an increasingly posthumous reality in visions of annihilation by nuclear war, overpopulation, pandemics, or climate change. Essential to humanity's experience of the globe, after all, is its simultaneously expansive and limited character. If the human species is too large to represent itself politically, it is nevertheless small enough to be controlled and even exterminated. Rather than the usual depiction of all things global as being marked by an almost infinite amplitude, crucial to it is the sense of tragic limits and humanity's inability to escape the threats that more and more define the globe.

This is why a global consciousness does not require traveling the earth. Such a geographical understanding remains trapped within

the swashbuckling tales of an imperial imagination. Torn between
the real and unreal, humanity is imagined in apocalyptic terms even
by those who have never been anywhere. Which is to say its looming yet uncertain presence in our times calls up the end of the world
as an old theological principle. And just as we find it difficult to
think about the species without contemplating its extinction, so, too,
have those invoking Islam as a global figure been haunted by visions
of its destruction. In colonial times it was the fear of conversion to
Christianity or the physical and cultural subordination of Muslims
that exemplified such annihilation. Recent forms of militancy like
Al-Qaeda link this fear to nuclear catastrophe and climate change,
whose risks its spokesmen attribute to the infidel West.

Whatever their precedents, however, these remain nontheological forms of apocalypse. And while militant movements in particular
may embellish them with references to angels, martyrdom, and the
afterlife, such invocations seem like desperate efforts to attach another world to this one. Is this why they become possible only in
moments of excessive violence, serving as wagers to force the appearance of the otherworldly by seeing its presence in the martyrdom of Muslims willing to forsake the kind of self-interest that is
meant to define ordinary life in the world below? I suggest it is the
absence of transcendence in the global arena, and therefore in Islam
as an actor within it, that serves as an impasse for the theological
imagination. Because the transcendental reference point of theology
cannot be found within global history, the risk of apocalypse may
well present the only route by which we can experience it.

This posthumous or prospective experience of humanity constitutes a perverse form of the theological. For by imagining the extinction of life on earth, we may even gain access to God in shifting
from the global to a planetary dimension. Modern Islam is thus
faced with two difficulties. The first is to conceive of political
agency at a global level, and the second is to retain theology and its
transcendence within such an arena. In both cases the Muslim community or *ummah*, itself a largely notional entity meant to be called
into being by Islam, becomes the experimental site at which these
problems are to be addressed. This community, in other words, is
nothing more than a vanguard for humanity. As such it redefines
traditional notions like conversion and even makes them irrelevant.

Like the human race of which it is a miniature, the global *ummah* exists empirically but not politically. Each faces the problem of how to assume political as much as theological agency.

A World Without Politics

The historian Cemil Aydin has argued recently that the Muslim world, both as idea and as reality, was founded during the nineteenth century only in the context of European imperialism.[33] And as we have seen in Blunt's sociological conception of it, such a world was defined neither in religious nor in political terms. In part this had to do with the impossibility of casting it in the role of a territorial polity. But just as important was the way in which Islam's own founding entailed displacing such traditional forms of authority. This is nicely illustrated in a popular Urdu novel about the education of Muslim girls published in 1873. In one part of the book its well-known author, Nazir Ahmad, describes a geography lesson in which various territories, some defined by political borders and others in cultural and historical terms, are identified on a map. The Arabian Peninsula is said to be an empty space infested by marauding Bedouin, one whose only significance lay in its historical role as the site of Islam's birth.[34]

In one sense this depiction of Arabia, as central and marginal at the same time, had long been a familiar one. While the peninsula owed its religious status to shrines like those in Mecca and Medina, these monuments and institutions had always been mediocre in their architectural quality as much as financial endowments—at least as compared with the splendid mosques, tombs, and seminaries found at the centers of Muslim power in Baghdad and Cairo, Istanbul and Isfahan, Delhi and Samarkand. Rarely visited by Muslim rulers, Arabia served instead as a place of exile for their enemies, as it still does for Ugandan dictators and Pakistani prime ministers. By the time Nazir Ahmad's novel was published, however, the peninsula had begun to assume a new kind of importance. As Ottoman power waned and British influence extended outward from its economic and military base in India, the Muslim world emerged as a category that provided a novel way in which to imagine Islam's cartography.

Arabia soon came to be placed by Muslims at the center of their geographical imagination. But Nazir Ahmad's geography lesson illustrates that this was no longer for ritual reasons having to do with pilgrimage. Crucial, rather, was the peninsula's historical status as the birthplace of Muhammad and so Islam. The pilgrimage was part of a quite different imaginary, its rituals referring to the story of Abraham, Hagar, and Ishmael, whose sanctity Muhammad was seen as having restored. This narrative, and its commemoration, was now folded into his role in the emergence of Islam as an abstract and universal agent. And it rendered the peninsula's shrines into sites of historical memory rather than of ritual practice. We have already seen the implications of this shift in Blunt's book, which foresaw the Muslim world's colonization by European powers and sought to bring Islam under the protection of the British Empire by transferring its center from a political capital like Istanbul to a purely historical location like Mecca.

This meant that Istanbul, capital of the only remaining Muslim power, had to be divested of its claim to the caliphate. Islamic authority, Blunt thought, should return to an Arabian Peninsula defended by the Royal Navy. He was among the first to make an argument that would eventually redefine the geography of Islam by placing Arabia at its center. His reasoning was based on two major premises. The first was faithfulness to Islam's history, which allowed him to claim that Istanbul and its Turkish emperor could never be true Muslim leaders, a role reserved for Arabs and their homeland. And the second was that India was crucial in the making of this new Muslim world centered on the Arabian Peninsula. Apart from India's large Muslim population, its armed forces, traders, laborers, and pilgrims had become crucial to the security, economy, and demography of Arabia even in Ottoman times. In many ways Mecca and Medina were, and to some degree still are, Indian or rather South Asian cities. The same is true today of Jeddah, Muscat, and more recently Dubai, Abu Dhabi, Manama, Doha, and Kuwait City, which have replaced colonial Aden as the great entrepôts of the region.

Indian Muslims were nonetheless eager to support Ottoman claims to Muslim leadership, until the new Turkish republic abolished the caliphate after the First World War. Yet Blunt's ideas about Arabia, no doubt developed in concert with Muslim thinkers, had made enough headway to redefine Islam and its cartographic imagination away from Istanbul and toward Mecca and Medina. The caliphate's Indian allies could justify their position, after all, only by invoking its protection of the Arabian Peninsula and its sacred cities as the permanent and cartographic center of an autonomous Muslim world standing apart from the very political authority required to protect it.[35] And this desire to return to historical origins rather than focus on the rites that had hitherto defined the holy cities would soon allow Muslims to abandon the Ottomans and their caliphate. Their desire would instead find its fulfillment in the Wahhabi movement and in particular its alliance with the family of Ibn Saud in the founding of Saudi Arabia.

From its emergence in the middle of the eighteenth century, the Wahhabi movement had inspired little but horror among Muslims in India, as elsewhere around the world. Its demolition of shrines and the tombs of saintly figures in the nineteenth century, for example, provoked outrage, followed by joy when the Ottomans sought to crush what was widely considered a heresy at the time. Yet attitudes were changing, and there was even a scare later in the century about an anti-British rebellion of so-called Indian Wahhabis, which showed that Muslim societies with weak or colonized elites were capable of falling prey to such puritanical forms of Islam well beyond Arabia. And by the twentieth century the British themselves had got into the habit of admiring the Wahhabis and even those who appeared to be their Indian followers, whom they saw as the Protestants of Islam out to destroy the decadence and superstition of their corrupt and therefore Catholic coreligionists.[36]

The movement's Muslim admirers included both conservatives and liberals who, like the English, saw the Wahhabis as rationalists willing to break with the authority of traditional religious authorities as well as that of Muslim kings. When Britain decided to support Ibn Saud and his Wahhabi troops in the 1930s, Indian Muslims were prepared to welcome the creation of Saudi Arabia. Ibn Saud himself was profuse in his gratitude to those among them who had contributed funds for his struggle, despite disagreeing with Wahhabi excesses that included massacres of Muslims who did not follow his creed. The ground for this welcome had been laid once Istanbul, or for that matter Cairo or Baghdad, was replaced by Mecca and Medina at the geographical center of Islam. As the historical site for an ideal Muslim society, Arabia became central to the Muslim imagination beyond its traditional role in the pilgrimage. It had also become the location of a prophetic utopia that was separated from both kingship and the caliphate as forms of authority that emerged only after Muhammad.[37]

The new geography of Islam was also a Protestant one, with Rome's decadence mirrored in Istanbul. For Blunt this new Rome had to be forsaken for Arabia's holy cities as versions of Geneva. At its birth, Saudi Arabia looked very much like the fulfillment of his vision, representing Islam's geographical center protected by Christian powers. The United States soon replaced the British in this role, while oil turned the peninsula into a crucial resource for Western capitalism. But its religious and economic centrality continued to be defined by Arabia's political marginality. Today this situation is beginning to shift, with Saudi Arabia like other Gulf states trying for the first time to claim political and even military supremacy in the Middle East. While such claims to dominance are directed against Iran's geopolitical agenda in the region, they are also made possible by the decline of Egypt as a Middle Eastern power, as well as the wars and invasions that have taken Iraq and Syria out of the running. Turkey remains the peninsula's only and as yet ambiguous rival apart from Iran.

Yet Arabia can assume political power only by putting its religious status at risk, defined as this has been by the peninsula's marginal role in geopolitics. And indeed, its rulers are asserting royal control over their religious establishments, whether it is by promoting "moderate" Islam, combatting terrorism, or allowing women to drive. Even Saudi Arabia is looking more like a "secular" than a "theocratic" state in which sovereignty has finally been claimed by the monarchy. And in varying degrees this is true of all states in the peninsula.[38] Whether this will succeed in remaking Arabia remains to be seen, but what will it mean for the modern geography of Islam? The Muslim world is being remade, and Saudi Arabia's emergence as a regional power might well signal the disappearance of Islam's geographical grounding. For this depends upon the peninsula's depoliticization, which serves to guarantee Islam's autonomy as an agent of history disconnected from any single power.

Might the dissolution of the Muslim world as we have known it lead to its fragmentation, just as the international order appears to be fragmenting in the shift from a unipolar to a regionalized rather than multipolar world? Or is it more likely that this dissolution will reinforce the sociological character of Islam by giving more prominence to the large and increasingly prosperous Muslim populations in Southeast Asia alongside the much smaller ones defined by the wealth and increasing political heft of the Gulf? The Middle East has maintained its status as Islam's historical and geographical homeland in large part because of its depoliticization, which is to say its subordination to Western geopolitics since the end of the First World War. As its status slowly changes, with Iran and now Turkey as well as the Gulf states claiming political autonomy, neither Arabia nor the region as a whole may be able to constitute Islam's geographical center for much longer.

CHAPTER TWO
A Prophet Disarmed

ONE OF THE MOST interesting examples of the way in which Islam emerged in the nineteenth century to displace older figures and authorities has to do with the term "Muhammadan." While Muslims may not themselves have used this appellation, or others like "Mohammedanism," when speaking or writing in non-European languages, they seemed comfortable with various renditions of the name well into the nineteenth century. They frequently used it in languages like English and French for themselves and their institutions, as well as in similarly adjectival forms like *muhammadiyya* or *muhammadi* in non-European ones. But though such terms continued to be deployed in colonial societies as administrative and sometimes academic categories into the next century, Muslims had by then abandoned them in favor of "Islam" and its grammatical derivatives. I have tried to show in the previous chapter how this shift was not merely a semantic one but entailed a new conception of Islam as a global presence and agent in history.

But repudiating the identificatory power of the Prophet's name in this way could also mean depriving him of any sacred quality and, in doing so, differentiating him from other religious founders, of whom Jesus stood as the classical example. Yet Muhammad's humanization as a simple medium for Islam's founding in the eyes of some but by no means all Muslims did not reduce him in their religious lives. On the contrary, his subordination to Islam understood as the true agent of Muslim history seems to have made the Prophet into an even more important figure in their devotions. Whether seen in profane terms as representing the genius heralding Islam as a new departure in human history, or in theological ones as God's final messenger, Muhammad became the subject of an unprecedented proliferation of biographical and devotional works from the nineteenth century.

Many of these publications were modeled on or responded to European writings and so foregrounded issues and events in the Prophet's life that would not have been relevant in earlier times. His relations with and treatment of women or religious minorities, for instance, became a major theme in such works, as did comparisons with other religions and their founders. From the nineteenth century, in other words, we have the production of a single and therefore nontheological canon of writing about Muhammad whose form was shared by believers and unbelievers alike.[1] And as we saw in the previous chapter, Muhammad became important in this way because he had replaced the caliphs, padishahs, sultans, emirs, and other kinds of ruler as an authority whose life and words could explain the inner meaning of Muslim societies. It was Islam, represented by its prophet, rather than any political authority, that now offered the key to understanding these people and places.

In premodern times it had become popular for Muslims to see the Prophet as unlettered so as to emphasize by contrast the miraculous nature of the Qur'an's beauty, whose divine authorship would therefore owe nothing to his efforts. But this did not detract from Muhammad's sacred qualities and powers as the privileged recipient of revelation. By a curious parallel it has become fashionable in modern times to stress the Prophet's humanity, often by depriving him of such powers so as to make Islam the only agent of history and focus of belief. Yet this has made Muhammad, but never God and rarely the Qur'an, into a lightning rod of controversy and violence since the nineteenth century. Did such stirs reveal and seek to interrupt his subordination to Islam as its representative, or did they occur because he required defense after the reduction?

The Prophet's humanization has received its deepest analysis by SherAli Tareen, a scholar of religious studies who traces the theological debate it prompted in nineteenth-century India.[2] He argues that Muhammad became central to the lives of believers in a new way there with the loss of Muslim political sovereignty in the British Empire. On one side of this debate stood those who blamed kings, aristocrats, and the culture of courtly as much as religious intercession they promoted for the loss. They thought this culture had led to the denial of God's sovereignty and so destroyed the Muslim solidarity that was achieved in obedience to it alone. Divine sovereignty had instead been replaced by relations of royal, saintly, and prophetic mediation, with Muhammad misunderstood as a miracle worker interceding for Muslims before God by way of dreams, rituals, and a sacrilegious devotion to his person.

On the other side were those who thought that to humanize Muhammad as the perfect Muslim was to insult him without any benefit accruing to divine sovereignty by way of compensation. In fact, the idea of God's absolute transcendence signaled his loss of reality in the believer's life. Both parties recognized the absence of sovereignty as the most serious problem facing Muslim societies. But they did not link it to the decline of monarchy and so call for its political renewal as they might have done in the past. Instead, the theologians Tareen studies understood God's sovereignty or the Prophet's share in it as necessary to unify the Muslim community in social terms rather than the state in political ones. This situation was typical of colonial rule, where religion and the social sphere it had been confined to came to constitute a site for native sovereignty. And it has resulted in a postcolonial politics where sovereignty cannot be confined to the state but repeatedly returns to society.

Those Muslims who sought to humanize Muhammad as nothing more than God's most perfect servant entertained a view of sovereignty whose unitary and transcendent form Tareen tells us closely resembled that of the modern state of European vintage. But having expelled this sovereignty into God's keeping, they rendered their obedience to it voluntarily and so were freed from its coercive force as represented by any religious or political institution. Others understood divine sovereignty as being shared or dispersed through the person of Muhammad to be experienced by Muslims in rituals and visitations. In this way they adhered in some ways to a premodern understanding of it. Their argument was therefore about whether Muhammad represents the transcendence or immanence of divine sovereignty in the absence of its political form. But might this debate actually conceal the possibility that neither divine nor prophetic sovereignty exists in modern Islam?

Whereas the theological debate Tareen traces with such sensitivity offers us alternative visions of Muslim sovereignty, we shall see that popular protests over insults to the Prophet are marked by its almost complete absence from the vocabulary of such protests. This is not because one set of controversies is lettered and the other unlettered. Rather, the two proceed along parallel tracks since theological debates have never led to popular demonstrations, though they may refer to the latter for justification. Popular demonstrations, instead, represent a fulfillment of the theologian's fear that divine sovereignty is no longer available to Muslims. And this is why Muhammad cannot assume his metaphysical role in such events either as a model Muslim subservient to God's sovereignty or as a sharer in it. Instead, it is Muslims who, in recognizing themselves as its heirs, are forced to repudiate this sovereignty as being sacrilegious.

God rarely if ever makes an appearance in such controversies, which are not therefore about his relationship to the Prophet at all. They are instead about the relationship Muslims have with Muhammad seen as an object of their protection rather than a subject in his own right. Is this because Islam, rather than God or the Prophet, has become the true subject of Muslim history, thus depriving them both of their roles as sources of sacredness and sovereignty? Having become Islam's representatives, in other words, these holy personages may have lost their own agency and so can suddenly be pressed into becoming objects in the narratives of others. I argue here that Muhammad's defenders not only protest his translation into such alternative narratives but are also unable to refashion him as a subject of theology. The controversies about insulting the Prophet that I discuss, therefore, bring Muslim clerics together with the representatives of colonial and secular states in a theological understanding of such events. But this understanding is overwhelmed by the quite different language of mass Muslim protest, which is defined by the absence of theology and the problem this poses in the career of modern Islam.

Bombay for Beginners

Insults to Muhammad have become a flashpoint for Muslim protest only in modern times, with the phenomenon starting in India during the middle of the nineteenth century. They went global with the controversy over the publication of Salman Rushdie's 1989 novel *The Satanic Verses*, which led to riots, murders, and death sentences around the world. Since then, there have been at least three global protests over such insults, each one giving rise to violence. Important about all these controversies is their concern with demeaning portrayals of Muhammad in the press rather than with any theological argument. On every occasion, in fact, it has been those opposed to such protests who have attached theological meaning to them. This they have done by invoking themes like Islam's supposed proscription of the Prophet's image in order to make sense of Muslim outrage, even though such a proscription has rarely if ever been at issue in such controversies.

The first two such protests, each descending into riots, occurred in colonial Bombay, one in 1851 and the other in 1874. In both we already see emerging the contours of all subsequent controversies over insulting the Prophet. Unlike the provincial society of North India, where religious controversy still took the form of theological debates between Christian, Hindu, or Muslim missionaries, in the great commercial center of Bombay it was the appearance of newspapers and books meant to entertain and inform a general public that caused offense.[3] The objective of these publications was not to proselytize or even to engage in polemical debate but to make profits by piquing the interest of or pandering to the prejudices of their readers. In one case it was a Gujarati newspaper and in the other a book in the same language, both published by Parsis (Indian Zoroastrians), that provoked Muslims to attack a community praised for its capitalist enterprise and urbanity.

In turning away from the supposedly traditional enmity between Hindus and Muslims as well as from the more familiar causes of religious conflict in desecration, missionary activity, or theological debate among believers in differing traditions, the Bombay riots of 1851 and 1874 already signal the making of a new context for controversy. Rooted in commerce and industrial capitalism with its anonymous mass of consumers, protests against insults to the Prophet could now only impute motives to his critics that were not theological but merely defamatory. The 1851 riots were occasioned by the publication in the *Chitra Dnyan Darpan* (Illustrated Mirror of Knowledge) of a biographical article about Muhammad drawn from Simon Ockley's eighteenth-century *History of the Saracens* together with a portrait. It was this portrait that was said to have offended Muslims by its disfigurement through a printing error, with the account itself deemed innocuous.

But this narrative of Muslims being stirred to fanaticism by a simple mistake (and interestingly not the supposed proscription of Muhammad's image) is put into question when we look at the biographical account. It begins by stating: "We have in our former papers given accounts of the career of some of those remarkable persons who have made great changes in society. We proceed to-day to give the account of the life of another famous man. No other person has so much altered the affairs of the world, or destroyed the lives and property of people, and led them to believe him as Mahomed has done."[4] More than a simple recension of Ockley's book, the article seems to have been published in response to Muslim slights against the Parsi prophet Zoroaster as well as the conversion of Parsis to Islam. Indeed, the violence between Muslims and Parsis flared as the former emerged from Bombay's great mosque leading one such convert in procession.

A complex event, then, had to be reduced to an example of Muslim fanaticism. But this was difficult to do. For instance, it had to be noted in the press and Parsi polemics that the Mogul or Iranian Muslim community in Bombay had been ordered by the Persian consul not to participate in the riots and that its members had indeed rescued a number of Parsis from violence. Or that the Gujarati-speaking Muslims who, like the Parsis, were engaged in trade and commerce, also did not take part in the riots. At fault, rather, were Hindustani-speaking Muslims from North India who belonged to the laboring classes and were unable even to read the Gujarati article they thought offensive. Meanwhile, Parsis had to defend themselves from accusations by British police of their own working classes instigating some of the violence. Viewed from another perspective, we can see the riots pitting workers against business owners. Eventually, the "respectable men" of both communities joined forces with the colonial state to control the poorer among their coreligionists.

The complicated sociology of this event meant that imputing a purely theological language to it proved impossible. Apart from general descriptions of Muslim fanaticism, the only effort to do so seems to have come from the *Telegraph and Courier,* which accused the prominent Muslim merchant and justice of the peace Mahomed Ibrahim Muckba of delivering a speech about courting martyrdom to defend the Prophet. This he denied in print.[5] The riots were soon subordinated to another logic, which had to do not with theology but with free speech. The editor of the *Bombay Times* wrote: "There are many things quite true, and which under certain circumstances may be expressed with the most perfect propriety, the propagation of which might under other circumstances have been most mischievous. When we discover from the fact that they have done harm— that mischief may arise from them—then they ought to be avoided."[6]

To this, the *Telegraph and Courier* responded:

> We fear that our contemporary has a dash of Irish blood in his veins. Else how could he tell us that when things, right in themselves, are *done* at such a juncture, or under such circumstances, that they produce mischief,—then they ought to be *avoided?* . . . We never heard anything more unreasonable. If Byramjee Cursetjee, or any other person, were, *at a period of popular excitement* knowingly to do aught calculated to increase the ferment in people's minds, and thus lead to a breach of the peace—then of course the act would be criminal. But from all we can hear, it was Byramjee's publication that caused the excitement among the Mohamedans: he did not find them already excited, and by an act of reckless folly, goad them into outbreak.[7]

The riots, in other words, had been fully absorbed into the vocabulary of liberalism, being understood by the critics of Muslim fanaticism as a result of mistaking the secular for the sacred.

Representing the first modern controversy about insulting Muhammad, the 1851 riots led to the repeated invocation of fanaticism as a theological principle without offering any example of it, apart from the violence itself, which was seen as being irrational. On the contrary, it illustrated the emergence of a new kind of controversy stoked by the press and spilling over into social life, where it was the injury to personal reputation and communal feeling that mattered. And it was not accidental that this injury looked very much like that caused to wealthier and more influential individuals by libel and defamation, with each type of hurt requiring the press and its publicity to occur. Indeed, as the historian J. Barton Scott points out, it was difficult to separate blasphemy from libel, defamation, or even sedition, all these crimes being interconnected in law as much as logic and disallowing any clean separation of religious and secular realms.[8]

By the twentieth century, Scott notes, Muslims protesting against insults to Muhammad in colonial India were themselves making reference to libel and defamation, invoking a famous British case in which a long-dead prime minister, William Gladstone, had his reputation protected by the courts from such insults. All of which goes to show how important nontheological arguments had become for Muslims who sought to defend their prophet. And this meant that the way to address such injuries, whether they were considered to be against the reputation of a person (Muhammad) or the feelings of a class of people (Muslims), was to weigh them against the wider public interest conceived as a market for commodities as much as of ideas and information. The discussion then became a technical one about the limits of a free market and the dangers of protectionism as opposed to its benefits.

While we have little information about Muslim views of the controversy in 1851, the riots of 1874 offer a much clearer picture of religious relations emptied of theology. Here the offending publication was a Gujarati book written by a Parsi titled *Renowned Prophets and Nations, comprising the Lives of Zoroaster, Moses, Christ, and Mahomed, an abridged history of the Ancient Arians, the old Parsees, and complete history of the Jews, the Christians, and of the Mahomedans, together with an account of the Creation of the World, (from the earliest period to the present time).*[9] We are told that despite its scope, this was a slim volume and that the offending portion of it, said to have been taken from Washington Irving's biography of Muhammad, claimed that he had a son by a "kept woman." Here it was an insulting reference to the Prophet's sexual life that caused outrage. As with the 1851 riots, the Muslims who protested this insult were not ones who could read the offending Gujarati text.

Fearful of trouble among the Muslim working classes, their "respectable men" came together to condemn the book and ask for it to be withdrawn by the police, which it duly was and the author held for safekeeping. Nevertheless, riots between Parsis and Muslims did break out, with the latter represented by Sidis or African laborers and Arab boatmen from the Persian Gulf as well as by Pathans from the Afghan frontier. Yet again, in other words, we see a very distinctive segment of the city's diverse Muslim population take part in the violence, and not its Gujarati or Konkani middle classes or elites, nor even its religious authorities, who strove to keep the peace. Joining the working poor engaged in the riots and looting were also low-caste or untouchable Hindus. These latter were subsequently let go by the courts on bail as they were not Muslims; thus the riot was defined in purely religious terms.

Yet, the acts of violence in this controversy featured attacks on liquor shops owned by Parsis whose looted stock was drunk down by Muslims. As in 1851, therefore, we see the city's Muslim elites struggling unsuccessfully to control its working classes while at the same time being obliged by their very claims of leadership to defend Muhammad from insult. And in doing so they set a precedent for all subsequent controversies. The *Times of India* makes note of this new argument in its report on a meeting held by Bombay's leading Muslims and addressed by their chief religious authority: "Cazee Abdool Latiff Saheb addressed the meeting at some length stating that complaints having been made to him by several members of the community as to a Goojratee publication by a Parsee containing language calculated to wound the religious feelings of the professors of Islam, he had, in company with some respectable people of the Jamat, called upon the Commissioner of Police, and laid the facts of the case before him."[10]

Following his statement, the qazi was thanked by the audience, and "Moonshee Ali Akbar Khan said that the Mussulman community ought to be very much obliged to Cazee Abdool Latiff Saheb, who had taken so much trouble in the matter, and he further suggested that a petition might be presented to Government for passing a law preventing persons from publishing any matter calculated to give offence to or wound the religious feelings of any community."[11] Crucial here for all future controversies are two themes. The first has to do with the invocation of hurt feelings or wounded sentiments. Not blasphemy, in other words, nor even an offense against the Prophet, but Muslim sensibilities were at issue here in much the same way as they would be in cases of libel or defamation whose injury pertained to the loss of reputation in the market of public opinion.

This language was taken from the Indian Penal Code, which, though composed some decades earlier, only entered into law in 1860.[12] Its author, Lord Macaulay, had replaced blasphemy, still a crime in Britain, with the injunction against deliberately hurting religious sentiments without regard to their truth.[13] Drawn from the utilitarian philosophy of Jeremy Bentham, with its criterion of avoiding harm, section 298 of the penal code still finds a place in Indian and Pakistani law. Concerned with "uttering words, etc., with deliberate intent to wound the religious feelings of any person," it is the last of eight sections dedicated to public nuisance. By shifting the offense from religious figures or truths to the sentiments of their followers whatever the religion involved, the Indian Penal Code did away with blasphemy. For unlike European countries, many with established churches, colonized ones were necessarily secular, given the lack of a common religious identity between rulers and ruled.

Muslim invocations of hurt feelings, then, involve no claims of a theological nature but are if anything appeals to utilitarianism's calculus of pain and pleasure. The second precedent set by the 1874 riots has to do with Muslim demands for legislation preventing such hurt, not only to their own sentiments but to those of all religious groups and again without reference to blasphemy. To this day such demands are discussed in the framework of market regulation, with any potential interference in the free circulation of ideas like goods debated in terms that would have been familiar to Bentham. Should religious sentiments be protected? Or would this set a bad precedent in reducing the free circulation of information and opinion in newspapers or books, which needed regulating only by the invisible hand of the market? In comparing their hurt to the kind of injury proscribed by libel, defamation, and, we shall see, counterfeit goods, Muslims have consistently argued for limits being placed upon the workings of the market.

By 1890, this argument took on global ambitions, with Muslims in Bombay meeting in their thousands to protest the staging of a play about Muhammad in London. In their petition to the secretary of state for India, the protestors wrote:

> That the Mussulman subjects of her Majesty in British India *alone* number about fifty millions and form an important section of the populace under her Majesty's dominion. That your petitioners have recently learnt with great regret that a theatrical performance was intended to be acted on a London stage, in which the Holy and Revered Prophet of Islam was to be represented. This news caused a great stir in the whole Mussulman world, and has shocked and wounded their religious feelings. . . . Your petitioners need not remind your Lordship that it has always been the anxious care of the *just* and benign British Government, to preserve strict neutrality in matters of religion, and to prevent acts calculated to wound the religious feelings and susceptibilities of its subjects.[14]

New about this argument was the claim that even without the franchise and so a say in the way they were governed, the sheer number of Muslims under British rule obliged the government to represent their views in a vaguely democratic way. And this was important because a refusal to ban the performance in London would amount to a violation of the state's secular credentials, based as they were on religious neutrality, since it would be tolerating what in effect was a Christian polemic against Islam. While the petition did not achieve its aim, crucial about it was the attempt to shut down an English play from India in the name of the Muslim world. And this effort at demonstrating Islam's global reach, moreover, took as its object the protection not of Muslim tradition but the British Empire's own secularism. However imperfect or disingenuous such an argument, it nicely illustrates the novel context in which insults to Muhammad had come to be placed.

If it was so easy to translate controversies about insulting Muhammad into the language of the marketplace in nineteenth-century Bombay, this was because he had already lost his theological character and sovereign agency. And while my attribution of this loss to the emergence of Islam as a global subject may not be immediately evident, a little reflection will suffice to show its massive presence as a presumption in the riots. We have seen, for example, that the divisions between Muslims in the 1851 and 1874 riots were based not on theology but on class and ethnicity. And that those who engaged in violence as well as those who didn't comprised groups with very different and even opposing theological traditions. To this day, such protests bring together Muslims of divergent theological views, suggesting not their unification on a certain understanding of religion but rather its irrelevance in these controversies. In fact, they could come together only by setting aside their religious rivalries and so theology as such.

All of the various denominations of Muslims supporting or opposing the Bombay riots were nevertheless identified as "Muslims" not only by the colonial state but in their own estimation. This is why the gatherings of "respectable men," which sought to address both the city's Muslims and the colonial state, were very deliberately made up of leaders from all the varied sects and schisms of Islam present in that great metropolis. Men who disagreed with each other on almost every theological particular were happy to come together as Muslims. The meeting held in 1890 to petition the secretary of state, for instance, included, "Borahs, Moguls, Memons, Khojas, Shias, and Sunis."[15] This was possible not on the basis of some general or ecumenical agreement about what they held in common theologically, but by ignoring such matters altogether since they were joined by Islam as a global agent that rendered the divisions between religious groups as well as the distinction of religious and secular domains irrelevant.

From Property to Personhood

It is the market that allowed for Islam's globalization, not so much by enabling the expansion of its following as by Muslim efforts to control the circulation within it of the Prophet's image as a commodity in newsprint. But why have his defenders never used the rich theological vocabulary that is to be found in the Islamic tradition condemning blasphemous statements against Muhammad (though no punishment is prescribed for them in the Qur'an)? In their arguments with colonial states as subjects and now with European ones as citizens, of course, Muslims have been obliged to rely upon a legal language not of their own making. But they have not drawn upon this theological tradition even in purely internal debates within Muslim countries either. Instead, we have to listen to their opponents for any references to theological categories and terms like "blasphemy" or "apostasy," both taken from Christian history.

This became clear during the global protests over insults to Muhammad that emerged with the publication of *The Satanic Verses*, despite the fact that its title and content referred to a venerable theological controversy. It stemmed from an incident where the Prophet sought to enable the conversion of an important tribe to Islam by agreeing to consider its goddesses intermediaries with God. The verses acknowledging them, however, were soon expunged from the Qur'an as satanic interpolations, with Rushdie using the event to reflect upon the ambiguities of authorship in a situation where the devil could apparently interrupt God. Yet this theological reference never became an issue in the worldwide protests against the book, which focused instead on a dream sequence where prostitutes are given the names of Muhammad's wives. We have already seen how such sexual themes had come to define Muslim protest in the 1874 Bombay riots without any theological issue being involved.

Not coincidentally, given the subcontinental origin of protests against insulting Muhammad, the first Muslims to be offended by Rushdie's novel were immigrants of Pakistani and Indian descent in Britain. Their demonstrations then spread to their ancestral countries before they took the rest of the Muslim world by storm. Important about the offense attributed to *The Satanic Verses* was both its ordinary and indirect character. It was not Muhammad himself who was insulted, as he might have been if protestors took the novel's title seriously, but his wives. And this insult, too, was a quotidian one that didn't require questioning the Prophet's theological status in order to be offensive. This was why the Muslims who spoke of their hurt sentiments to the press repeatedly placed the insult within the context of their everyday lives by comparing Muhammad and his wives to their own relatives. It was the familiarity of the offense rather than its theological exceptionality that made it so hurtful.

The Prophet was vulnerable to such ordinary insults not only because he had become human, but because his role had been taken over by Islam. Over the course of the nineteenth century, he had become a figure who could stand as a model for Muslims in his role as a father or husband as much as a statesman even for those who also believed in his miraculous powers. This new relationship to the Prophet was the direct result of Islam's emergence as a subject of history in its own right, with Muhammad like all Muslims seen as one of its representatives. But this also made Muhammad into an ambiguous figure. How was his quotidian presence as a model for Muslim behavior to be reconciled with the Prophet's sacred role as a recipient of divine revelation? The problem, in other words, was that his theological status no longer appeared self-evident.

On the one hand, Muhammad took on the role of Muslim property in these protests, with his circulation as a generalized commodity in the market of public opinion posing a problem of ownership for his followers. This is why Muslim demands have since the nineteenth century been directed at disallowing or at least controlling the dissemination of apparently incorrect or counterfeit narratives about him. But on the other hand, he represented Muslims themselves, and so insults directed at the Prophet hurt them or at least their reputations, as in cases of libel and defamation. Shabbir Akhtar, then a doctoral student at Cambridge who led the intellectual charge against *The Satanic Verses* in Britain, notes in his book about it that Muslims there were outraged because, in identifying with Muhammad, they saw Rushdie's novel as a slanderous attack on them.

Akhtar wrote: "According to English law, what is not prohibited is permitted; but many things are explicitly not permitted: blasphemy, obscenity, sedition, treason, incitement to racial hatred, breaches of national security, subversion, contempt of court and of Parliament, and libel. . . . Is it unreasonable to extend this concern to the prohibition of the publication of books like *The Satanic Verses* which are likely to inflame, through defamation, the feelings of a given section of society and, in doing so, to provoke public disorder?"[16] The issue had nothing to do with theology or even with free speech. Indeed, he claimed it was the Muslim argument that was never allowed a hearing in the press and so had to be demonstrated in other ways on the streets. Is Muhammad, then, the subject or object of Muslim feeling? The vacillating relationship between ownership and identification in these controversies tells us that at their heart lies a question of how to be religious in the globe conceived as a market.

Akhtar pointed out that Muslim protests in places like Bradford and London had started out criticizing the novel itself as a commodity and asking for its withdrawal. At that point, therefore, claims over property, circulation, and ownership defined the controversy. But he tells us that when the Ayatollah Khomeini entered a now global debate to issue a call for Rushdie's execution, the focus suddenly shifted from the book as a commodity in the publisher's market to its author. Indeed, the Ayatollah did not even call for the book's banning.[17] This meant that now at stake was not the question of claiming ownership of Muhammad and controlling his circulation in the market, but of defining his role in representing the Muslims who identified with him. Having hurt Muslims themselves, rather than their prophet, Rushdie had suddenly become their enemy whether or not he chose to apologize and withdraw his novel.

Khomeini's sentence against Rushdie and all those involved in publishing his novel is remarkably brief and states:

> I am informing all brave Muslims of the world that the author of *The Satanic Verses*, a text written, edited, and published against Islam, the Prophet of Islam, and the Qur'an, along with all the editors and publishers aware of its contents, are condemned to death. I call on all valiant Muslims wherever they may be in the world to kill them without delay, so that no one will dare insult the sacred beliefs of Muslims henceforth. Whoever is killed in this cause will be a martyr, God Willing. Meanwhile if someone has access to the author of the book but is incapable of carrying out the execution, he should inform the people so that [Rushdie] is punished for his actions.[18]

Its Persian text is prefaced by an Arabic aphorism, "We are from God and to God we shall return," that is generally uttered in commiseration for someone's death. It is likely that Khomeini used it in reference to recent riots over the book in Pakistan and India, in which at least one person was killed and hundreds were injured. These incidents may well have changed his opinion about the controversy, which he had hitherto dismissed as a pointless irritant.[19] In this sense Khomeini can be seen as sentencing those associated with *The Satanic Verses* for the deaths of Muslims protesting it. No longer a question of who owned the Prophet in the marketplace of ideas, his sentence served as retaliation for the first deaths, unmentioned and unmourned in the West, related to the controversy. It was a sentence that showed up the West's hypocrisy about who deserved protection and who didn't.

For all Khomeini's authority as a Muslim jurist, however, his decision to call for Rushdie's killing was not simply a theological one, his decree being a *hukm* issued by a head of state rather than a *fatwa* or legal opinion, as it is routinely mistaken for being. And, in fact, a *fatwa* is not even the same thing as a judicial sentence, which derives its authority from the ruler or state. In keeping with Shia procedure, Khomeini's statement does not cite the Qur'an, traditions of the Prophet, or any jurisprudential principle and precedent to make its case. Indeed, no argument is made at all. This suggests that Khomeini issued it on the basis of his own sovereign decision as Iran's supreme leader, and in doing so set aside not only Islamic theology and law but the sovereignty of God and Muhammad. Interesting about his statement, for instance, is that it names Islam as the novel's first target before Muhammad and the Qur'an, which can thus be understood as its representatives.

Yet none of these figures is said to have been insulted by it, but instead, Muslim beliefs or sentiments in Macaulay's terms. In the Persian original the phrase used is *muqaddisat-e muslimin* or "the sacred things of the Muslims," where sentiments are implied in the reference to objects in their possession. It is true that Khomeini turns to theology when describing those who might give their lives to kill Rushdie as martyrs; but this was immediately counteracted by Iran's parliament offering a reward to anyone who carried out the act without losing his life, which turned the possible murder into a risky economic transaction. It was a bounty of the kind familiar in US history to encourage the killing of native peoples, recapture escaped slaves, or deliver speedy justice to terrorists worldwide. In this way Khomeini's sentence as modified by Iran's parliament did not represent the state's exclusive right to sovereignty but rather opened it to the claims of others. The Ayatollah had lifted the protests out of the market in which Muhammad's ownership was contested to see Rushdie's offense as being directed against Muslims. But by offering a reward for the novelist's murder, his own parliament returned the issue into the market's keeping, in a good example of the back and forth between personhood and property in these spectacles of outrage.

By intervening in if not hijacking the controversy, of course, Khomeini was no doubt also making a case for his own and Iran's Islamic credentials to the global audience created by it. This may have involved competing with Saudi Arabia for the right to speak on behalf of Islam as an historical subject. But these calculations were contingent, making the controversy available as an opportunity for other kinds of aims. Similarly, we can say that it was made possible by immigration and the attempt of British Muslims to find a public voice for themselves, or by the advent of twenty-four-hour news cycles and the global distribution of their television content, or by the emergence of struggles over issues of identity with the end of the Cold War. None of these factors, however, could give rise to a global debate in their own right but had to be subordinated and lend strength to the nineteenth-century one about Muhammad in the marketplace.

Globalized through the market, Muhammad represents Muslim property as well as personhood. Both possibilities involve the risk of his falsification and also disappearance. On the one hand, after all, the Prophet's reproduction and circulation as a commodity escapes the reach of his putative owners to become the property of others. And on the other hand, his availability as a representation of the ideal Muslim means that Muhammad risks being reproduced by anyone who would claim him and so lost to his followers in another way. The debates we have been looking at so far move from the discussion of property to that of personhood, with the struggle of Muhammad's defenders being to remove him from the commodity's world of reproduction and circulation and stabilize the Prophet as a representation of the Muslim self. But the process can also be reversed, with debates about the Prophet's personhood turning into arguments about property.

It is the latter trajectory that can be seen in the persecution of the Ahmadis, a community originating in nineteenth-century Punjab that was the first to embark upon a global mission to proselytize for Islam in places like Europe and North America.[20] Drawing upon the methods of Christian missionaries, as many religious groups did when faced with them in European empires, the Ahmadis were lauded by fellow Muslims as long as they took the fight for Islam into the Christian or Hindu camp. It was once they turned their attention to Muslims themselves that things became difficult. For unlike other sectarian disputes among the Prophet's followers, the Ahmadis did not quarrel over matters of ritual or practice and continued to behave in the most orthodox of ways. It was their ideas that were radical and their public insistence that only those who accepted their founder were true Muslims.

It might have been the fracturing of Muslim families in the Punjab by quarrels over the status of Mirza Ghulam Ahmad that first made the Ahmadis controversial. But they came to inspire paranoia largely because it was impossible to tell Ahmadis apart from other Muslims. Intimacy and so the fear of impersonation is therefore crucial to anti-Ahmadi polemics, and this accusation of deception was soon attached to Ghulam Ahmad's alleged claim to be a prophet. Since Muhammad is meant to be God's final messenger, this much-disputed claim has been understood as putting him in Muhammad's place and so beyond the pale of Islam. Ahmadis have thus been declared non-Muslims in Pakistan and a few other countries. Identifying with Muhammad, then, which was what those who protested against the circulation of insulting statements about him did, runs the risk of reproducing him in other ways so as to deny the Prophet's finality.

It should be no surprise that Ghulam Ahmad was himself a staunch defender of Muhammad, constantly engaging in polemics with those he believed were insulting him and predicting their deaths as divine punishment.[21] Yet by attributing the violence visited upon those who offended the Prophet to divine chastisement,

Ghulam Ahmad was not deploying a theological argument. On the contrary, he sang the praises of the British Empire as a secular order that, by allowing religious freedom to all its subjects, had created a marketplace in which persuasion and consumer choice rather than force would determine people's faiths. And this meant it was the invisible hand of the market that decided which religion won and which lost, as well as who lived and who died to demonstrate its truth. The theological element in this reasoning, then, was internal to the market rather than a transcendental intervention into it.[22]

But if a defender of the Prophet like Ghulam Ahmad could be attacked for insulting him, was it because Muslims had to disavow identifying with or owning Muhammad, even as they did both? Telling about the polemic against the Ahmadis is how religiously impoverished it is. It was not enough to claim they denied Muhammad's finality on theological grounds. They also had to reason it through in the historical, political, and philosophical ways that had come to define Islam as a global subject. This is why the chief argument used by all Muslim groups against Ghulam Ahmad comes from the philosopher Muhammad Iqbal, who came himself from an Ahmadi family. Having broken with the Ahmadis while retaining much of their style in thinking, Iqbal wrote several refutations of their beliefs in the 1930s. In them, he stated that Islam was the first postmetaphysical faith, representing the shift from religion as a way of establishing divine authority by occult means to one guaranteeing human freedom: "[T]he Prophet of Islam seems to stand between the ancient and the modern world. In so far as the source of his revelation is concerned he belongs to the ancient world; in so far as the spirit of his revelation is concerned he belongs to the modern world. ... In Islam prophecy reaches its perfection in discovering the need of its own abolition. This involves the keen perception that life cannot for ever be kept in leading strings; that in order to achieve full self-consciousness man must finally be thrown back on his own resources."[23]

By claiming to be the fount of divine wisdom, therefore, Ghulam Ahmad was allegedly dragging Muslims back to a metaphysical dead end by reviving occult forms of authority while at the same time denying their intellectual and political freedom. Iqbal's vision of human liberty looks very much like the Ahmadi understanding of secularism and the religious choice or reasoning it allowed, though without the Ahmadis' focus on the market, which Iqbal despised as a site of capitalist inequality. Interesting about this polemic is that both sides denied themselves the theological repertoire meant to accompany such debates. For even Ghulam Ahmad's miracles and predictions, we have seen, rely upon the market's hidden hand for their explanation. If for him the Prophet could become a focus of identification to such a degree as to enable the reproduction of Muhammad's authority, for Iqbal he represented no miracle worker but the ideal of human freedom.

The process of disavowal is clear in these debates. Some of Ghulam Ahmad's critics are shocked at his audacity in claiming prophetic status because it is too exalted for ordinary mortals. Yet, they are happy to identify with Muhammad in seeing him as a model father, husband, or statesman who is also vulnerable to insult and injury. Others deny the Prophet's status as a miracle worker while being horrified that Ghulam Ahmad might claim to share his ordinary function as a Muslim leader. Iqbal claims that it is Muhammad's historic role in closing the period of occult authority and opening one of human liberty that is threatened by the Ahmadi founder, who, however, had made a similar claim for himself. The threat of insult and impersonation is therefore internal to Muslim discussions about owning Muhammad as much as identifying with him. And this suggests the Prophet remains trapped within a marketplace whose logic he cannot escape.

Having been excommunicated in the 1970s, the Ahmadis come to pose a different kind of problem, which is no longer one of identification but goes back to the question of ownership. They are now accused of misleading believers by offering up a counterfeit or simulacrum of Muslim piety that might seduce those believers unawares. It is no longer the claim to prophecy that is important, at least not directly so, but the ownership of Muslim forms of identification in their own right. Since the 1990s, then, Ahmadis in Pakistan have been prevented from uttering Muslim greetings, praying like Muslims, calling their places of worship mosques, or even looking like Muslims. And although there is certainly an element of impersonation here, it is not the Prophet who is the target of such proscriptions but the ordinary Muslims who also identify with him and thus close the circle between what is and is not acceptable in the believer's relationship with Muhammad.

The Prophet occupies an impossible position as person or property in debates about Muslim injury set within a global marketplace. But in recent developments these Muslims have themselves emerged as subjects who can be counterfeited to become objects in the ownership of others. This is why the Ahmadis can be seen to subvert Muslim identification so easily. In *Zaheeruddin v. State*, then, the 1993 case penalizing Ahmadis for practicing even the most acceptable Muslim rituals, the Pakistani court assimilated their offense to that of violating copyright or patent. In doing so, it even cited as precedent cases like *Bollinger v. Costa Brava Wines*, in which the latter company had illegitimately copied the former's brand of champagne. No less theological an argument can be conceived, one that returns by a different route to the economic origin of Muslim protests against insulting Muhammad.

If Mirza Ghulam Ahmad is accused of impersonating the Prophet, his followers are suspected of counterfeiting Muslims. And this is possible because there already exists a relationship of imitation between Muhammad and his followers. To copy one is therefore to copy the other. This logic of circulation and reproduction belongs, of course, to the marketplace and suggests that not just the Prophet but his devotees, too, have been pulled into it as subjects who can also become objects. The loss of Muhammad in such reproduction then becomes a loss of oneself, and it is the fraught connection between the two that gives rise to anxiety. Is this why the vocabulary describing insults to the Prophet in Pakistan is identical to that used for ordinary people? There is no theological specificity to words like *tauheen* (insult) and *gustakhi* (insolence) against Muhammad's *namus* (honor) and *hurmat* (respectability). In fact, the theological term *sabb* (to insult or revile), which does refer to offenses like blasphemy, is never invoked in such controversies.

Despite Islam's rich vocabulary of imprecations, the theological element in these discussions invariably comes from Christianity and tends to be deployed by the critics of Muslim hurt and injury as much as by its proponents. Of these, blasphemy, rather than, say, sacrilege, is the chief one, and during the Rushdie affair it was cited

not only to describe what offended Rushdie's critics, but also to acknowledge that these Muslims in fact wanted their sentiments to
be covered by England's own blasphemy law. Their declared aim,
in other words, was not to impose Islamic law in the West but to
be included in an existing if by then recondite piece of legislation
that protected Christianity alone. This did not happen, of course,
and Britain eventually did away with the law altogether. But efforts
to have Muslim sentiments covered by Christian provisions for
blasphemy have continued.

In Search of the Sacred

When he was Pakistan's prime minister, Nawaz Sharif campaigned
to have an Irish law on blasphemy serve as the model for a global
moratorium on insulting all religions, only to have the Irish alter it
to one protecting religious freedom as one of several human rights.
In this way, Pakistan has served as the inadvertent agent of Europe's
secularization. The last effort of this kind was made by another
Pakistani prime minister, Imran Khan, who, however, invoked not
blasphemy but rather the Holocaust as a precedent and model for
thinking about insults to Muhammad. In his speech delivered to the
seventy-fourth session of the UN General Assembly on September
27, 2019, he said: "In Western society, the Holocaust is treated with
sensitivity because it hurts the Jewish community. So that's the same
respect we ask for; do not hurt our sentiments by maligning our
Holy Prophet (PBUH). That is all we ask."[24]

While it may owe something to the lack of theological precedents from which Khan could draw in speaking to a global audience, more interesting about this reference to the Holocaust is how
it shifts the discussion from one vision of the sacred to another. It is
as if he realized that suffering, especially on a genocidal scale, constitutes the only real taboo both in the secular societies of the West
and for the international order. But in the process, he conflated
the proscription of insults directed at Muhammad on the basis of
his exalted theological status with those defiling the memory of an
historical event. Apart from attenuating blasphemy's theological
character in this way, Imran Khan's statement compared the injury
of Jewish and Muslim sentiments and in doing so, like Macaulay,

referred to the truth of people's feelings and not the content of their beliefs. Rather than seeing his reference to the Holocaust and Jewish history as opportunistic, we should note that Khan's political career has long been dogged by anti-Semitic accusations from some of his rivals. Khan's first wife and the mother of his children was the British socialite Jemima Goldsmith, whose Jewish faith was repeatedly invoked in Pakistan to claim that Imran Khan was an Israeli agent.

Despite and perhaps because of this history, he latched on to the Holocaust and the injury its denial inflicted upon Jewish sentiment as an example and precedent for banning insults to the Prophet. In a letter he wrote on October 25, 2020, to Mark Zuckerberg, the CEO of Facebook, and posted on Twitter, Khan made the comparison between anti-Semitism and Islamophobia.[25] Suggesting that just as anti-Semitism had led to the Holocaust so too might Islamophobia lead to genocide, the prime minister pointed to examples of discrimination and violence against Muslims in countries like India as well as in the West but not Pakistan's ally China, which had also been accused of persecuting them. He urged Zuckerberg to ban all such expressions of hatred on the same principle as Holocaust denial had been banned, singling out insults to the Prophet among these expressions. Blasphemy has been downgraded here from an offense in its own right to one that might lead to violence against Muslims by adding physical injury to their hurt sentiments.

By comparing insults to the Prophet first with the injured sentiments of Jews who had to endure Holocaust denial and then with the perils of tolerating anti-Semitism, Imran Khan sought to lay hold of a theological principle that was simply not available to him by way of Islam—and this despite his overtly Islamic demeanor, complete with quotations from the Qur'an and proposals to turn Pakistan into a version of Muhammad's government in Medina. Although he referred to the Holocaust to attract the attention of non-Muslims internationally, Khan repeated the same comparison to Muslim audiences in Pakistan because he had no more authentic argument to propose. He even claimed that permitting such insults would only lead to the radicalization of Muslims, which turned the proposed ban into a way of preventing crime rather than protecting the Prophet. His predecessor had done the same by grasping at what remained of Christian laws against blasphemy, but Khan's move to exit the arena of religion altogether demonstrates Islam's nontheological character.

There were, of course, specifically political considerations behind some of Imran Khan's statements. For much of this period, after all, he had to deal with violent demonstrations in Pakistan by a new political party that had begun its career by supporting him. Named the Tehreek-e Labbaik Pakistan ("I am Present Pakistan," referring to Muslims calling out "I am present, O Prophet of God" when on pilgrimage to Mecca), this party had been founded among the populous group of Muslims following the Barelvi creed specifically to protect Muhammad from insult. And in 2021 it had campaigned for the expulsion of the French ambassador on the grounds that his country refused to ban offensive cartoons of the Prophet published by the satirical magazine *Charlie Hebdo*, which had then led to a massacre in Paris. Khan was forced to ban the party while proclaiming his loyalty to Muhammad.

But the Pakistani prime minister's views about blasphemy predated the party's emergence, and the point I want to make is that whatever the individual intentions involved, which we can never know with any certitude, more important is the narrative arc such events traverse. It is the familiarity of this trajectory that allows historical events, each with its specific context and character, to cohere one with another and so become meaningful at a global level. Imran Khan's case is no different, since apart from contributing a new twist to this narrative with the invocation of the Holocaust, he adhered to its now rather banal form like all the others who have protested insults to the Prophet. It is equally true to say, of course, that those who object to such protests also possess a stereotyped narrative focusing on free speech and the opposition of secular and theological principles.

It should come as no surprise, then, that on April 19, 2021, the prime minister delivered a televised address to the nation in which he again mentioned the Holocaust and asked why certain European countries insisted on tolerating insults to Muhammad in the name of free speech despite the hurt they caused. But then he went on to say, "When 50 Muslim countries will unite and say this, and say that if something like this happens in any country, then we will launch a trade boycott on them and not buy their goods, that will have an effect."[26] While nothing came of this proposal, widely reported though it was in the Muslim world, it took as its precedent the sanctions regimes validated by the international order though in reality put in place only by Western countries against those outside their number.

Among the few experiments in sanctioning that had the West as their target were OPEC's oil embargo of 1973 and the Muslim boycott of Danish goods following the 2005 publication in Denmark of cartoons about Muhammad during the Global War on Terror. But Imran Khan's proposal also referred back to the founding of protests against insults to the Prophet as a genre. For in suggesting it he returned to understanding these insults in terms of the market, where it was property and not people that took pride of place. And so, we see yet again how the debate about offense and injury shifts between ownership and identification, being unable to stabilize the Prophet as either an historical actor or the sovereign subject of theology. Instead, he is constantly in the process of morphing into his own Muslim followers on the one hand or their property on the other.

I have spent so much time examining Imran Khan's views on blasphemy not for their intrinsic importance so much as because he actually did offer some kind of sustained argument about the proposal to ban it. Conventional and contradictory as it may have been, this was still an argument, while others protesting such offenses against Muhammad tend to have none, besides invoking Macaulay's hurt sentiments and through them Bentham and his utilitarian philosophy. Apart from demonstrating yet again the absence of a theological narrative in these controversies, we need to ask why they fall so short of arguments while brimming over with the most eloquent expressions of outrage and injury. In one sense, of course, this is due to the fact that Muhammad cannot be extricated from standard liberal arguments about free and protected markets, as I have suggested. But I suspect there is another reason for this Muslim rejection of reasoning.

If Muslim protestors have so much to say about their feelings and so little about the Prophet they claim has been insulted, it is because they have rarely paid much attention to the provocations that offend them. To make an argument about blasphemy, in other words, one would have to attend to the offensive image or text, but although a few such analyses exist, they rarely become part of the controversy. I can think only of Iqbal's criticism of the Ahmadis. We have seen how those who rioted against insults to Muhammad in nineteenth-century Bombay were unable to read the texts they found offensive. Similarly, the protests against Rushdie were full of Muslims who refused to read his novel. A book about *The Satanic Verses* written by one of Iran's former culture ministers, therefore, was not only a rarity but played no role in the controversy.[27] And while the Danish cartoons were far more accessible, even these were not available in much of the Muslim world protesting them.

What caused Muslim outrage and injury, then, was not the actual experience of an offensive image or text but rather the rumor of its circulation. And that might also be why so many incidents of blasphemy in Pakistan take as insults apparently innocuous acts like tearing down commercial posters that happen to have Muhammad's name printed on them. Or accusing people of offending the Prophet without describing what they are meant to have said, as this would itself be insulting him. In some famous cases, people have been lynched on the mere rumor of insulting Muhammad. Such events, of course, proliferate in Pakistan and not elsewhere in the Muslim world because it has expanded Macaulay's provision against hurting religious sentiments to make accusations against insulting the Prophet much easier to prosecute, and thus encourage the routing of other conflicts into charges of blasphemy.

The more visible that such crimes against the Prophet become, the less apparent are the insults that define them. And this rise in the circulation of rumors whose details cannot be known makes experiencing their offense impossible. But more than this, it suggests that Muslim outrage is not even linked to the insulting words or pictures that are said to have provoked it. Instead of a visible or audible text that can be taken out of circulation to be analyzed, what causes offense is merely the news of its circulation. Without its circulation as rumor or news the insult does not exist. In some way, of course, we are back to the market here, but one that has been modernized by replacing physical commodities like newspapers and books with immaterial ones like rumors. Or rather, what counts as offense is uncontrolled circulation itself as the market's very essence. The irony, of course, is that Muslims can control this market only by repeating its action in the uncontrolled circulation of their outrage and injury.

The fact that Muslim accounts of the things they find offensive are brief to the point of nonexistence is surely tied up with Muslims' refusal to see or hear them. But if Muslim injury and offense do not result from the experience of an insult to the Prophet, then where does it originate? By separating Muslims' hurt from the words or images said to have caused it, we can arrive at something like an answer. The Muslims' sense of injury, while it may well be linked to larger historical factors such as colonial rule, being an immigrant minority, or subjection to war and oppression, possesses its own logic in the genre of insults to the Prophet, as we have seen. And at the heart of it lies a gap between Muslim complaints and actions. After all, why should insults to Muhammad that are compared with offenses against everything from one's family to the Holocaust lead to such passionate protest?

None of the examples proffered by the protestors themselves to make sense of their hurt matches up to their action. Nor do they have any specifically Islamic argument that can account for it. The complaint, in other words, is prosaic and even banal because it lacks any theological character. But the offense it prompts is often exceptional and entirely out of keeping with this complaint. It is at this inexplicable gap that the Muslim narrative breaks down because there are no words to cross over it. And since they have no words to describe their injury, Muslim protestors may turn to violence. This gap in the logic of Muslim offense represents the absence of the theological in Islam as an agent of history. Passion and violence therefore take the place of the Prophet's missing sovereignty without ever being able to replace it in the infinite cycle of ownership and identification. Perhaps it is the inexplicable intensity of Muslim hurt, which bears no relationship to its proclaimed causes, that has come to represent the only form of transcendence available under the reign of Islam.

From Blasphemy to Desecration

While insulting the Prophet has come to comprise one of the chief grounds of Muslim protest, especially in Europe and North America, it is not the only public offense against their religious sentiments. If blasphemy, to use the Christian term, has taken pride of place in controversies over such offenses, desecration has a much longer and more widespread history. The two most common forms it takes are physical attacks on mosques or shrines and the besmirching or destruction of sacred writ. But here, too, we are faced in modern times with the disappearance of any theological argument on the part of offended Muslims. I have suggested that cases of alleged blasphemy often result in violence because no theological language exists for them in public protest. And I now want to claim that acts of desecration seem to rehearse the sacred element that is otherwise missing from even the most passionate Muslim protest.

The most famous case of desecration of a mosque in modern times is the 1992 destruction of the sixteenth-century Babri Masjid or Babur's Mosque in the North Indian town of Ayodhya.[28] Claimed to have been built on the site of a Hindu temple marking Rama's birthplace, the Babri Masjid was pulled to pieces by a massive crowd after more than a year of violent mobilizations in many parts of the country. Credited with bringing the Bharatiya Janata Party and its Hindu nationalist ideology to power, this campaign and its culmination in the mosque's destruction resulted in well over a thousand deaths, the majority being of Muslims. Yet those who sought to defend the mosque in court and the press rarely if ever made theological arguments. Instead, they disputed the historical claims about a temple having stood in its place, while at the same time referring to India's secular constitution and laws protecting the ownership of private property and the unhindered use of existing religious sites.

The Hindu nationalists calling for a temple to be built on the site also acknowledged the absence of any theological element in the Muslim argument, claiming that mosques were not sacred sites for Muslims and that the Babri Masjid was not even an architecturally significant monument. The mosque's destruction and replacement some thirty years later with a temple, therefore, created a sacred site where one had not existed. But it could only do so by redefining Hinduism in Islamic, or better still, in monotheistic terms. To build a shrine on the site of a sacred figure's birthplace, after all, is not part of any Hindu tradition but is common to Judaism,

Christianity, and Islam. This is why there are no other temples in India marking the birthplace of any deity. The proto-archaeological imagination required to reclaim such sites is also familiar to monotheism. For Muslims have traditionally done so by discovering saintly remains under the ground while Hindus find *swayambhu* or self-produced *lingams* above it.

The first modern instance of religious conflict in Ayodhya occurred in 1855 and had to do not with the Babri Masjid but with a Sunni claim that the Hanuman Garhi temple was built on the site of a mosque.[29] The Shia principality of which Ayodhya was part decided against the Sunnis and in favor of the Hindu ascetics who occupied it. Quite apart from providing Hindu nationalists with precedents, such Muslim claims were recycled in other ways. Those supporting the new temple in Ayodhya, for instance, frequently refer to it as the Mecca or Vatican of Hinduism, thus seeking to create a single religious center for all believers on the monotheistic model. And the temple's pan-Hindu character was reinforced not only by the early funding it received from all over the country, but also by its design, with a South Indian idol of Rama installed in the sanctum. Hindu nationalism is thus locked in a mimetic relationship with its enemy and must literally replace it in a ritual act of sacrifice that reintroduces or reinforces sacredness to Islam.

More common than the desecration of religious monuments are defacements and destructions of the Qur'an. Perhaps its most famous recent example is from the United States, where a pastor named Terry Jones achieved notoriety between 2010 and 2012 by threatening to burn and burning copies of the scripture to protest the alleged imposition of sharia in the United States. He livestreamed the performance on social media, causing much outrage in parts of the Muslim world. There also exists a whole Scandinavian subculture of Qur'an burnings, in protest against Islam or Muslim immigration.[30] This shift in the Nordic countries from the more common debates about blasphemy to desecration is curious. And it has occurred despite the fact that one of the most widespread and damaging controversies over alleged insults to the Prophet started in Denmark in 2005, when the newspaper *Jyllands-Posten* published cartoons of Muhammad that gave rise to violent protests in many parts of the world alongside a boycott of Danish products.

What brings these acts of blasphemy and desecration together are their self-attribution as tests of Muslim tolerance or secularism, which are meant to demonstrate the ability of immigrants to live as good citizens in European democracies. By protesting against such acts, in other words, and thus proving their unwillingness to abide by laws protecting free speech on the one hand and the free use or disposal of private property like Qur'ans on the other, Muslims automatically disqualify themselves from citizenship. In this way such tests operate very much like the kinds of citizenship tests that many European states require of immigrants, though of course in much cruder ways. And, indeed, the latter kind of tests are sometimes put in place to take into account concerns raised by the former. Interestingly absent from this debate about tolerance, however, is any consideration of protest as itself a democratic value that is best represented by Muslim immigrants.

Anti-Islam protests, after all, are sometimes as offensive to public opinion as Muslim ones defending Muhammad or the Qur'an, both occasionally breaking the law in the cause of some higher ideal. And these ideals cannot easily be differentiated between secular and religious ones, since the invocations of free speech on the one side are reflected by claims about freedom of conscience on the other. The right to criticize defended by one party is counterposed with the right to live free from insult or injury by another. The problem with this debate is that the religion meant to be at its center is nowhere to be found. While they may be devout, after all, Muslims protesting against insults to Muhammad or desecrations of the Qur'an tend not to make theological arguments when doing so. And this often leads to their opponents having to argue that Muslims are dissimulating their true intentions. But then the latter also accuse their critics of being disingenuous in their defense of free speech.

Qur'an burnings inherit the free speech vocabulary that had characterized controversies over depictions of the Prophet, even though they make little sense where acts of desecration are concerned. Indeed, burning or banning books like the Qur'an has historically been understood as an example of censorship and so an attack on free speech. And the incoherence of extending this argument from depictions of Muhammad to desecrations of the Qur'an suggests that the shift from one form of criticism to the other is more substantial than superficial. Now the fact that Qur'an burnings must take their justification from insulting depictions of the Prophet only recognizes the latter's priority. For by appropriating and destroying some physical object, such desecrations give rise to a similar kind of argument about ownership as about blasphemy. Does the text "belong" to Muslims in some generic fashion even if particular copies of it do not?

Since anti-Islam activists purchase the Qur'ans they burn, these acts of destruction are also acts of sacrifice. Like the desecration of religious sites, in other words, burning Qur'ans accomplishes much more than claiming possession over them. The act of desecration is the mirror image of a ritual of consecration. Burning the Qur'an, after all, is also an acceptable way of disposing of it since fire is an agent of purity as much as of destruction. But more than this, I argue that in ritually setting the Qur'an alight, its critics are in fact introducing a truly religious and even theological practice into a controversy that lacks both. Given the secular language of Muslim protest, which as we have seen gives rise to much suspicion about the real intentions of such protests, there is a need to make religion visible in the debate. If Muslims will not or cannot deploy a religious vocabulary, then their opponents will have to do so in acts of negative theology that acknowledge the Qur'an's sacred status in the effort to extinguish it.

Here, then, is the ritual element missing from Muslim arguments and protests, where it is manifested in emotion and occasionally violence. In Pakistan, of course, such violence has become endemic for blasphemy as much as for desecration and represents popular sovereignty as mob rule. The act of iconoclasm, we know, repeats and reverses rituals of worship. And the precedent for these acts in countries like Norway is arguably the burnings of stave churches as part of the black metal music subculture of the 1990s. Both cases involve a criticism of religion, though church burnings did not serve as a test of Christian tolerance and were not linked to immigration. Yet, they did seek to avenge a pre-Christian culture, just as anti-Islam activists want to protect a Christian one. While

I am not positing any direct connection between these phenomena, what is interesting about them is the focus on ritual and religion, which in both cases can be retrieved from an opponent only in an act of negative identification.

Capitalism's Religion

Muhammad's vacillating status as person and property, I have argued, tells us about the way in which the vanishing of political and theological authority with the modern emergence of Islam has led to the dominance of a market logic in their place. I conclude this chapter by looking at how this logic ends up destroying even the commodified products of such a market in the name of iconoclasm. But this puts at risk the very history that Muhammad's biography is meant to represent. We saw in the last chapter, for example, that the site of Islam's founding in Mecca came to be valued for its historical role in the career of this new subject. For the rites of pilgrimage had little to do with Muhammad's mission. But what happens when the remains of this history are themselves effaced in the holy city? Does it become a story unattached to any external reality, but rather embodied by the pilgrim as its only medium? This is a question that presents itself to any visitor to both Mecca and Medina.[31]

When in the nineteenth century the Wahhabis started demolishing shrines and other structures associated with the Prophet, his family, and companions that had for centuries been objects of reverence, a thrill of horror passed through the Muslim world, providing an Ottoman army with the best of justifications for dealing with members of the sect as heretics. But in more recent times complaints over Saudi efforts to refashion Mecca have had little traction, and this despite the fact that the alterations to Islam's sacred city are more extensive than any in the past. Hills have been flattened, the houses of Islam's founding figures have been destroyed, and attempts have even been made to interfere with the Kaaba's structure, to say nothing of the rites of pilgrimage. Much of this change is justified by arguing that rebuilding is required to accommodate the ever-increasing number of pilgrims to Mecca, and this might well account for the wide avenues, air-conditioned tunnels, and light railway constructed for easing the traffic of devotees.

But what about replacing sites associated with the Prophet by structures like the American fast-food chains lining the perimeter of the Great Mosque, or a five-star hotel surmounted by a gigantic clock tower looming over the Kaaba? Is Mecca cashing in on its status as one of the world's most important seasonal destinations by reinventing itself as a center of religious tourism? But what kind of tourism is possible in a place whose monumental history is constantly being altered? I suspect the Wahhabi anxiety about idolatry that is expressed in these alterations is intimately connected to the Saudi tolerance of a capitalist culture of impermanence. For rather than turning Mecca into an old-fashioned historical site, one whose monuments become aesthetic and antiquarian fetishes of the kind that are so plentifully available in Rome or Jerusalem, the city's refashioning is meant to accomplish just the opposite. Forbidding idolatry means the loss of awe in the face of something stable and authentic. It is the difference between the pyramids of Giza and those in Las Vegas.

Whatever it is that pilgrims feel in Mecca, then, it increasingly appears to be a city built upon the erasure of historical authenticity. And by ridding itself of such an imagined and idolatrous stability, Mecca, like Medina, offers the visitor an experience that is as abstract as capitalism itself. A good example is Medina's Masjid al-Qiblatayn or Mosque of the Two Directions, which possessed prayer niches facing different directions, one toward Jerusalem and the other toward Mecca. It is said that there, Muhammad changed the direction of prayer from one city to the other. In 1987 the mosque, dating back to the Prophet's time, was torn down and rebuilt in a nondescript modern style ostensibly to accommodate more worshippers. But the new building now contained only one prayer niche, facing Mecca. And yet it is still called by the old name and visited by pilgrims eager to pray in an historical site despite its lacking anything from this past. Only its name and the pilgrims' presence are there to call it up. This is true of many such "historical" mosques in the holy cities, including that of the Prophet himself.

Now Mecca and Medina had always been great marketplaces, so the commercial aspect of the pilgrims' peregrinations is not new, but rather the lack of any historical object in the cities' urban spaces apart from the worshippers' experience itself. And in this way the abstraction that has always been part of modern Islam joins hands with capitalism to produce the most rational and indeed futuristic of religions. Is it this achievement that allows Mecca's transformation to go unremarked by the millions who in visiting it are schooled in the lessons of modernity? Visible forms of religiosity, like Muslims' veils, caps, and beards, that make Islam appear as an "alternative" culture in the capitalist West tell us little about the West's apotheosis in Mecca. Instead, think of the Saudi or Emirati woman whose fashionable European clothes are hidden underneath her "traditional" Muslim garments. Whether seen as a concession to public opinion or not, what is interesting about this sartorial combination is that it takes the products of Western capitalism into the most intimate part of the Muslim's life.

In earlier times, by contrast, Muslims and others who had to contend with Europe's colonial powers often took on a Western appearance outdoors or in public while reserving traditional modes of apparel and comportment for their private lives. For many Muslims today, however, whether minorities in Europe or majorities elsewhere, the situation is reversed, with clothing and other signs of tradition or authenticity on display only to the outside world, while the modern West is brought into the innermost recesses of their lives. It thus becomes difficult to determine what exactly is profound and what superficial in the making of pious Muslims today, because in however conservative and moralistic a way, their embrace of Western media, technology, and fashion marks Muslim devotees as being far more modern than their Christian or Jewish counterparts. And in this sense their visible distinctiveness in Europe belongs in the same generic category of subculture as that defining punks, goths, or skinheads.

While Muslims visibly marked by their dress and comportment may seem to comprise one of many alternative subcultures, unlike many others they do not usually aim to counter the capitalist cult of commodities by their distinctively alternative status. Whereas other subcultures inevitably fall prey to commodification the more popular they become, Muslim difference begins as a commodity in the marketplace. If pious female, but now also male, attire requires the existence of specialized shops that turn it into fashion, everything from dietary restrictions to beard lengths calls for the marketing of specialized services. Even more telling are the sharia-compliant financial instruments of Islamic banking and the increasingly institutionalized procedures of halal certification for a fee. Rather than attempting to escape capitalism, these Muslim practices revel in it. While the Western commodities consumed by pious Muslims find their way unremarked into the most intimate parts of their lives, in other words, such Islamic goods and services are celebrated as markers of identity.

But does attending to the commodity's particularity as representing Muslim identity not contradict what I have been describing as Islam's abstraction? It is possible to say, of course, that the commodification of Islamic attributes simply reduces them to the abstraction of capitalism. For they are all valued in terms of a cash equivalent, whatever emotional or symbolic power such items also possess. In this sense the very effort to manufacture a distinctive Islamic identity entails its subordination to the marketplace. Muslim difference therefore becomes an illustration of the social uniformity made possible by capitalist relations of production and consumption. Rather than mitigating or even dissimulating the abstraction of modern Islam, the concrete particularities of Muslim practice actually ground it. And we shall see that the commodification of Islam in the making of an apparently particularistic Muslim identity goes along with the destruction of all noncommodified forms in the name of iconoclasm.

Abstraction is what connects the iconoclastic aspect of Islam manifested in Wahhabism to capitalism. This is not an entirely novel argument, with the German philosopher Hegel, for instance, claiming in the nineteenth century that it was Islam's abstraction and rejection not simply of images, but of all things solid and stable, that made it into the most modern of religions. Abstraction, he maintained, led to fanaticism defined as the attachment to a pure idea, something that he thought was revealed in the French Revolution as, in some sense, a Muslim event.[32] Whatever the merits of this argument, it tells us that there exists a long and respectable tradition that would link Islam to what is most modern about Europe, in both its positive and negative aspects. In general, the attempt to banish one idol inevitably ends up installing another in its place, if only in the form of the commodity fetish. But what if it is capitalism as a whole rather than the sum of its commodified parts that is worshipped in Mecca?

Deployed though they are on flags, architecture, and the like, abstract symbols of Islam like the crescent and star, the calligraphic name of God, or verses from the Qur'an rarely become objects of veneration in their own right. And in the absence of other permissible figures, Muslim iconography in modern times relies heavily upon buildings, the Qur'an itself as a book, and any other object on which the name or words of God have been inscribed. Among these objects I find the clock most interesting, since even without being etched by some divine pen it has become one of the most popular of Muslim icons. As a sign of modern technology, of course, clocks and clockwork were popular in eighteenth-century Europe as well as Asia and Africa, with the Deists' God himself being called a clockmaker. The profusion of clocks that continue to be embedded in the gateways of mosques and shrines, installed in towers, and otherwise hung on the walls of religious and secular edifices, however, suggests another kind of obsession in the Muslim world.

Given the call to prayer, clocks seem to be redundant, even if they may represent such themes as the transitoriness of the world or the coming end of time. Modeled on Big Ben in London, though much bigger than it, the Makkah Clock Royal Tower mentioned above is surely the perfect idol for modern Muslims, its moving parts and relationship with numbers representing the marriage of entity and abstraction. This giant clock is set atop a luxury hotel, from which the Kaaba becomes an expensive view. It dominates the city not only as its great alternative attraction but also as a kind of metronome for all that occurs there. Indeed, the ceaseless revolution of its hands can be said to mirror Mecca's most important ritual, the circumambulation of the Kaaba viewed as the central point of a living clock. The clock tower is a visible symbol of the mechanized labor and endless consumption that Saudi Arabia's resource economy makes possible.

Its massive physical presence also diminishes the Kaaba and its sanctuary without claiming any sacrality of its own. But then the clock tower's task is precisely to destroy any such sacred quality or at least to replace its historical permanence with the impermanence of consumption as a form of the commodity's pleasurable destruction. And with the elimination of any visible sign of the Prophet's life in Mecca and Medina, what survives of it is only the Muslim's imaginative reexperience of this past. Evicted from the external reality of any monumental or historical trace, to say nothing of relics like his grave in Medina, which is impossible to access, Muhammad is now available to his followers through their own experience of his biography and career in narrative and pilgrimage. And in this way he has become an intimate part of their lives, if only to reprise the now familiar roles of a figure who can be either identified with or possessed.

CHAPTER THREE

The Idols Return

W HY DO INSULTS TO the Prophet and on occasion the Qur'an sometimes provoke global outrage but offenses against God never do? Shabbir Akhtar, whom we met in the last chapter at the head of Rushdie's critics in Britain, claimed it was because Jews, Christians, and Muslims shared the same God, while the "endorsement of Muhammad's prophethood was the distinguishing feature of the Muslim outlook."[1] In other words Muhammad as God's final messenger was vulnerable to attack because he belonged to Muslims alone. And this despite the fact that God is undeniably the more sacred figure of the two and in fact the ultimate subject of theology. Blasphemy as such is therefore not an issue in these debates, but rather contestations over some form of intellectual property. Yet we shall see that God, too, has been appropriated into the narrative of Muslim ownership here and there, in a sign of his own theological disappearance as a transcendent being.

Starting late in the last century, for example, two controversies about who owns God have emerged among Muslims, one in Pakistan and the other in Malaysia. The earlier but also less important one politically has to do with altering a centuries-old Persian expression of farewell, *Khuda hafiz* ("Lord keep you"), to *Allah hafiz* ("Allah keep you") in Pakistan and to a much smaller extent in

India. An example of the Islamizing policies adopted by the military dictator Zia ul Haq in the 1980s, the new expression was preferred because while "Khuda" supposedly referred to anyone's God, and even a human lord or master, "Allah" was supposedly the specifically Muslim name for him.[2] The near-universal adoption of this new expression, at least in public, was meant to stress the specifically Islamic identity of its users since it repudiated the older one's courtly and secular contexts and could be uttered only when speaking to other Muslims.

While the debate over God's ownership in Pakistan occurs only between Muslims, however, the more recent and dangerous controversy in Malaysia has to do with Christians using the word "Allah" for God. Leading to lawsuits and attacks against churches in 2009, this debate remains confined to Malaysia despite the fact that in neighboring Indonesia, too, with a very similar language, "Allah" remains one of two standard terms for God across religious boundaries. Indeed, it is controversial there only among Christians themselves, because of the emergence of a Zionist church that advocates using the Hebrew Tetragrammaton for God instead. And it has been argued that the situation in Malaysia is so distinctive because the Malay ethnic group needs to consolidate its bare majority in the country by fetishizing all signs of Malay identity, among which religion has come to be seen as one of the few remaining survivors.[3]

Whatever their specific circumstances, however, what is interesting about both debates is that while they both have to do with ownership, as did the controversies over insulting Muhammad, neither involves identifying with God in any way. And this means that unlike his prophet, God has not become vulnerable to attack, even if the use of his name by non-Muslims can allegedly seduce true believers into confusing him with other deities. Important about these regional and fairly low-grade controversies, therefore, and distinguishing them from the ones about insulting Muhammad, is their focus on making "Allah" into a proper name. Yet in Arabic it is not a name at all but simply the word for "God," which is why the use of "Allah" by Christians in the Middle East remains uncontroversial. Why, then, has "Allah" become a proper name elsewhere?

It is not his messenger with whom God is associated in these debates but Islam, which we saw in the first chapter had to be turned into a proper name before it could become an actor in global history. The fact that God also needs to be made into such a name, however, turns him not into a subject in his own right but instead into the object or property of Islam as the only true agent of history. This is why his defenders in places like Pakistan and Malaysia are so keen to do what is otherwise unacceptable by questioning Allah's transcendence and universality in confining him to Islam and so Muslims. He has become the personification of Islam as an abstract actor and in this way shares in its subjectivity while remaining subordinate to it. Whereas Muhammad's subordination to Islam opened the possibility of his impersonation, however, God's allows for the return of his opposite in the figure of the idol.

One way of distinguishing between the threat of Muhammad's impersonation and God's replacement by idols is to reflect upon a popular Persian expression that provides Shabbir Akhtar with his book's title. "Be careful with Muhammad" is the second half of a venerable saying that begins "Be crazy with God" and that Akhtar ignores, as he does God, throughout his book.[4] Seeming to acknowledge the intimacy possible with God but not his messenger, something that has long been true in a number of Muslim literary traditions, this expression is often deployed by those defending the Prophet from insult. Yet it is misplaced since Muhammad has become intimate as a figure of identification for them while God is nowhere to be seen. Meanwhile, the use even today of apparently blasphemous statements about God in poetry, such as comparing him to women, idols, and unbelievers, would be unacceptable for the Prophet in verse.

As a prophet and so lawgiver Muhammad is associated with the social order he is responsible for establishing, while God transcends this order and is more closely linked to its end in the apocalypse. It is therefore God's very transcendence in Muslim tradition, one that is radically antinomian or beyond the reach of law, that makes an intimate relationship with him possible outside and even against its social order. Because he is absolutely different from human beings, God can be known only by his opposite in the figures of idols, women, and infidels, with poets describing their relationship with him in terms of proscribed worship, illicit love, and drunken passion.

Rather than comprising some hedonistic genre, such verses with their multiple meanings were quoted in the most serious theological tracts. Comparing God to kings, men, or believers, on the other hand, would be blasphemous, even if divine authority has always been known by analogy to monarchical and patriarchal rule.

Unlike the Prophet's impersonator, in other words, the idol who threatens to replace God belongs in a very different genealogy. While the early days of Islam saw the appearance of a number of false prophets, those prophets never came to represent important literary or even theological figures in Muslim history. Idols, however, are to be found in profusion, their defeat and destruction permitting them to be incorporated into Muslim literary tradition as figures of antinomian attraction alongside infidels and women. All of these personages, for example, come together in an Urdu couplet by the last Mughal emperor, Bahadur Shah II, who wrote under the pen name of Zafar, or victory. It was a name that had its own pathos and irony, given that the emperor was removed from his by then largely decorative throne and sent into exile by the British after allowing himself to be made the figurehead of a mutiny by their own Indian troops in 1857.

In translation the couplet reads, "for God's sake, puritan, do not lift the Kaaba's veil, lest that pagan idol appear."[5] The Kaaba is a cubical building draped in black cloth that stands in Mecca at the heart of Muslim devotion, since believers prostrate toward it in their ritual prayers several times a day. Before it was emptied by Muhammad, the Kaaba had supposedly housed many idols, of which the three most powerful were female ones called Al-Lat, Al-Manat, and Al-Uzza. Zafar compares the building to a woman and rhetorically warns his more puritanical coreligionists not to lift her veil in case the idol underneath is revealed. The Prophet had placed an empty shrine at the center of Muslim devotion, with its veil concealing a void as the perfect sign of an invisible God. But Zafar suggests that in becoming a site of Muslim devotion the Kaaba had itself become an idol and thus represented the return of one of the goddesses Muhammad had ousted from it.

Zafar's verse possesses a number of aesthetically pleasing implications. Since women are not allowed to veil during the pilgrimage to Mecca and therefore in the sight of God, it is the Kaaba that has taken on their female identity. And yet its veil is meant to conceal the idolatry at the core of Islam and thus the infidel's survival within it like a bit of spolia. Zafar seems to be saying that it is impossible to get rid of the idol or infidel from Islam, just as it is impossible to exclude women from the world of men. For the very act of iconoclasm (destroying idols), conversion (saving infidels), or concealment (protecting men from womanly seduction) ends up lodging these idols, unbelievers, and women in the innermost life of Islam. Their inseparability had made these poetic figures into coevals, each one capable of standing in for the other and for God. And this way of thinking about idols as part of a triad was likely the most common form in which they appeared in the Muslim literary imagination for centuries.

One of the couplet's suggestions is that revealing the idol at Islam's heart could lead to her forsaking the Kaaba. Indeed, the hemistich I have translated as "lest that pagan idol appear" can also be read "lest that pagan idol leave," since the word "appear" (*nikle*) can be used to mean "leave" in the same way that the English phrase "to turn out" can mean "to end up as" or "to expel." To unveil the idol is therefore to lose it, Zafar seems to be saying, in a characteristic reference to premodern ideas about the esoteric or hidden reality of literary as much as political and theological narratives. These could be spoken of only allegorically and so preferably in poetry or philosophy. While still available as a specialized delectation in old-fashioned verse, this way of thinking no longer retains a more general or philosophical import, and so the idol, too, can no longer remain within Islam but must be hunted down and destroyed in sometimes obsessive and violent ways.

It was the loss of Muslim power in the nineteenth century that allowed the idol and infidel (if not the woman, as we shall see in the next chapter) to escape the aesthetic and philosophical tradition of Islam's imperial past. SherAli Tareen argues that the loss of political sovereignty in India resulted in efforts to purify Muslim lives of courtly and pagan practices while at the same time imitating this lost sovereignty by hardening religious boundaries between the communities inhabiting a newly colonized society.[6] And it was in this situation that idolatry suddenly came to represent a living rather than merely an historical threat. Iconoclasm, of course, has had a long if uneven career through both Muslim and Christian history, its first modern manifestation being the Salafi or Wahhabi movement of the late eighteenth and early nineteenth centuries. The term "Salafi" refers to the *aslaf,* or pious forebears who are to be emulated; and "Wahhabi," to Muhammad ibn Abd al-Wahhab, the most important Salafi thinker in Arabia.

The kind of iconoclasm that defines Salafi practice focuses on physical objects as idols and ritual practices as idolatry. Particularly important are courtly and other ceremonies including acts of obeisance to kings or even the Prophet that should be reserved for God alone, as well as pilgrimages to shrines or the tombs of saintly personages long venerated by Muslims. In more recent times pre-Islamic monuments, too, have been condemned as idols, not because Muslims revere them, but because their very existence stands as a reproach to Islam. This form of iconoclasm has been picked up by militants in our own day and has led to the destruction of antiquities in a criticism of the priority the West is alleged to give dead monuments over living Muslims. But such conceptions of idolatry are neither very widespread nor interesting. Far more important intellectually as much as politically has been the effort to identify modern institutions and ideological abstractions rather than old-fashioned objects and practices as idols.

Abstraction is fundamental to modern Islam not only in the ideas it is associated with, but also in the physical manifestation of those ideas in design and architecture. Abstract modernism as a European art form has been so popular in the Muslim world because it rejects the idolatry of images for geometry. One of the more interesting aspects of Muslim social life, then, has been the way in which it has incorporated the cultural forms of high modernism and transformed the traditional arts of calligraphy and the arabesque in the process. But abstraction has a much deeper meaning for Islam, which we have seen has itself come to be imagined as an abstract system. What threatens Islam or is capable of posing as its rival, therefore, is not any kind of idolatrous object or ritual but another abstract and global subject. Beginning early in the twentieth century, then, ideologies like nationalism and communism, or institutions like monarchy and democracy, come to be described as idols.

In his Persian epic of 1935 called the *Javid Nama* (Book of Immortality), for instance, Muhammad Iqbal describes the "assembly of the gods of the ancient peoples." Its idols have come alive again not only because of the archaeologist's and the orientalist's work in recovering ancient civilizations, but because such artifacts and histories were then taken up as sources for the narrow new ideologies of racism and nationalism. These have replaced the philosophical and so universal ideals of all religions with material desires fostered by a modern civilization founded on capitalism. One of these idols, Baal, sings of how "the days of joy have returned to the world, religion has been routed by sovereignty and lineage. ... Ancient gods, our time has come!"[7] Iqbal was one of the earliest thinkers to attend to the idolatry of what we might call abstract materialism, of which he thought communism the most powerful exemplar since it sought to destroy the idol of commodities by a superior version of materialism. But he was not the only one to do so, and soon Muslim thinkers of many intellectual persuasions had made such ideologies the chief new form of idolatry even as they described Islam itself as an ideology.

Doing Without God

In the quotation above, Iqbal names sovereignty or the state (*mulk*) as a new idol leading people astray, and it soon became the most important one in Muslim thought. This is in part because sovereignty forms the basis of every political order and ideology and so can represent them all. But more importantly, it involves delivering even the most abstract of social systems into the keeping of one or more human beings, however exceptional or temporary their authority may be. While communism, for example, might be Islam's rival, what really makes it unacceptable is the sovereignty its general secretary, politburo, or party exercises. The absolute authority of any human being over others is what Muslim thinkers found objectionable because of the tyranny contained in the very idea of sovereignty. They imagined Islam as a self-regulating system, much like the economy, that required only administration and occasional fixing rather than sovereign power.

Iqbal himself did not think along these lines, his criticism of sovereignty being rather its unequal distribution among human

beings and so reliance on the obedience of some to others. It was
bad enough if this obedience was enforced tyrannically, but even
worse if it came to be accepted voluntarily since this meant that the
sovereign had really become an idol. But the great critic of sovereignty in Muslim thought was a fellow Indian who had communi-
cated with Iqbal and professed to have been guided by him. Abul
Ala Maududi was a journalist who moved to Pakistan after independence and became the founder of the Jamaat-e Islami or Islamic
Society, the most important Islamist party in all three of British
India's successor states. Himself the leading Islamist thinker worldwide, Maududi's ideas were developed in the aftermath of the First
World War at a time when Indian nationalism became a mass
movement for the first time under Gandhi's leadership.

In those days and like most of his coreligionists, Maududi was
part of this national movement, which had made common cause
with Muslim efforts to protect the status and sovereignty of the caliph after the Ottoman defeat. He even wrote an adulatory biography of the Mahatma, which the British banned before it could be
published. And though he parted ways with Indian nationalism
eventually, Maududi continued to be influenced by its Gandhian
form in a number of ways that included the idea of noncooperation. Like Gandhi as much as Iqbal, he was deeply suspicious of the
state as a political form, the violent logic of whose sovereignty all
three men thought was most perfectly manifested in colonialism.
Already in 1909, for instance, the Mahatma had famously compared nationalism understood as a quest for Indian sovereignty to
the desire for English rule without Englishmen.[8]

In other words, although anticolonial struggles are seen as
claims by subject peoples to assert their political sovereignty, this
vision ignores a remarkably powerful tradition that distrusts the
state both as a product and as an agent of empire. It was a tradition
that drew upon anarchism, itself the dominant form of radical politics at the turn of the twentieth century. This is not surprising for a
time when antistatist ideas were popular the world over, having already taken on a religious aspect in the work of men like Tolstoy
and Gandhi. Anarchism died in the West after the First World War,
at least in part because communism assumed its radical role with
the establishment of the Soviet Union. But it lived on in colonized

societies and among religious groups for which the state was considered illegitimate. Gandhi and Maududi, then, can be seen as res-
cuing the principle of anarchism from its Bolshevik appropriation
in Lenin's development of Engels's theory about the "withering
away of the state."

In colonial India the debate about anarchism took the form of a
choice between social reform or political power as a national priority. It was a choice that represented a disagreement between those
Indians who thought that political liberty should precede social
equality and bring it about, and others who feared that such liberty
if achieved without a social transformation would only perpetuate
inequality by empowering majorities and the powerful at the expense of minorities and the powerless. This difference not only
characterized the relations between religious communities, primarily Hindus and Muslims, but also came to define those between
higher and lower castes. Both sides adopted the liberal notion that
a gradual process of education and legislation was required to create a nation made up of equals in India, whether this was to occur
by way of social reform before the achievement of political freedom
or after it.

Those opting for the precedence of political freedom, mostly in
the Indian National Congress but including revolutionaries on the
Marxist left and the Hindu right, entertained a prospective vision
of this pedagogy and the fraternity it was meant to achieve; while a
diverse range of groups, led by the Muslim League but including
Indian liberals as well as conservatives and low-caste leaders, entertained a proleptic understanding that saw tyranny and violence in
the achievement of political liberty without any prior commitment
to social equality. Muslim and low-caste leaders voiced this argument most eloquently, claiming that the Congress advocated political freedom at the expense of social reform to place the powerless
in a new kind of democratic bondage to the powerful. Each side
also blamed the other for bad faith. The Congress accused its rivals
of loyalty to Britain, while the League blamed its opponents for
wanting to replace British with Hindu colonialism.

Without being detained by the accuracy of these polemics, we
can see that they represented opposing political principles. Maududi
staked his position in the social camp but in a far more radical way

than most of his compatriots, including those in the Muslim League, which he condemned as a party of secular elites who simply wanted a nation-state of their own. The problem that occupied him, in other words, was not the conventional one of how to recover sovereignty but the even more difficult question of how to remain free by renouncing it. This he wanted to do because he thought that sovereignty was a theological rather than a political category and so belonged to God alone. Having studied the works of its European theorists, including Jean Bodin and Thomas Hobbes, Maududi came to the conclusion that sovereignty's unitary and absolute form could never be instantiated in political life. For no human agency, individual or collective, was able to exercise such power. And it was precisely because the ideal of sovereign power could never be fulfilled that tyranny entered the world to compensate for its shortcomings.[9]

Instead of merely accusing those who claimed sovereignty of usurping a divine prerogative, Maududi argued that their inevitable failure to do so gave rise to violence as a way of closing the gap between sovereignty's ideal and its reality. By reserving it for God, therefore, he was in fact expelling sovereignty and, with it, theology itself from the world of humanity. Gandhi had dealt with the problem of sovereignty by dispersing it among all the individuals in society, where it took the shape of their willingness to make nonviolent sacrifices for principles at the cost of their interests and even lives. Maududi, however, did not trust even this fragmented if truly anarchistic idea of sovereignty and wanted to get rid of it altogether so as to replace what Lenin, after Engels, had called the "government of men" with the "administration of things." And whereas Lenin had pushed this withering away of the state into an undefined future, Maududi thought it could be achieved very quickly by deploying Islamic law against the state.

What made the sacred law so important for Maududi was not just its moral truth or legitimacy among Muslims but the fact that it was hidebound and archaic. Since the law was apparently impervious to human alteration and founded so long ago as to be free from present-day accusations of bias, he thought it was neutral to the influence of contemporary interests. It might even be said to constitute the detritus of a divine sovereignty whose active agency had vanished from the world. And this meant that the law could not easily be changed or manipulated by the state or any other authority and thus served as a check on the human desire for sovereignty that Maududi considered a form of idolatry: "All persons who exercise unqualified dominion over a group of men, who impose their will upon others, who make them their instruments and seek to control their destinies in the same manner as Pharaoh and Nimrod did in the heyday of their power, are essentially claimants to godhood, though the claim may be tacit, veiled and unexpressed. And those who serve and obey them admit their godhood even if they do not say so by word of mouth."[10]

The sacred law, then, was meant to be interpreted in a narrow and purely administrative way by religious scholars outside the ambit of the state and its legislative, executive, and judicial institutions. In this way, it represented some version of the separation of powers as a constitutional principle. Apart from his institutional solution to the problem of sovereignty, which we have seen relies on the expulsion of theology from politics, Maududi offers an interesting historical account of its disappearance. In his 1966 book *Khilafat-o Mulukiyyat* (Caliphate and Monarchy) Maududi grapples with the problem of how to manage the sovereignty conventionally attributed to the caliph even after the institution's abolition.[11] To begin with, he describes the caliphate as a divine trust limited in its power and confined only to the most pious individuals. Not satisfied with these restrictions, however, he goes on to praise the decline of the caliphate into a symbolic office well before the rise of European empires. For however despotic they might have been, the kings who took power from the caliphs were unable to claim the latter's theological status and therefore sovereignty. And this meant that religious scholars became the protectors of Islam as a purely social entity.

The decline and final abolition of the caliphate was therefore providential, for it preserved the institution as an abstraction whose ideals could be fulfilled by presidents, parliaments, and the people. Yet these people and institutions could do this only variously and piecemeal, without any of them ever assuming the office itself. And in this way the caliphate was reduced to a function within a system, its sovereignty the mere shadow of an absent God.

Indeed, one reason why God had to be expelled from human affairs along with the sovereignty that belonged to him was because
the existence of both was premised upon the vesting of absolute
power in either a person or a class of people. And this way of
thinking about power stood in opposition to Islam as a system
whose agency was purely abstract in a way that couldn't be identified as being either sacred or secular. These categories, after all, depended upon the division of society into domains like the public
and the private that were irrelevant to Islam conceived as a global
subject.

Because sovereignty and therefore politics itself as an autonomous field of action has been expelled from human affairs along
with God, conflict becomes impermissible in Maududi's vision of a
moral society. This is because its escalation beyond or outside the
law would threaten to bring the idol of sovereignty back to life.
Like Gandhi in this respect, Maududi's social or rather antipolitical
ideal is defined by an obsession with segregation and parallelism in
order to prevent the emergence of such conflict. For the Mahatma
as much as Maududi, therefore, this meant conceiving of relations
between men and women, upper and lower castes or classes, and
Muslims and non-Muslims in terms of a harmonious interaction of
separate functions in which the possibility of competition and so
conflict was minimized. Each man, of course, had his own idea of
what these relations should look like, but both of them envisioned
a society divested of antagonism and so politics as we understand
it. This was the conclusion to which their development of anarchist
ideas had driven them.

If Maududi's ideas emerged in the context of Indian nationalism and were of a piece with those of his contemporaries like Gandhi, he was nevertheless singularly responsible for globalizing these
notions by way of Islam. In many ways what has remained a minor
tradition of social and political thought in India assumed a truly
global countenance through Islamism. The Mahatma, of course,
had no desire to place limits on the state and its sovereignty in any
institutional fashion, as Maududi did, and he relied instead on the
dispersed and sacrificial sovereignty of individuals defending the integrity of the social realm against the political. Maududi, however,
though he never managed to control the new Pakistani state to his

satisfaction, was nevertheless largely responsible for having all three iterations of its constitution reserve sovereignty for God and thus expel it from the grasp of human beings. In this way, Maududi and with him the Pakistani state sought to exit the logic of political theology. As deployed by figures like the jurist Carl Schmitt from the middle of the twentieth century, this term refers to the historical translation of theological categories into secular politics, with sovereignty being the chief example of the process.[12] Islamism, and perhaps modern Islam itself, resists this logic and as we shall see attempts to shut political life off from the theological by making the latter unavailable in Muslim life.

Pakistan is probably the first and only modern state to explicitly renounce sovereignty. Its first constitution, from 1956, includes as the initial sentence of the document's preamble a text from the Objectives Resolution of 1949, which states that "sovereignty over the entire Universe belongs to Allah Almighty alone and the authority which He has delegated to the state of Pakistan, through its people for being exercised within the limits prescribed by Him is a sacred trust."[13] This formulation was retained in the 1962 constitution but altered slightly in the one from 1973, which omitted mention of the "state of Pakistan" as the medium through which some version of divine sovereignty was delegated to its citizens.[14] While the authority and instrument of this delegation remain unknown, its limits are repeatedly stressed in the body of the constitution, which requires all laws to be in conformity with the Qur'an and the Prophet's tradition. But making the people an indirect because institutionally unanchored recipient of God's sovereignty as a trust leaves it a free-floating power that can be claimed by anyone in their name.

Clearly the result of a political compromise, Pakistan's constitution has been interpreted differently by its secular leaders and religious authorities since 1956, when the country became the world's first Islamic republic. In good liberal style the former have freely drawn the most general ideals from scripture, while the latter have typically focused on specific provisions of Islamic jurisprudence. Rather than a quarrel between modern and traditional Muslims, both sides agreed that Islam's role in the state was ideological (*nazariyati*) since they conceived of it as an abstract system meant to

produce human freedom. This is why Islam was so frequently compared to communism as its chief model and rival. In Lenin's view, of
course, sovereignty was a temporary power held by the communist
party as it sought to destroy the state through the dictatorship of
the proletariat. And he used the word "dictatorship" to signal the
transient and necessarily violent form that sovereignty took as a
weapon seized from the capitalist order to be turned against it.

While nobody in the Pakistani debate on sovereignty envisioned it as an instrument to be used against the state in this way,
Maududi's conception of the Islamist party as the Leninist vanguard of a coming revolution does lend that party the potential
role of running a temporary dictatorship. Yet this would mean laying claim to a more fulsome version of sovereignty than Maududi
himself wanted, and so it had to remain institutionally disconnected even in theory. We can see this in the Pakistani constitution,
where despite the president being invested with the power to suspend or override the law in times of emergency, neither the president's nor any other office of state has been formally vested with
sovereignty. It remains, in other words, a free-floating power in the
constitution since God alone can exercise such power in an unfettered manner. And I suspect its unsettled or constrained status in
Pakistan is what paradoxically allows sovereignty to assume its
most extreme form there in the coup.

It is not that Pakistan's coups and suspensions of constitutional
freedoms have been caused by its renunciation of sovereignty or
refusal to vest it in any office. Rather, the constitution's effort to
limit sovereignty, even if only rhetorically, ends up making it an ex-
traconstitutional power in the political imagination. Military
coups, for example, are brought into a constitutional framework
once legitimized by Pakistan's supreme court, but they begin outside it without presidential assent as required by the constitution's
emergency provisions. Similarly, the constitution's Islamic provisions, because they, too, are not fully vested in any authority or institution, routinely provide the justification not only for coups in
the name of moral renewal, but also for mass protests in causes
such as blasphemy. The attempt to limit sovereignty, in other
words, results in its spectral return as limitless violence insofar as it
is justified in the language of the very constitution it breaks apart.

Sovereignty Reclaimed

By the time Iran entered into history as the world's second Islamic republic following its revolution in 1979, Maududi's conception of a state limited in its sovereign power had changed drastically. Already in 1970, the Ayatollah Khomeini had delivered a set of lectures in the Shia shrine city of Najaf that came to be published as a celebrated treatise called the *Vilayat-e Faqih* (Guardianship of the Jurist).[15] Eventually absorbed into the new Iranian constitution, its thesis was that the jurists who represented religious authority in the absence of the Hidden Imam, until his messianic return, should also administer the state. Unlike Maududi's vision of a state constrained by such scholars from the outside, in other words, Khomeini not only put them in direct control of it but seemed to have no interest in the withering away of its sovereignty. And yet, like Maududi, he, too, was harshly critical of the idolatry manifested in the sovereignty of the shah, who was overthrown by the Islamic Revolution.

Describing the shah and other illegitimate claimants to sovereignty by the term *taghut*, or tyrant, Khomeini compared them to figures like the Pharaoh who persecuted Moses and claimed divinity for himself. The *taghut* was therefore also an idol, and Khomeini repeated Maududi's anarchistic claim that no human being should be in a position to rule over others since God was the only sovereign. In practice this meant that "law is actually the sovereign [*hakim*]," with government requiring not legislation but interpretation. Yet he was willing to put jurists in charge of the state.[16] In part this had to do with the fact that unlike the divided and unorganized Sunni religious leadership Maududi had to deal with, Khomeini could count on an institutionally coherent class of Shia jurists to assume office. In this sense his idea of a revolutionary vanguard was much closer to the communist party than Maududi's. But as in the latter's political theory, the Ayatollah had them exercise a supervisory function over the people's elected representatives.

Khomeini could so easily insert jurists into the state because it had come to represent Islam as a system rather than threatening God's sovereignty. The jurist, in other words, did not impersonate God, the Prophet, or the Imam by assuming sovereignty but instead performed their duties as a set of institutional functions (*vazifeh*) divorced from their spiritual status (*maqam*). These sacred figures were no longer even seen as persons but had been reduced to their roles within a system, and it was these abstract and institutional duties that the jurist took on. This way of thinking differed radically from traditional conceptions of divine delegation, in which religious authorities were seen as the Hidden Imam's deputies (*vakil*) and saintly ones as inheriting his charisma either by blood or through a Neoplatonic chain of emanations. That is why any qualified person could perform the functions Khomeini describes and in doing so literally take the place of the Prophet or Imam as his successor. Instead of reneging on Maududi's argument against claiming sovereignty, therefore, Khomeini actually fulfilled it by divesting such power of any personal status to make an institutional function out of it.

But Maududi's ghost was not so easily laid to rest. In January 1988, the man who would succeed Khomeini as supreme leader referred in the Friday prayers that he led in Tehran to a recent debate about the revolutionary state's economic plans. Ali Khamenei sought to interpret Khomeini's opinion that the state could oblige the owners and managers of businesses to deal more justly with their workers even if this broke the conventions governing private contracts in Islamic law. Khamenei states that "this work, this measure by an Islamic government does not mean smashing accepted Islamic laws and decisions."[17] Khomeini responded in an open letter a few days later disputing this interpretation: "It seems from Your Eminence's declaration in the Friday Prayers that you do not consider proper the absolute velayat [guardianship] which was given by God to the Noble Prophet (Peace and blessings be upon him!) and is the most important of divine commandments and takes precedence over all commandments of the sharia."[18] Instead of the specific provisions of the sacred law, in other words, Khomeini was interested in the authority of the Prophet to set them in place as well as to act outside them on his own cognizance. And it was this authority, or rather its function, that he thought the Islamic state should have at its disposal.

Khomeini went on to argue that if the Prophet's authority was no longer required because it had been displaced by the law he brought, then surely it had been reduced to a merely historical incident with no further meaning: "If a government's authority was within the framework of the secondary divine commandments, I must submit that turning over divine government and the absolute velayat to the Prophet of Islam (Peace and blessings be upon him!) is an empty and meaningless phenomenon and point out the consequence of this, that no one has any need of it."[19] The Prophet, in other words, could be a living figure in Islam only by the state perpetuating his political function. And this authority took precedence over the law itself, with Khomeini going so far as to claim, "I must submit that government, which is a branch of the absolute velayat of the Prophet of God (Peace and blessings be upon him!) is one of Islam's primary commandments and takes priority over all secondary commandments, even prayer, fasting, and hajj."[20]

In one sense the Ayatollah's audacity here bears comparison with nineteenth-century liberals, like Syed Ameer Ali, who had subordinated the particularities of the law to what they thought was its spirit, ideal, or intention. But Khomeini doesn't follow such an interpretive strategy and instead derives the imperative of sovereignty from a process of juridical reasoning. And yet he is able to do so only because, like Ameer Ali as much as Maududi, he understands Islam as an historical agent that takes the abstract form of an ideological system. Islam and the revolutionary republic that represents it thus have interests (*masalih*) that take priority over the law: "The government may unilaterally dissolve legitimate treaties which it made with the people should they be contrary to the interests of the country and Islam. It may prevent anything which is contrary to the interests of Islam, whether it must be followed unquestionably or not, as long as this is the case. It may temporarily prevent the hajj, which is an important divine obligation, should it be against the interests of the Islamic country."[21]

This vision appears, for the most part, to mirror modern ideas of sovereignty as a power that underwrites the political order without having to be manifested. It is only at moments of crisis that sovereign power reveals itself as an exception to the norm, whether this involves asking citizens to die or kill for it or temporarily restricting their short-term liberties in the long-term interests of the state. But that is not quite true of Khomeini's political thought. For unlike the notion of sovereignty associated with the work of the jurist Carl Schmitt, the Islamic Republic's power to suspend the law is not inevitably linked to the sacrifice of everyday rights and liberties. In fact,

we have seen how Khomeini invokes the sovereign exception precisely to institute such quotidian freedoms.[22] That is why the economic and administrative examples he offers are so banal, ranging
from clearing roads to limiting the oppressive conditions of labor
contracts. Sovereignty, in other words, can establish a welfare state
as well as suspend it and is therefore indifferent to a political imagination structured around the fear and management of emergencies.

Schmitt considered sovereignty to be the perfect example of
what he called political theology, because its logic of exceptionality
was premised upon the exercise of absolute and unaccountable
power. This suspension of the law and its normative order not only
mimicked God's action in the world, being comparable in this respect to a miracle, but also manifested divine power in what he
thought was its necessarily violent and sacrificial character. Khomeini's vision of sovereignty, on the other hand, while also exceptional in its suspension of the sacred law, did not depend on such a
narrative of sacred violence. Its exceptions could therefore last in-
definitely in order to permit the making of another kind of norm
in the shadow of Islamic law. Because it was the sharia that stood
for God's will in the world, then, suspending it gave rise to a norm
without divine authorization in its own right even as it might be
established by invoking the Prophet's sovereign authority.[23]

All of this means that it is impossible to understand the relationship between the sovereign exception and the legal norm by
analogy to that between the sacred and the profane. For each one
can embody God's will, though at different levels of meaning and
abstraction. Khomeini, however, seemed to think that both the
sharia and its suspension served to hold back the messianic fulfillment of Islam in the apocalypse. Their task, in other words, was to
prevent the final victory of a theological narrative in political life.
We see this in his treatment of the Hidden Imam. Unlike in the
Vilayat-e Faqih, it is not the Imam whose functions the state inher-
its in Khomeini's later work but only the Prophet's. Why is this the
case? On the one hand, of course, Muhammad is a more ecumenical figure since his authority is acceptable to all Muslims and not
just the Shia. But more important, perhaps, is the fact that both the
Prophet and the state that performs his function have in some way
been divested of theological meaning.

Islam's theological character has instead been given into the Imam's keeping, for he is the harbinger of the apocalypse in which the law will forever be abolished in a kind of permanent act of super-sovereignty. Like God, therefore, the Imam represents the end of politics, and Khomeini discusses this messianic role in his political testament of 1982, which was published only after he died in 1989. The prologue to this text opens with a famous tradition of the Prophet regarding the two trusts (*thaqalayn*) he was leaving behind.[24] One was the Qur'an and the other his household or family, as represented by the Imams, who are seen by the Shia as the true if unacknowledged and persecuted heirs of Muhammad. The Prophet's tradition maintains that these two trusts are inseparable and will return to him at heaven's lake following the apocalypse. But Khomeini's interpretation suggests that they have in fact been separated by tyranny throughout history and will come together only in some mystical fashion at heaven's lake. And this of course implies that there can be no divinely sanctioned political order on earth but rather a fundamentally human appropriation of Muhammad's authority.

Khomeini's political thought, then, diminished the role of theology in one way while augmenting it in another—for it is meant to stave off the Imam's messianic return and thus serves as an example of the biblical *katechon*, a restraining force pushing back the apocalypse. Indeed, Khomeini explicitly refers to this idea in his testament, warning Muslims not to behave in such a way as to hasten the coming of the Mahdi and with him the end of the world and humanity's political role in it. What he accomplished, in effect, was the relegation of Islam's sacred figures to a kind of messianic time while retaining their abstract functions for Muslim use in the present. And this allowed Khomeini to continue writing mystical treatises and poetry in which such personages could still be grasped through Neoplatonic chains of emanation, even as they had been reduced to easily replicated functions within Islam conceived of as an abstract system.

The King Is Dead

Maududi and Khomeini argued that the individual as much as collective personification of power in forms of government like monarchy and democracy was idolatrous. This was because their impossible desire to manifest the sovereignty of God could only result in tyranny. Maududi tried to avoid this fate by expelling God and therefore God's sovereignty from the doings of humanity, only to have this power haunt the Islamic Republic of Pakistan in the coup as its purest form. Khomeini, on the other hand, appropriated divine sovereignty in the most fulsome way, if only by separating it from the sacred figures who had once embodied it and reducing them to functions. In either case, Islam has become history's true actor as an abstract system, with God, Muhammad, and the Imam rendered into its predecessors and precedents. This is why they had to be set aside, with Khomeini willing to suspend the law they authorized not in the name of God but of Islam and the state representing it.

In his testament, the Ayatollah even replaces God with Islam by describing the latter in terms that had been conventionally reserved in poetry for the former. He therefore hopes "the enlightened face of Islam should be revealed to the world's peoples, because if this face with that beautiful appearance which the Qur'an and Tradition in all their aspects have invited (us) to is allowed to appear from beneath the veil (cast over it by) the enemies of Islam and by its uninformed friends, Islam will be world-conquering and its proud flag will fly everywhere."[25] But this comparison of Islam to a beautiful woman who must be unveiled is immediately followed by another in which it is said to resemble a commodity. He compares Islam to a jewel that, despite being universally sought after, has been neglected and ignored by Muslims themselves, who have therefore been unable to offer it to others. And so, we return to the economy as Islam's true model insofar as it is understood as a system. These disparate ways of portraying Islam tell us that it has not been personified so much as taken on some of the characteristics of the sacred figures it has either absorbed or replaced.

But the eviction of divine persons and therefore of theology itself from the working of Islam as a system meant opening it up to multiple and even democratic forms of Muslim occupation. Already in his *Vilayat-e Faqih*, Khomeini had noted that while the state's guardianship was reserved for qualified jurists, none of them could have any authority over the others. This was, of course, the way in which the Shia clerical class operated outside the state, and the Ayatollah seems to have envisioned their occupation of it in a similarly plural and even anarchistic mode. And while he instituted and inhabited the position of supreme leader following the revolution, Khomeini continued to expand the list of those who could lay claim to sovereignty, from the president and parliament to the people for whom he used the old imperial title "shadows of God." He was not shy about inserting the people and even humankind into scenes that had previously been reserved for the sacred figures of Islam. When invoking the two trusts (the Qur'an and the Imams) left behind by Muhammad, for example, the Ayatollah added that "it must be said that the cruelty which tyrants have done these two trusts left behind by the gracious Prophet, peace be upon him and his descendants, has also been inflicted upon the Muslim community, and indeed upon mankind, so (much so) that the pen cannot transcribe it."[26]

This vision of a sovereignty devolved laterally to other offices of state as well as downward to individuals has lodged antagonism at the very center of government in Iran. Far more than a constitutional separation of powers, in other words, what we see happening within the Iranian state is the violent struggle to share a sovereignty that has been radically divided between its institutions as well as notionally made available to its citizens. Although this struggle is often described as factionalism within Iran's governing elite, what interests me is how closely it follows Khomeini's effort to split and disperse sovereignty within and beyond the state even if only theoretically. Crucial about it is the repudiation of the kind of sovereignty that Carl Schmitt described as being theological because it is unitary and absolute. Maududi, of course, did hold to this vision of sovereignty, but by expelling it from the world he also ended up leaving Islam open to multiple claims of authority. Like Gandhi, he had wanted to roll back the modern state so that society could administer itself. Coming from a place where Muslims were a minority, he was also suspicious of democracy as the instantiation of majority rule. He therefore opened Islam to occupation in an antistatist way.

Apart from the anarchist precedent in repudiating such unitary ideas of sovereignty, the most important attack such ideas have suffered in modern times has probably been during the Cultural

Revolution when Mao set the Chinese people against their state while nevertheless occupying a key role within it. This is very much the kind of role that the supreme leader, or guardian of the revolution, as he is also known, occupies in Iran as both the head of state and its possible nemesis. But like Mao and unlike Schmitt's sovereign, whose authority is manifested in deciding on exceptions to the established legal norm during moments of emergency, the supreme leader is meant in theory not to absorb such transgressive power within the state but instead disperse it to the people outside of it. This is why he is called the revolution's guardian, for as with Mao's Cultural Revolution, the Islamic revolution of Iran is envisaged to be a continuing and even permanent process that should not be stifled by the state it has established. It is the very reverse of the Bolshevik revolution's establishment of a party-state.

The guardian's relationship to the people, therefore, is among other things meant to exclude and circumvent the state so as to limit the state's reach and correct its abuses as Khomeini had done. But how could the Islamist desire to foreclose all human claims to sovereignty and to restrict its operation end up dispersing it among ever greater numbers of people? What impelled figures like Khomeini and Maududi to countenance such a fragmentation, even if only inadvertently, was their thoroughgoing criticism of mediation as both a political and spiritual mode of consolidating authority, which they identified with idolatry. This involved imagining authority as a line of individuals or offices in which each granted access to another higher up in the chain of command. Although they were happy to acknowledge such forms of linear authority when it came to the Prophet or Imams, Islamist thinkers were unwilling to do so for social and political relations between people aside from instances of expressions of courtesy toward elders and the learned.

If anything, they insisted that Muslims rebel against their own parents, families, and communities should these latter contravene the dictates of Islam. With God, the Prophet, and the Imams having been set aside, as we have seen, and kinfolk as much as kings displaced from their mediating roles in a hierarchy, Muslims were brought face to face with Islam as an abstract system exercising historical agency. But Islam cannot be personified or serve as one link in a hierarchical chain of authority, comprising as it does a totality that acts in its own name. Muslims could relate to it only directly and as individuals instead of being funneled through a chain of mediators to salvation. Their relationship to Islam was like that of industrial workers to a machine that required their disciplined action to work as an agent in its own right. And if a machine or system, to invoke the economy again as an example, had come to replace the individual authorities of the past, this was due to the wholesale criticism of monarchy as much as sainthood that Muslim liberals and fundamentalists had launched starting in the nineteenth century.

This criticism was so effective that while sainthood may still preserve its mediating role, kingship has forsaken it entirely even where the rituals of mediation are still invoked, as in Morocco. The Muslim world might still be full of kings, from Southeast Asia to the Middle East and West Africa, but with the exception of Morocco and Oman, these are all colonial monarchies going back to the nineteenth century at the earliest. They have largely been modeled on the princely states of British India and adopted their titles, with numerous highnesses interspersed with a few majesties. Extraordinary about these royal houses is the fact that, like their European peers, they no longer produce political thought even when exercising real power. And this is because a millennium-long tradition of thinking about kingship in genres such as the mirror for princes was abandoned in modern times along with most of its vocabulary. Unlike the West, where categories like sovereignty were inherited by new republics from their kingly past and pressed into service for describing popular authority, Muslim thinkers seem to have dismissed their own political traditions either for European ones or by mining a new kind of authority out of Islam newly conceived as an historical subject.

The distrust of mediation as a form of idolatry, then, is linked to Islam as a system that acts as a whole through the simultaneous functioning of its many parts. Mediation stretches out the working of authority in time as much as space since it involves the believer moving from one figure such as Muhammad to another like God in an allegedly idolatrous fashion. Islam, however, invites believers to work its machinery or fit into it directly and in one go. And this means that even as it acts in history, Islam permits the telescoping of time so that Muslims can access the past immediately and identify directly with its heroes, or rather their functions, in the present. An identification that had previously required lengthy mystical training was in this way turned into one accessed through politics. And Khomeini was eloquent in describing this telescoping of time. We have already seen how he insisted upon the jurist being not just the deputy of Muhammad or the Hidden Imam but their true heir and even replacement. This was one way of removing the mediation of time as much as authority from his relationship to Islam.

In his testament Khomeini goes further and compares the sacrifices and bravery of Iranians during the revolution to the virtues of Muslims in the time of Muhammad and the first Imams: "I claim with courage that the Iranian people and its masses of millions today are better than the people of the Hijaz during the time of the Prophet, peace be upon him and his descendants, and the people of Kufa and Iraq in the time of the Prince of Believers and Hasan bin Ali, upon whom be the peace of God."[27] Given the high theological status of the Prophet and his successors, as well as the supposed purity of those who had the good fortune to live in their times, this was an extraordinary and even scandalous statement to make. And Khomeini followed it up by noting that many among the first generation of Muslims had in fact neglected their duty to Islam even when in the presence of the Prophet and Imams. Their charisma, in other words was neither sufficient in their time nor necessary in ours to ensure the making of a just social order.

But this meant that the revolution's success was due to the very absence of such sacred figures, with the superiority of the Iranian people over earlier generations of Muslims resulting "from their love, attachment and great faith in the exalted Lord and (in) Islam and life everlasting, even though they are neither in the auspicious presence of the gracious Prophet, peace be upon him and his descendants, nor in the presence of the infallible Imams, upon whom be peace. And their motivation is faith and trust in the unseen."[28] Khomeini's speculations on the political effect of absence and ignorance here bear comparison with the thought of the early twentieth-century syndicalist Georges Sorel on what he called the myth of the general strike as a mobilizing force. Unlike political utopias, Sorel argued, which could be analyzed in purely theoretical ways, myths worked politically because they had been severed from ideologies to become standalone principles in whose name people were willing to act. Unlike many utopias they were also not messianic, let alone apocalyptic, but meant to bring about a new social order.

For both Sorel and Khomeini, furthermore, political action was explained not just by what exists, whether interests, grievances, or oppression, but by what does not exist in the figure of the myth. Political consciousness, elaborate ideologies, and objective conditions alone cannot explain the contingency of events—for example, why a popular uprising occurs today rather than yesterday or tomorrow—and so we tend to diminish the importance of such moments by consigning them to the realm of the accidental. But Khomeini was concerned precisely with this contingency as a mystery in which he recognized the religious nature of political action. It was not simply the oppression Iranians faced but their belief in the unseen or absent figures of theology that inspired them to rise up against the shah. And yet, as my comparison with Sorel is meant to illustrate, this deeply religious vision was at the same time quite indifferent to theology because it could always be understood in a purely philosophical not to say political way as Khomeini himself seems to have done by one interpretation of his words.

To prefer God's absence to God's presence is not such a strange attitude in the poetic and mystical tradition Khomeini had inherited. It was commonplace in this literary tradition to prize the yearning and desire that constituted the very essence of love over the merely domestic bliss of cohabitation with the beloved, whether human or divine. And it might well be that Khomeini transferred this attitude from a mystical and poetical realm to the political one. Crucial about it, however, was the expulsion not just of the beloved from everyday life, but of all mediators as well. Once upon a time the idol, woman, or infidel could serve as mediators for an invisible God in poetry, overlapping in this way with the role played by the saint and the king in mysticism and politics. But now they have all been displaced as figures of idolatry to join an already absent God as the mere shadows of divine sovereignty. And instead, we have Islam as an abstract system that literally allows Muslims to take their place.

In one sense, therefore, Islam makes possible the democratization of Muslim authority and practice. And yet in doing so it also places a huge burden of responsibility upon believers, since they are now capable of claiming far more in the way of divine characteristics than any king or saint ever could have. No longer a singular personage or monument, similarly, the idol can now be anyone and anything. This leads to a hermeneutic of suspicion, where the dispersal of authority results in a variety of efforts both to reclaim and to disclaim it. Indeed, the two claims go together, since even those who assert their Islamic authority are compelled to deny their status as idols who falsely grasp at divine sovereignty. Meanwhile, ordinary Muslims must live with the suspicion, even if only in their own minds, that they might be trespassing upon the privileges of an absent God rendered even more inaccessible by his lack of any mediators apart from themselves.

It is almost as if we are seeing a perverse expansion of the old philosophical and mystical idea of the sage who becomes a perfect man capable of sharing in the divine essence. It is perverse because the whole point of doing away with the idolatry of mediation was to prevent such experiences or at least the claims to authority they might entail. But as Zafar's couplet with which I began this chapter suggests, banning the idol only leads to her taking lodging in the heart of iconoclasm. By permitting the removal of royal and saintly mediators from Muslim life, Islam has put believers into a direct relationship with God's sovereignty, if not person. And in doing so, it has short-circuited the lengthy process of mediation that had once allowed for the making of saintly or kingly authority. This new power or possibility in the hands of ordinary Muslims, then, had to be controlled even as it was deemed a necessary part of Islam's democratic or perhaps anarchist future.

The Atheist's God

The inability of Islam to permit either a fully theological reasoning or an acquaintance with God does not mean that such ways of thinking and experience have simply disappeared from Muslim lives. They now occur beyond the boundaries of Islam in vernacular practices that have survived its historical agency. But it is not only these remnants from the past to which we must look for such modes of apperception, so I conclude this chapter by showing how apostasy, and especially the turn to atheism, may be among the most productive sites for a Muslim theological imagination today. This is in keeping with the newly individualized and unmediated character of Muslim relations with God, which in some ways align very nicely with a certain kind of Protestant theology. And as we saw in the last chapter, Christianity has in any case increasingly come to provide the theological language that is lacking in modern Islam.

Any kind of transformative experience can be understood as a conversion in the Christian sense, and so remain theological even when it describes a turn from religion to atheism. I suggest that it is this sort of transformation that has come to characterize not the fidelity to Islam as much as Islam's repudiation. But this is not such an unusual situation in a time marked by the global efflorescence of new identities, especially dissenting and minority ones that require the traditionally religious practices of struggle, sacrifice, and testimony for their manifestation. The single-minded adoption of a profane identity, in other words, can be even more theological in its absolutism than the acceptance of another religion. And it may well be that such deeply held identities, whether personal or political, are coming to join if not replace religious belief around the world. We may be living at a time when the experience of transcendence is migrating from religious to secular life rather than simply being imitated by the latter in art.

One of the consequences of Europe's refugee crisis has been the increasing spate of conversions to Christianity among Muslim migrants. While numbers are difficult to obtain, a 2016 article in *The Guardian* was one of many to offer evidence.[29] These included a church in Berlin whose congregation increased in size from 140 to 700, the newcomers being Muslim converts from Iran, Afghanistan, and Central Asia; and mass baptisms held at a municipal swimming pool in Hamburg. Interesting about these anecdotes are the mixed motives of the converts, unlike, as we shall see, the much more absolute commitment of those who opt for atheism. Whether due to migrants' revulsion against the violent forms that Islam has taken in places like Syria or Afghanistan, or in order to ensure their welcome, security, and legal recognition in Europe, these conversions have occurred quietly and without much drama. In fact, they rarely seem to have resulted from any effort at proselytism and do not tend to be accompanied by any great transformation in the appearance, behavior, or language of the convert.[30]

In parts of the Muslim world, of course, but also in a number of non-Muslim countries like India, converting from Islam, Hinduism, Judaism, or Christianity to another religion, or even to another denomination, may be discouraged if not forbidden and invite legal punishment as much as popular censure. Nevertheless, conversions still do occur and tend not to follow the model of transformation we have inherited from Christianity. This is classically described in the story of St. Paul receiving a vision of the cross on the road to Damascus while he was on his way to persecute the fledgling Christian community. In recent years, for instance, a number of poor Muslims have been "returning" to Hinduism, their "homecoming" staged for the media by groups seeking to proclaim India a Hindu nation. Not only is there no talk of transformation and belief in these cases, but also no attempt by any of India's Muslims to persecute these converts, who are generally seen as having changed their faith for instrumental reasons having to do with gaining material support and social recognition. Although we may not know why exactly these conversions occurred, it is fair to say that they cannot be described as a transformation of belief and so character.[31]

Muslims also become atheists, and there is a long history of atheism in Muslim societies. Some famous medieval scientists and philosophers were known to be unbelievers, but though they may have argued with their more observant friends and relations, these men remained respectable members of their communities. It would never have occurred to them to renounce Islam and proclaim atheism as a mission, which would have simply catapulted them back into the theological world they had supposedly abandoned. But the curious thing about some of today's atheists is how theological their rejection of religion can be, involving sacrifice, transformation, and a new belief that they find as difficult to conceal as any faith calling out to be preached. In Europe and North America, many of these men and women call themselves ex-Muslims, a name that models the renunciation of Islam upon that of addiction, alcoholism, or even crime. Conceived as a kind of illness from which they are recovering, Islam for these individuals still dominates their identities by being present in their name.

Could it be that by retaining Islam in their chosen name, ex-Muslims are not simply emphasizing their identity as victims of their societies or families, but also in some sense recognizing the theological character of their renunciation? Their victimization is very real, as the stories of threat, oppression, and outright violence many ex-Muslims have faced reveal, and maybe this accounts for the highly religious way in which their renunciation of Islam is accomplished. A common storyline has to do with the initially doubting Muslim trying to reinforce his or her faith by reading the Qur'an, which of course only makes things worse, eventually precipitating a decision to forsake Islam altogether.[32] Since the proliferation of printed editions from the early twentieth century, the Qur'an has become a handy reference for ordinary believers, allowing them to contest the authority of clerics in a Protestant way. But printing and other technologies, together with literacy, have also supported the expansion of clerical authority to rural parts of the Muslim world where it had rarely enjoyed any popularity.

In the past the Qur'an was only read by religious authorities on the one hand and recited by schoolboys on the other. In neither case was it considered a unified narrative, and it was consulted only in fragments for specific ritual, juridical, or mystical purposes that required training to be accomplished. The Qur'an was not, in other words, ever read as an expository text with a single meaning, and indeed never read at all by the majority of Muslims, whose religious practices bore only a tangential relationship with it. But today the Qur'an has for many become the fundament of Muslim belief, and like the evangelical's Bible must be read either to be believed or, as with ex-Muslims, to be rejected as unbelievable. In both cases the procedure involved is identical, as is the presupposition that belief should be based upon the reading of scripture. It is in such ways as this that the name "ex-Muslim" reveals its truth as an identity unable to escape Islam. Conversion remains a vibrant practice in the Muslim world, though it tends to be invisible to outsiders. Apart from the numbers garnered by Christian missionaries, there have been significant conversions from Sunnism to minority forms of Islam, often involving grave risks rather than material benefits. In Iran, similarly, Bahaism made deep inroads into Shiism during the nineteenth century.

A 2012 WIN–Gallup International poll, for example, showed that 5 percent of Saudis identified as atheists, more than in the United States, while 19 percent did not consider themselves religious—in a country that punished unbelief with death.[33] The rates are similar if not higher in other parts of the Middle East. Apart from the secularists and socialists of the mid-twentieth century, however, atheism in the Muslim world has ceased to be a politically defined phenomenon. It retains, instead, a highly individualized form as a personal identity. At most, atheists in countries like Saudi Arabia or Pakistan try to form secret communities. Unlike ex-Muslims, these men and women, who meet in internet chat rooms and sometimes in unnamed physical locations, are not interested in cultivating their victimhood as part of a recovery process. Instead, they seem more like the philosophers and mystics of old, who produced esoteric knowledge that criticized conventional religious beliefs and organized themselves in secret societies, as Freemasons did in the West.

Driven as this new atheism may be to secrecy out of fear, we should not dismiss its esoteric dimension with its long history in Muslim societies. For these men and women appear to reject the theological obsession with revelation and a universal mission to focus instead on the kind of knowledge that dissents from popular opinion instead of seeking simply to replace it. They are in this way part of a great tradition that contests all authoritative claims in the name of freedom. But perhaps the most spectacular refusal of Islam in recent times came during the 2016 terrorist attacks on an upscale restaurant popular with expatriates in Dhaka.[34] Militants claiming allegiance to ISIS held dozens hostage there and killed twenty. Muslims were asked to identify themselves by reciting bits of the Qur'an and then could go free. A young man and woman decided not to do so and died alongside their non-Muslim friends. Had they claimed for themselves the kind of sacrifice that is otherwise used by militants to showcase their theological purity?

CHAPTER FOUR

Women on the Verge

ORN TO SECULAR JEWISH parents in New York, Margaret
Marcus spent her disturbed youth searching for religious
meaning in various forms of Judaism and then in Islam as
Judaism's closest relation outside the intellectual hegemony
of Christianity.[1] Following a lengthy correspondence with Abul Ala
Maududi, the Pakistani founder of Islamist thought, she ended up a
convert to Islam at his hands in 1961. Moving to Lahore and becoming the second wife of a member of Maududi's party, the Jamaat-e
Islami, she took the name Maryam Jameelah and went on to become
the first and arguably most influential female exemplar of Islamism.
Jameelah then began a career writing excoriating accounts of the
modern West and its Muslim admirers in English that were translated into other languages for a global audience. And yet she was
never seen or heard in public, either in person or through broadcast
media. Her persona was a purely textual one.

A global icon for what was then known as Islamic fundamentalism, Jameelah was feted not only because of her gift for polemic,
but equally for the very past she had apparently renounced. Her
Jewish and American identity, in other words, continued to define
Jameelah in the eyes of her Muslim readers. Each of her books
drew attention to the fact that if a Jew and an American like herself
could recognize the truth of Islam, that truth should be blindingly

evident to those who had the good fortune to have been born Muslim. She can also be placed in the long line of Jews who "rediscovered" the truth of Judaism in Islam, from the heresiarch Sabbatai Zvi in the seventeenth century to the Galician writer and sometime Pakistani politician Leopold Weiss in the twentieth. Muhammad Asad, as the latter came to be known, was, like Jameelah, keen to save Islam from what he saw as the fate of modern Judaism, which both of them considered a faith defeated and absorbed by Christianity.

Ending up criticizing Maududi himself for being too Westernized, Maryam Jameelah was unafraid to represent Islam in her own right both as a convert and as a woman.[2] She turned the Muslim woman into a public yet at the same time a paradoxically private person, one whose life was unknown to the world but who was yet capable of representing Islam in her own voice and by speaking from its very center rather than as a marginal figure. I argue here that as subjects of this kind, women have even gone on to displace men as generic Muslims in the imaginary of modern Islam. We shall see that this story goes back another hundred years, but Jameelah's triumphal illustration of it allows us to recognize very clearly the problem posed by its narrative. For although she was defined as a generic Muslim by her rejection of all the particularities of dress and behavior from a non-Muslim past, this very history nevertheless remained the only way in which such a woman could be known in the present.

Each one of Jameelah's books contains a frontispiece with a portrait of the author in which she is shown covered from head to foot in a black veil. Below the image appears the following text: "Thus do I, an American-born convert, speak through this picture to my Muslim-born brothers and sisters misled by an education hostile to all that Islam stands for and blinded with its false standards and ideals." Such a portrait is in effect a piece of irony rather than an alternative form of representation, since it proclaims that the Muslim woman must be seen not to be seen. It tells us not only about the absolute dominance of visual representation as a form of truth-telling, but also about its vacillation, for what exactly is the truth being revealed here?[3] This play of visibility and invisibility was crucial to the making not only of Maryam Jameelah but of the Muslim woman herself as a subject of discourse. Because her life as a Muslim couldn't be known, Jameelah's non-Muslim past became the only way in which her biography could be understood, while the inability to see or even hear her made clothing and writing the only ways in which she could communicate.

Jameelah herself was very clear about the problem posed by visibility in the making of the Muslim woman. For by offering up her veiled image as a repudiation of ocular veracity, she sought to withdraw the female body from masculine knowledge both of an informal or salacious kind and in its public manifestation as an instrument of the state's efforts to discipline and regulate citizens. In doing so, Jameelah argued, she was simply refusing the objectification of female bodies for male pleasure, knowledge, and exploitation, including their deployment in advertising and consumerism. This appropriation of feminist argumentation went on to become crucial in Islamist polemics all over the world and was much deployed during and after the Iranian Revolution. It illustrates a reasoning that possesses little if any theological character, but it also follows very nicely from historical efforts by colonized subjects to avoid European forms of knowledge and so control.

Any effort to avoid the objectification of such visual targets of desire, of course, lends itself to being commodified as well. Not only are veils commodities in their own right, for instance, but they also encourage the fetishism of the eyes and faces, hands, and feet, which often remain the only visible parts of the pious Muslim woman's body. This suggests that the piecemeal eroticization of women's bodies is as likely to occur in a conservative Muslim society as in the capitalist West. This fragmentation is evident not only in poetic and other literary tropes from the past, but also in the vogue for nose jobs and other kinds of cosmetic surgery in places like contemporary Iran. Initially popular with women, these largely facial procedures are now common among men as well. They may demonstrate how in some ways women have become model or generic Muslim subjects. Like women and following their precedent, after all, some Islamist and especially Salafi men have also adopted forms of clothing and comportment that visibly mark them as devout Muslims.

I shall return to the issue of surgical and other corporal alterations and ask whether they illustrate the detachment of Muslim subjects, male or female, from their biologies to deny the latter as sites of a specifically Islamic identity. Yet they cannot do without these bodies either, which insist on representing the subject's truth even as the objects of its instrumentality. By making the Muslim woman knowable only in her sartorial appearance and vanishing every other aspect of her personality, Maryam Jameelah, for example, externalized her gendered identity away from the body. But in doing so she also made Islam into a superficial marker of the subject's truth, since the Muslim woman's appearance in public had little if anything to do with her dress or comportment in private. The two were instead distinct, with the domestic arena of a woman's life ostensibly unregulated by dress codes or anxieties about foreign influence.

Is the most intimate part of the Muslim woman's life, then, the domestic sphere in which she is not bound by most sartorial and many behavioral restrictions in the name of Islam? And does she therefore only represent her religion in the public arena as a largely external marker, especially in the capacity of someone who must be seen not to be seen? Jameelah's Islamist narrative seems to enforce a hard distinction between public and private, since the veiled woman as she represents her is necessarily a public rather than a private figure. Yet insofar as she is set apart from sight and touch and therefore rendered unknowable, she remains at the same time a manifestation of the private or domestic sphere. The appropriately accoutered Islamist woman even serves to fragment the private realm and disperse it through her mobility within public space, thus undoing any purely spatial distinction between the two. She could maintain her invisibility in public life, while enjoying its culture and commodities in her domestic existence.

Of course, such women might well be disciplined into thinking and behaving as pious Muslims across their public and private lives, in Islamist representation as much as reality. But my point is that their inner lives are not meant to be accessible outside the family, with Islamism seeking to empower patriarchal society by setting strict limits to the modern state's interference in domestic life. And this was simply one way in which it was meant to roll back the disciplinary and regulative controls of the state seen as a colonial and Western institution to privilege the autonomy of a social domain instead. Such a strategy has never been entirely successful, with Islamic states encroaching upon family life just as families appeal to it for intervention. But the restrictions on women's biopolitical citizenship remain very real and prevent their full integration into such states as objects of knowledge in practices ranging from statistics to surveillance. And this also prevents the complete hegemony of such notions of citizenship in general.

More important about the making of the Muslim woman as a subject in Islamist narratives, however, is that her virtue differed little from that which was recommended for men; and this meant that it couldn't become a way of defining and distinguishing between gender roles. Instead, it was precisely the external and in that sense superficial marking of distinctions in clothing and comportment that allowed for the separation of genders. Because it was literally so flimsy, this kind of distinction had to be rigorously policed, since it threatened to unravel into various kinds of sexual ambiguity. We shall see that the threat of indistinct gender divisions loomed large over Islamist narratives, which did not rely upon biology to define identity; and it was this threat that made appearance so crucial in marking gender roles for men as much as women. While such regulations were often retrieved from medieval codes of conduct, however, they have taken on a quite different meaning in modern times.

Domesticating Islam

We saw in the last chapter how women in the literary canon of languages like Persian, Turkish, and Urdu were routinely paired with idols and infidels, all understood as pleasingly seductive threats to the social order. Their very distance from or negation of this order, however, permitted these figures to be paired, in turn, with God, who not only transcended it in another way, but was also bound eventually to destroy such a social order in the apocalypse. For existing as he did above the law, God could be compared to such figures who were seen as being outside it in other ways. Some aspects of this pairing are still evident in everyday Muslim life, for example in the use of the word "idol" (*sanam*) as a popular woman's name, while "infidel" (*kaffir*), too, can serve as a term of endearment for coquettish women and mischievous children. In this world of references, then, women did not stand alone and could not be said to exist as subjects in their own right.[4]

Similarly, in the tradition of social and juridical thought, women were often placed alongside children and slaves or other menials as legal minors, for they all belonged to a domestic sphere as the wards of free and adult men. While the poetic world in which women could be paired with idols, infidels, and therefore God continued to exist as a literary archaism, however, women had to be extricated from its social and juridical equivalent to become subjects in their own stead. This happened starting in the second half of the nineteenth century in colonized societies like India and Egypt, and with the advent of the modern nation-state in countries like Turkey and Iran.[5] Although each of these places possessed its own unique history that determined how women emerged as subjects, common to them all seems to have been a redefinition of Islam's role in the public and private domains of social life.

In colonial societies, for example, the establishment of a secular state and public sphere well in advance of Europe resulted in Islam's displacement from political life and the corresponding diminution of its theological debates there. For these debates along with Islam itself now had to be shifted to the new arena of private life. This entailed locating Islam among the remnants of what had once been the old regime's public arena, often conceived as a moral city in a tradition dating back to ancient Greece. Since that public arena was deprived of its courts, barracks, and palaces by the colonial state, however, the mosques and seminaries that remained had now become little more than the private institutions of a religious community. Given the moral city's fragmentation and the loss of power suffered by its institutions, they were no longer able to ground Islamic norms and practices in the absence of royal authority. This meant that Islam now had to be established in a parallel process of native colonization, which took Muslim domestic life as its target.

Resistant as many Muslim movements were to the colonial or nation-state's interventions into the domestic arena, they did not hesitate to conduct a similar if entirely private project of their own in this direction. For with the partial destruction of Muslim public life, the men who had once represented it were suddenly thrown into relations of the closest proximity with women, children, and menials, all now defined as members of a merely religious community lacking political power of its own. This led to a series of reform movements among the new middle classes who proved to be the beneficiaries of colonial rule. They sought to remake masculine Muslim authority apart from the old world of kings, saints, and clerics on the one hand, while extending such a reformation to women on the other. And to accomplish this mission, the Muslim men who now represented Islam had to separate these women from children and menials by making them for the first time into subjects in their own right.

This effort at Islamizing women, who might hitherto have been permitted all kinds of vernacular and even pagan practices and beliefs, began as always with the Muslim liberals in a middle-class milieu.[6] But it soon moved on to the world of clerics and subsequently Islamists from the same class background. They all agreed that women were meant to be educated so as to provide companions for their husbands, thus keeping their menfolk away from the courtesans and dancing girls who had been such an essential part of the old aristocratic order in many parts of the Muslim world. They also needed to be educated so as to teach their children how to be good Muslims and to manage their households without falling prey to the dishonesty and malign influence of servants. Clearly a middle-class enterprise, this reformist project was directed against aristocratic as much as saintly culture, the one deemed to be decadent and the other superstitious.

The novelist Nazir Ahmad wrote several books on the making of good Muslim women. One from 1877, called *Tawbat un-Nasuh* (Nasuh's Repentance), concerns a gentleman's renunciation of aristocratic practices following his infection with cholera in an epidemic then sweeping Delhi. In his fevered state, Nasuh dreams of meeting his father, come up from hell to warn him about the torments awaiting his reprobate son. Upon making a miraculous recovery, Nasuh embarks upon a mission to reform his wife and children. He tells them: "that man who is the oldest in this house is in the position of an emperor, and the house's other inhabitants, like subjects, are commanded by him. . . . The most dangerous fault I see in my domestic kingdom is this, that me and my subjects, which is to say you people, are ready and fitted out for rebellion and mutiny against the emperor of the two worlds."[7]

At this, his oldest son, Kalim, grumbles, "If to think oneself an emperor isn't madness, then what is it?"[8] Interesting about this vision of domestic virtue is that it has appropriated the very aristocratic categories Nasuh otherwise repudiates, except they now exclude kings to link ordinary heads of family directly to God as his representatives. And this accounts for the absolutism of Nasuh's mission as much as the shadow of madness that dogs it. He thus tells his wife: "this state is for you one of trial. Faith and children are two separate things, and it is a most unfortunate fact that a union of the two does not seem possible because our children are enemies of religion and faith. If we incline toward the children, then religion and faith abscond; and if we protect faith, then the children abscond. You thus have a choice to take whichever one you want."[9] This is an extraordinary statement, because it separates women from the very functions that otherwise define their virtue. The woman forced to choose between her recalcitrant children and her faith, in other words, has become a subject in her own right and for her own sake here.

Kalim, against whom his mother, Fahmida, is asked to harden her heart, is as enamored of a declining aristocratic culture as his father once was. He complains, "now one hears this new talk, of course, to sit in line at the mosque, not to play, not to meet any friends or acquaintances, not to go to the market, not to participate in festivals and spectacles."[10] When his father's admonitions become unendurable, Kalim leaves Delhi for a princely state whose young ruler was gathering worthlessly cultured companions about him in an effort to make his court like the Lucknow of old. But he arrives too late, as the colonial state had already deposed the prince and put the affairs of state in the hands of a committee. Kalim then joins the local army, is wounded ingloriously, and dies repenting of his sins. This extreme end seems to be necessary to destroy the powerful seductiveness of aristocratic ideals. A grieving Nasuh has his son's mock-aristocratic rooms opened and destroys their contents, including burning the books.

Nasuh is more successful with his remaining children. His younger son, Salim, is dissuaded from consorting with common boys from the bazaar, while his daughter, Naima, fights a losing battle against her father's efforts to rid his household of the kind of seraglio intrigue that British observers often saw in Muslim households. This was attributed to undifferentiated gatherings of women, children, and servants, which Naima remembers fondly: "Neither has the earth remained nor the sky. . . . There is neither that laughter nor that interest. Not that conversation, not that fun, not that laughter. A certain unhappiness is spread about the house, otherwise not a month ago the neighborhood's women used to be here all day. One would be singing a song, another telling a story. Our neighbor Ajuba is such a hearty soul that she would set us laughing uncontrollably by coming up with new caricatures every day. Now no-one comes in the house even to spit."[11]

Interesting about the novel is that its author puts credible challenges to his own vision of reform into the mouths of its intended objects. Naima thus tries to push back against Nasuh's program of a female education in virtue by linking her autonomy to an acceptance of gender inequality: "I know that for women a lot of prayer and fasting is unnecessary. Their worship is only this, that they should see to the housework. Watch over the children. When do they get the time from such domestic chores to pray? For men, of course, there are no cares of cooking, no fighting of children; they can worship as much as they please. . . . You can say what you will, there will never be equality between woman and man. God certainly must have granted some kind of ease to women."[12] The equality between genders that was claimed by the advocates of modern Islam, in other words, turned out to be more oppressive in this view than the old narrative of inequality.

The poet Akbar Illahabadi went much further in claiming that the project of educating women to become good Muslims was all about squeezing labor out of them in a situation where the middle classes were being organized into nuclear families. He attributes the following sentiments to a Muslim reformer who sought to ameliorate and so modernize the status of women: "But it is necessary that her upbringing be appropriate; from which our worth and station in the community might increase. She should always be expert in the necessary skills; follower of her husband and slave for the children. If too educated she won't remain under control; she'll even put the Creator to her work. Learn to do the household accounts yourself; it isn't good to leave this task to strangers. What's the pleasure if she doesn't know how to cook; this is a great jewel for women. Sewing is a special womanly skill; one must watch out for the tailor's thefts."[13]

While the reformed Muslim woman separated from her children and servants had a particular burden to bear, she was nevertheless considered to be a man's equal in virtue. And this was borne out in her education, which did not distinguish between the sexes. What did its discipline aim at? We can find out by comparing a few model curriculums. The theologian Ashraf Ali Thanvi's *Bihishti Zewar* (Jewelry of Paradise), first published in 1905, embodies an entire female curriculum in itself, from the alphabet to modes of letter writing, polite conversation, recipes, medicines, household accounts, sewing, and, of course, the rules of religion. These latter are so extensive and detailed that mastering them, declared the author, would make women equal to ordinary clerics.[14] Nazir Ahmad similarly instructed women in household affairs but did not emphasize religion to such an extent. He did include in his curriculum, however, subjects such as geography, of which Thanvi disapproved as being likely to excite cloistered women needlessly.

The pioneering girl's school in the North Indian town of Aligarh taught Urdu, mathematics, Qur'an, embroidery, cooking, games, Indian history and geography, and, after 1914, English.[15] That part of Altaf Hussain Hali's model curriculum that does not include domestic management in his tract of 1874 called the *Majalisunissa* (Gatherings of Women) is described by its heroine, Zubayda Khatun: "By the time I was thirteen, I had studied the *Gulistan* and *Bostan*, *Akhlaq-e-Muhsini*, and *Iyar-e-Danish* in Persian, and in Arabic the necessary beginning grammar, in arithmetic the common factors and decimal factors and the two parts of Euclid's geometry. I had also studied the geography and history of India, and had practiced both *naskh* and *nasta'liq* calligraphy and could copy couplets in a good hand. At that point, my father began to teach me two lessons a day. In the morning we read *Kimiya-e-Sa'adat* and in the evening *Kalila wa Dimna* in Arabic."[16]

Apart from their typical emphasis on domestic duties and concern about the amount of education to be allowed women, what is striking about these curriculums is that they faithfully reflect the various ideals of men's education in vogue at the time. Thanvi's curriculum sets out the practice of the religiously inclined person; Nazir Ahmad's and Hali's describe the education of any worldly gentleman; and the curriculum of Aligarh's girl's school, with its inclusion of English, prescribes for women the education of a modern man. In fact, all these courses of study were meant to do for women what they did for men—produce a virtuous subject. It was also a process of conversion, very similar to that which brought infidels into the fold of Islam. And just as the convert no longer posed a threat to Islam's social order, so, too, was the reformed Muslim woman unable to challenge this order as she had once done.

But if the Muslim woman could no longer be represented as a source of disorder, the Muslim man in the new public sphere had now become both the victim and the agent of its corruption. She therefore had to be secluded from this impure world not only to save her from it, but also to render her into a sort of guardian of tradition whose task was to save men from the wickedness of public life. Only in the nineteenth century did women become moral influences of this kind. As such, they were often cast as nonsexual and maternal figures, and in reformist literature the aggressively sexual woman was replaced by a pathetic or suffering one. This image of an uncomplaining and silently suffering woman was used to justify her education in didactic works like Hali's *Chup ki Dad* (Homage to the Silent).[17] And while such an image might well have been used in the beginning as propaganda for women's education, it soon became an ideal of Muslim femininity.

The Ideal Muslim

The figure of an idealized Muslim woman who represents Islam while calling for masculine protection marks the remarkable reversal of a long-standing gender narrative. Her new role also bears comparison to that played by the Prophet, which suggests how she might have become an ideal or generic Muslim subject. The anthropologist Arsalan Khan, for instance, describes how the Tablighi Jamaat or Missionary Society in Pakistan, which forms part of the world's largest Islamic movement, upholds women as models of subjectivity.[18] The Tablighis compare their relationship to God as being like that of a woman to a man, with the Prophet providing the perfect example of this soft and pliant subjectivity ready to be instructed in virtue. They also conceive their mission of preaching as being set against the stubbornness of male agency and meant to create a feminine ethics of care in the household. It is now men, in other words, who represent in their very gender the principle of disorder (*fitna*) that had once been attributed to women.

This comparison is taken very far indeed, with the movement's members likening women in the home to men in the mosque, both of whom are meant to attend to the needs of their families. Preaching itself is described as a mother giving birth to faith, which has to be nurtured like a child. God similarly inseminates the preacher's heart as men do women's bodies, so that the missionary becomes pregnant with divine agency. And like women, these men's pious practices consist of living communally and serving one another in conventionally feminine ways like cooking and cleaning. While they are not without some precedent in Sufi devotion, these ideas and habits are novel in their explicit criticism of masculinity as a violent form of agency recalcitrant to divine command. Women, by contrast, are understood as model Muslims not because of their education as much as their gender. For they are not agents in their own right but instead represent Islam's agency. Given that God had previously been seen either as a powerfully sexualized woman or as an equally potent king in Muslim literary tradition, his transformation into a middle-class paterfamilias here is remarkable.

The Muslim woman's emergence as a subject, in other words, is paradoxically premised upon her disappearance as an agent, which is why it is she rather than a man who can best represent Islam. Of course, the Tablighi Jamaat does not stand in for Islamic movements more generally. But it shares with them a focus on the domestic arena, not only as a target of reform, but as a model for society as well. Resulting, as we have seen, from the capture of public life by the colonial or national state and the fragmentation of older ideas about the moral city, the emergence of the household as a model for Muslim social life also indicates its depoliticization. By appropriating the household for Islam, then, its followers were able to make women into virtuous subjects. But in doing so they were also faced with the difficulty of drawing any significant distinction between private and public realms. And it is the diminution of such a distinction that allowed women to emerge as generic Muslims.

Now it is true that the household has from ancient times offered a model and precedent for thinking about political life, though women and children were never seen as anything more than the wards of men in it. Different about Muslim visions of the household is the fact that it refuses to stay in place and threatens to take over the public arena with its own categories of personhood and forms of interpersonal relations. This is in part because Islam is no longer firmly attached to political or religious authorities and can therefore speak through even women as its privileged mediums. But more important is the fact that it has increasingly come to be grounded in the social rather than political domain. And this means that even when a state is declared to be Islamic, it must derive its legitimacy not just from scripture but however disingenuously from the patterns of everyday life.

The establishment of a virtuous domestic sphere is thus crucial for any conception of modern Islam. Though this private realm is meant to serve as an autonomous domain of Muslim authenticity, however, it often needs to be regulated by the state if only so as to retain its role as a model of virtue that supposedly stands outside politics. This is not so different from what happens in liberal societies. And it sometimes leads to contradictory policies in Islamic states, as the anthropologist Ziba Mir-Hosseini points out in her work on the changing practice and law of divorce in Iran.[19] She shows how the Islamic Republic's early repudiation of Pahlavi-era family laws that had sought to protect women was eventually replaced by efforts to reinstate those laws in more Islamic terms. But this gave men control over divorce and polygamy while also enabling women to challenge them, in the process making strained marital relations more intractable rather than less so, as Islamists had wanted.

The Islamization of the household, and especially of the women who were its chief denizens, called for a new justification of gender difference. While Muslim modernists starting in the nineteenth century had used apologetic arguments to reinterpret their traditions in more or less liberal terms, Islamists in the twentieth attempted to legitimize old hierarchies in far more conservative but equally European ways. Maududi's book *Parda* (Veiling), first published in 1939, offers a good example of this.[20] Drawing upon the work of figures like the French sociologist Paul Bureau, who wrote about changing sexual mores and the dissolution of old social orders, Maududi located gender relations within a theory of civilization that had nothing to do with theology. Indeed, he invoked scripture and its authoritative commentaries only at the end of his book in a purely illustrative way to legitimize its otherwise profane argument.

For Maududi, the global dominance that the West had achieved by way of imperialism imposed a model of gender relations upon the world that was destructive of civilization. Because Christendom had been so oppressive for women in its denial of sexual pleasure, when its hegemony was finally overthrown during the Enlightenment, this ascetic ideal was replaced by its opposite in the form of hedonism. Although it was meant to have freed both women and men from the church's unnatural bondage, however, this new hedonistic spirit ended up being even more degrading for women. They were saved from being men's chattel only to become objects of their exploitation through capitalism and democracy. The one bought and sold them as commodities, and the other stripped them of honor and protection. Women, in other words, had moved from one extreme to another but remained the victims of male desire.

Like every other Muslim reformer, liberal or conservative, Maududi breaks with tradition by attributing sexual license and its destructive consequences to men alone, while seeing women merely as their victims. He acknowledges that women's bondage might have served some purpose in the making of early human societies, but as with the liberals thought that the growth of civilizations required the equal participation of women. And Islam, of course, which he saw as maintaining a balance between oppression and license, represented the perfect form that civilization took. To understand the meaning and purpose of this balance, Maududi turns to the laws of nature, which had been established as a criterion for judging the veracity of religious doctrine by the nineteenth-century modernist Syed Ahmed Khan. Rather than referring to nature as something ingrained in animal life, however, these laws represented a kind of providential design.

Unlike other animals, Maududi wrote, the sexual urge in human beings was not tied to procreation alone. Its constant presence suggested, rather, that sexual attraction and pleasure were meant to create permanent bonds of love and companionship between men and women so that they might establish families, giving rise to social life and thus civilization itself. This also explained why gestation was so extended for human beings, as well as why babies needed nurturing for such a long period of time. Since it was the woman who was primarily responsible for the birth and early upbringing of the child, a responsibility that left her uniquely vulnerable and dependent on others, the love and attraction she elicited from her male partner was what made him sacrifice his natural egoism to protect the fledgling family. And this meant that it was women and the sexual attraction they exercised which made men virtuous. Departing from Christian or for that matter Sufi asceticism, then, Maududi made sexual attraction into the basis of virtue as much as civilization itself.

Women were therefore crucial to the making of social life by prompting feelings of altruism and self-sacrifice in men that religions then came to reinforce in often more negative or punitive ways, by criminalizing incest, fornication, and adultery as well as sexual perversions; encouraging marriage and the establishment of families; and requiring women's segregation in public life to protect the sanctity of these institutions. For the family, Maududi emphasizes, is meant to serve as the seedbed for all moral virtues, which were elicited from men by women through the working of sexual attraction expanded into the love of wives and children and then to society at large. As a description of sublimation and the repression of destructive male urges in the interests of civilization, Maududi's text bears comparison to Freud's *Civilization and Its Discontents*, which had been published nine years earlier but was unlikely to have been known by the Islamist thinker.

In Maududi's theory of civilization, then, women and the family were far more important to the making of an Islamic society than public institutions and authority. This is what made gender relations so crucial to Islam. But having established the family as what he called the workshop or factory (*karkhana*) of civilization and so Islam itself, Maududi was faced with the problem of how to regulate the relations of men and women within it. His use of the term "factory" for the family is important because the gender relations Maududi describes are modeled on the economic division of labor. In order for them to possess the common interests required for the family to survive, husbands and wives could not compete with one another. Just as they had differing biological functions, then, men and women should have separate vocations. The former were further meant to be the active partners and the latter the passive ones in all their mutual relationships.

Of course, Maududi was quick to note that describing women as passive and men as active did not imply any moral hierarchy between them. Indeed, neither could do without the other, and their interaction was required for the benefit of civilization. He uses the arguably feminine example of sewing to illustrate what he means, with a needle representing the active element and cloth the passive one. This vision of equal but differing duties was intended to stave off competition and was familiar among nineteenth-century moralists responding to capitalism in Europe. It also had a long afterlife in colonial India, with Gandhi, for example, convinced that the caste system worked in exactly this way. Maududi himself was equally concerned with labor disputes, unions, and strikes. And this showed that his understanding of gender relations both drew upon and informed other kinds of social conflicts, demonstrating how the public and the private were open to one another despite his efforts to separate them.

The Body in Question

At several points in his narrative Maududi turns to biological reasoning. This is intended to show that the Muslim woman's role as a wife and mother, the very things that make her crucial to the development of Islam as a civilization, also render her unfit to take on roles that are reserved for men. The examples he proffers are taken from the canon of Western misogyny, and Maududi focuses in particular on menstruation and the physical and emotional disabilities it allegedly entails. But in doing this, he departs from the juristic literature he would have been familiar with, for which menstruation is not a uniquely female trait. It belongs, instead, in a list of conditions, including such things as involuntary bleeding, sneezing, coughing, and urinating, that indicate the subject's loss of control over his or her own body. It is the breaching of corporal boundaries that makes such people, whatever their gender, ritually impure and so unable to pray or conduct other religious duties.[21]

By picking out menstruation as a defining feature of women's biology, Maududi dispensed with the ritual continuum of which it had traditionally been a part so as to make women into distinctive and autonomous subjects. The irony of their sexual autonomy, in other words, was that it was premised upon women's subordination in new and very modern ways that are familiar to us with the emergence of other identities such as race. Familiar though Maududi's reasoning may be, however, it is interesting how superficial it remains. This is not due to Maududi's incompetence as a theorist as much as to his apparent unwillingness to propose a more substantial biological argument. Instead of claiming that women are inherently and by their very nature different from men, as is the case for misogyny in the modern West, he dwells on some illustrations of their temporary departure from an otherwise common corporeality.

We have already seen another example of Maududi's ambiguous approach to biology, when he distinguished between the reproductive role of animal sexuality and the civilizational one of human beings. And while he does not tell us why he holds back on a more fulsome biological account of gender relations, I suggest it is because Maududi, like other modern Muslims, was unable to suggest any deeper distinction between men and women by the very logic that established Islam as a subject of history. As we saw in the first chapter, Islam was distinguished by its apologists from other civilizations in part because it was seen as being free of biological hierarchies like those of race and, for Indians like Maududi, of caste as well. He therefore criticized Hinduism for assigning social roles on the basis of birth, while remaining oblivious to the fact that he had himself deployed the same kind of reasoning to justify the distinction of such roles by sex.

Maududi's blindness likely derived from his ostentatious repudiation of biological determination and distinction in the name of
Islam. Indeed, the biological reasoning of his book was counterposed by the privilege he gave to sociological factors in its argument. This included seeing the family as a factory and God as a
master engineer for the universe understood as a machine. Maududi's narrative was thus far more mechanical than it was organic. For
crucial to Islam was the intellectual work of ideas and beliefs rather
than the corporal functions of biology in bringing about a virtuous
social order. This was also why Muslims were able to pivot from
conceiving of Islam as a civilization in the nineteenth and early
twentieth centuries to imagining it as an ideology or structure of
ideas after the Bolshevik revolution. Maududi was a bit late in up-
dating his vocabulary in this respect, but by the Cold War he had
become one of the chief spokesmen of Islam as an ideology, which,
like Soviet communism, had no truck with biological determinism.

Given these circumstances, what role did biological reasoning
play in imagining modern Islam? For one thing, of course, bodies
and the urges that instrumentalized them had to be set aside in
order to have Islam function as an ideology. This is what justified
gender segregation and sequestration, which were meant to enable
the operation of a public life dominated by reasoned debate rather
than bodily desire. And while such a vision does have some links to
the history of Muslim political thought before colonialism, it also
takes as a presupposition the liberal idea of a public sphere characterized by rational discussion. In this sense the body, however powerful its illicit desires, represents little more than a distraction that
can and must be controlled. But biological reasoning also plays another kind of role in Islam, and this has to do with shoring up a
gender binary that is forever threatening to come apart.

The ideal Muslim as a representative of Islam, after all, has always been conceptualized as a generic figure set against the hierarchies of monarchical and mystical models of social order. And it is
precisely as a mouthpiece for this unitary form of Islam understood
as the true subject of history that the Muslim woman can become
such a figure. But this also means that she may escape her gendered identity, which therefore needs to be reinforced constantly.
The incomplete and even half-hearted references to her biological

nature that we see expressed by writers like Maududi provide one way of doing this. But however draconian the implications of such reasoning as far as women's autonomy and freedom are concerned, it does not suffice to provide an intellectual foundation for gender hierarchy. This is perhaps why Maududi has recourse to scripture at the end of his book, though in justifying his argument by appeal to theological authority he only weakens its own intellectual credibility, which was premised upon a sociological understanding of interactions between the sexes.

Is it also the insufficiency of biological reasoning in providing a foundation for gender hierarchy that leads to demands for it to be supplemented by sartorial and spatial distinctions? While they may be an inheritance from the historical past, after all, gendered regulations regarding clothing and comportment work here not only to protect Muslims from their own biological urges, but also by marking gender distinctions outside and beyond the body. As both the most visible and the most commonly experienced manifestation of gender hierarchy in some Muslim societies, such practices displace the body that is apparently their ultimate point of reference to define sexual relations in more or less disembodied ways. The very proliferation of gendered arguments and identifications demonstrates not just an anxiety about maintaining sexual difference but the inability to do so. And I suggest that this is because it cannot be naturalized in Muslim debate.

One reason why it might have been so difficult for writers like Maududi to naturalize a binary and heteronormative vision of sexuality had to do with its sheer novelty in Muslim societies. After all, the literary tradition to which Maududi was heir had been dominated by the celebration of male homosexuality as well as illicit love more generally. But such themes were not confined to literature and characterized the aristocratic culture of the Mughal, Safavid, and Ottoman empires in very public ways. Yet same-sex relations were not understood as occurring between people defined by distinctive sexualities and did not preclude them from engaging in heterosexual ones. These were also societies in which eunuchs were important figures at court, unveiled courtesans occupied public space, and people who had been born male or intersex lived together as women and were called upon to celebrate weddings, births, and circumcisions.

In Pakistan members of this *hijra* or *khwajasira* community are officially recognized as a third sex with certain positions and privileges reserved for them. In 2023, for example, Chandni Shah was elected as the Jamaat-e Islami's representative for a seat on the Karachi Municipal Corporation that had been reserved for third gender individuals.[22] The Jamaat, of course, was founded by Maududi and remains the country's oldest and most important Islamist party. Because Shah, whose birth name is Muhammad Junaid, presents herself as a woman though without being defined as one, the gendered dress codes otherwise enforced by the party she represents do not apply to her. She is thus able to move in public and interact with men as an unveiled woman might, something that would not ordinarily be tolerated, and with even more freedom than the latter. Classed as neither a man nor a woman, her dress and comportment elicit no rebuke and do not, apparently, threaten the gender distinction that such sartorial and behavioral codes are meant to enforce in a society defined as Islamic.

While these cultures of sexual multiplicity and ambiguity by no means lacked hierarchy or violence, their very existence made the imposition of a binary division of the sexes difficult. In this sense Islam came to serve as a medium for Western ideas of sexuality, if only in order to destroy the aristocratic culture that had housed such different visions of gender.[23] This still incomplete shift to a nineteenth-century European understanding of sex can be seen in the way in which an old juridical category, that of the hermaphrodite, has been repurposed to address transgender people and gender reassignment surgery since at least the 1960s. In juristic and other texts from the past, however, it was not so much who hermaphrodites were but where intersex individuals belonged that was important. Did they stand with men in the mosque or with women? Did they inherit what male descendants did or female? How should they dress and who might they marry?

These kinds of questions did not take individuals as objects of knowledge, nor seek to define their identities in purely sexual terms. They were concerned instead with how hermaphrodites might relate to other classes of people in social life. Depending on their physiological characteristics and bodily functions (such as menstruation, penile erection, or ejaculation), hermaphrodites could be characterized as male, female, or neither of the two, thus putting any binary view of sexual difference into question. And since a number of the physiological characteristics that could help classify intersex individuals emerged only at puberty, hermaphrodites could also change their sex over time even without medical intervention. Even as it gave rise to classificatory anxiety, in other words, the large literature on hermaphroditism in Muslim tradition demonstrated a recognition of intersex individuals and sought to attribute genders to them not on the basis of an impossible biological uniformity, but in order to deal with them as legal persons.

Once sex-change operations became possible, Muslim authorities approved them on the principle that, like determining hermaphrodites' legal status in the past, these interventions were meant to ascertain their correct gender. The Ayatollah Khomeini, for instance, had issued such a legal opinion in 1964:

> It seems that the sex-reassignment surgery for male-to-female is not forbidden (*haram*) [in Islam] and vice-versa, and it is also not forbidden for a *khuntha* (hermaphrodite/intersex) undergoing it to be attached to one of the sexes [female or male]; and [if one asks] is a woman/man obliged to undergo the sex-reassignment surgery if the woman finds in herself [sensual] desires similar to men's desires or some evidence of masculinity in herself—or a man finds in himself [sensual] desires similar to the opposite sex or some evidence of femininity in himself? It seems that [in such a case] if a person really [physically] belongs to a [determined] sex, a sex-reassignment surgery is not . . . obligatory (*wajib*), but the person is still eligible to change her/his sex into the opposite gender.[24]

Although Khomeini's statement begins by permitting surgery to correct the hermaphrodite's sexual ambiguity, it moves on to consider non-intersex individuals who may also change their gender. In 1988, when a male medical student in Cairo underwent a surgical procedure to become female, the doctors' syndicate objected, and as part of the debate that ensued, the chief mufti, Sayyid Tantawi, was asked for an opinion. He, too, relied on the figure of the hermaphrodite to approve the procedure, "as long as a reliable doctor concludes that there are innate causes in the body itself, indicating a buried (*matmura*) female nature, or a covered (*maghmura*) male nature, because the operation will disclose these buried or covered organs, thereby curing a corporal disease which cannot be removed, except by this operation."[25] Though he appeared to confine himself to the problem of intersexuality, Tantawi knew he was not dealing with a case of physiological ambiguity. His description of surgery as a way of discovering hidden sexual organs drew upon the discourse of hermaphroditism to recast the procedure as a form of discovery rather than creation, and thus turned biology into metaphor.

In 1987, after meeting a transgender person who was not a hermaphrodite, Khomeini issued another opinion permitting reassignment surgery: "In the name of God. Sex reassignment surgery is not prohibited in sharia law if reliable medical doctors recommend it. *Inshallah* you will be safe and hopefully the people whom you had mentioned might take care of your situation."[26] Apart from reaffirming his earlier opinion, this time without mentioning hermaphroditism, Khomeini, like Tantawi the year before, added to it the requirement of medical authorization. Iran has since become a world leader in gender reassignment surgery, second only to Thailand in the number of procedures conducted. And these are framed by an extensive medico-legal apparatus underwritten by the state, in which counselors, psychiatrists, pharmacists, and doctors support the transitioning individual over sometimes long periods of time until surgery is deemed appropriate.

The anthropologist Afsaneh Najmabadi has written a pioneering ethnography of transgender lives and their management by state institutions in Iran.[27] She notes in it that the expertise in plastic surgery needed to carry out reassignment procedures had been developed during the Iran–Iraq War of the 1980s to treat wounded soldiers. After the war, it was repurposed for civilian use in cosmetic and other forms of plastic surgery. Iran's recognition of transgender persons is often attributed to the desire of its clerical establishment to enforce a binary understanding of sexual identity and relations, but Najmabadi shows us how much more complex the situation is. Instead of encouraging homosexuals to transition

in order to enforce heterosexuality, moreover, all the juristic opinions and medical procedures dealing with transgender issues insist
on doing exactly the opposite and making sure people do not resort to reassignment merely for reasons of sexual inclination or
pleasure.

Just as with the hermaphrodite, then, the process of identifying
a gender is conceived of as the correction of a natural fault, and
this is why it is so easily medicalized. Homosexuality, on the other
hand, is seen as a sinful desire that, like all such urges, including
heterosexual ones, can and should be controlled by Muslims in
their capacity as moral agents. And in this sense same-sex relations
are still understood to be very much like their apparent opposites,
as the choices of moral actors and not a product of nature or even a
kind of disease. Despite these differences between the legitimate
lives of transgender people and the illegitimate ones of homosexuals, however, Najmabadi describes the ways in which they nevertheless overlap. Sometimes the former even provide cover for the
latter in the preoperative stage of transitioning, when an indefi-
nitely drawn-out course of counseling allows doctors and patients
to conspire in making homosexual lives publicly possible even if
under a different name.

Whatever the intentions of the state, in other words, or at least
some parts of it, ordinary Iranians are still capable of making their
own sexual and gendered lives, and these can be remarkably fluid
and flexible, as Najmabadi demonstrates. A binary vision of gender,
as I have been arguing, might be so ferociously upheld by the authorities precisely because it has effectively been dissolved by those
who themselves speak for Islam. Najmabadi tells us, for instance,
that some religious authorities describe gender dysmorphia in
terms of the soul and the body. It is the soul that is the true site of
gender identity, and if it finds itself in the wrong body, reassignment surgery is appropriate to change the latter. This means that
the body is in effect understood as a superficial marker of such an
identity. And, in fact, once its reassignment has been legitimized,
gender must be detached from biology to become a spiritual subject and in this way potentially a far more religious one.

When women were first enlisted to the cause of Islam in the
nineteenth century, it was in part due to the diminishing power of

both secular and sacred Muslim authorities and so the fragmentation of their public world. Having been freed from the ruins of this
moral city as an agent in its own right, Islam now took up its abode
in Muslim households, within which women were of course the
most important inhabitants. But making women into virtuous
Muslims meant turning them into some version of men, and this
led to a new kind of anxiety about regulating gender relations.
From figures of temptation threatening the world of male reason,
after all, women had come to be seen as victims of masculine un-
reason. It was they who now represented virtue in the household
newly designated as Islam's fortress. In these circumstances it
proved impossible to draw an absolute and especially a biological
distinction between men and women.

But relying upon sartorial and other disembodied forms to
draw such distinctions also fitted rather well with precolonial understandings of agency, which tended to focus on juristic persons
and for which sex did not represent the individual's truth. On the
one hand, then, the emergence of Islam was linked with the adoption of European ideas about women as subjects in their own right
and therefore about heterosexuality as a binary relationship occurring within a nuclear family. This was characteristic of its middle-
class origins. Yet on the other hand Islam also allowed for the
eradication of biological reasoning, initially with regards to race
and then for gender differences. Najmabadi, for example, points
out that there is no way of distinguishing between sex and gender,
or indeed even between genre and sex in everyday language. The
word used is *jins*, the Arabic form of "genus" or "kind." And this
suggests that biology really has not come to determine the classifi-
cation of identities, both in Iran and in many other Muslim countries as well. The Islamic authorization for surgical procedures to
change or rather reaffirm gender identities, therefore, served to
confirm the repudiation of biological sex.

Doing Without Politics

Olivier Roy has noted that relations between women and men have
come in modern times to be seen as constituting the most important cleavage in many Muslim societies. He attributes this to the

fact that Islamists in particular would like to depoliticize all interactions of class or ethnicity among Muslims and reduce them to
forms of social self-regulation.[28] Such relations were thus meant to
be defined not by competition but complementarity, as we have
seen was also the case with Maududi's view of gender. And as he
also made clear, sexual relations came to comprise the foundation
and model for every other kind of interaction between Muslims.
But the very effort to deprive these economic and other relations
of political character made them into incredibly fraught ones, both
in Islamic thought and in social reality. Not only did gender, and so
women especially, become key to thinking about social order more
generally, in other words, but it also came to represent an alternative vision of the generic Muslim subject.

The social life of sexuality, then, by no means comprised a distinctive department of Islamic thought but served rather as a
model for the larger depoliticization of Muslim society. In this way
it bears comparison both to the relations of labor and capital, as we
have already seen, and to those of Muslims and non-Muslims.
SherAli Tareen, as we saw in the previous chapter, has argued that
the breakdown of Muslim political and religious authority in colonial India led to the socialization of sovereignty in Muslim lives.[29]
By this he means that the sovereign power to draw distinctions between right and wrong and also between friend and enemy was detached from the institutional politics of the state to become part of
efforts at social ordering in civil life. Crucial to this shift were attempts to mark out new ways of considering the interactions of
Hindus and Muslims in a situation where neither held political
power.

It was not any presumption of the innate and inevitable differences between these groups that prompted this concern, in other
words, but the inability to draw such distinctions which led to the
anxiety that Muslims might inadvertently fall prey to Hindu influence and lose their autonomy in the process. And this is what made
friendship with non-Muslims such a delicate and contentious issue
for the clerical authorities Tareen studies. But friendship or love
also represented one of the great themes of precolonial Muslim
ethics. There it had often been approached through the figure of
the prince in advice literature, and through that of the beloved in

poetry. The two genres were in fact linked, since mirrors for princes routinely cited verses about the beloved, while lyric poetry treated the prince as one. The paradox both literary traditions addressed was about how to reconcile the political as much as erotic necessity of intimacy with the inequality of power or passion that made it impossible.

It is not just that the prince was unable to have the boon companions he required for trusted and honest advice because he possessed so much more power than they. Even beyond the political realm, after all, friendship and love were both necessary yet contentious sentiments because they deprived one or both parties of their judgment and so moral autonomy. Yet this loss of self-control was also capable of being enjoyed as the most intense form of self-realization, one that brought the impassioned subject wisdom and pleasure of a superior and even transcendent or mystical kind. The connection between the political and the erotic in these ways of thinking was typical of courtly culture. But their world of reference was dismantled in colonial times by translating the old problem of an individual's moral autonomy and therefore rational judgment into a collective duty to maintain the sovereignty of the Muslim community in purely social terms.

And yet something from these earlier narratives about moral agency seems to have survived within the apparently practical discussions about protecting the supremacy of Muslim communal identity that Tareen so nicely describes. For there is something excessive about the anxieties that inform clerical disquisitions on Hindu-Muslim friendship, which presume the possibility not simply of everyday prejudice clouding the believer's judgment, but something akin to the Muslim's erotic dependency upon infidels. I shall return to this love that dare not speak its name in the next chapter, whose twinning of fraternity and fratricide has received an exemplary analysis in the work of the Cambridge historian Shruti Kapila.[30] For the moment it is enough to note how familiar these efforts to distinguish between Hindu and Muslim were. For their focus on sartorial, ritual, and other ways of maintaining communal difference bears a striking similarity to debates occurring at the same time about the importance of distinguishing between men and women within Muslim society.

The loss of Muslim political power had rendered the relations between Hindus and Muslims as well as between men and women ambiguous and called for their redefinition. Efforts to prevent Muslims from being unduly influenced by Hindus therefore paralleled attempts to prevent women from being seduced or exploited by men. In both cases the loss of autonomy that resulted from such improper relations was attributed to differences in power or love between the parties involved. It was therefore considered necessary to separate those parties into distinct and marked categories whose relationship should be one of civility and sometimes even of equality but never again include the kind of intimacy that risked the loss of moral independence. Muslims and women were no longer meant to tolerate the kind of mastery, either amorous or political, that had once been such an important part of aristocratic culture.

The link between communal and sexual relations, I have argued, was defined by the colonial context they both shared. But this made them nonbinary by definition, for the colonial state, if not the idea of the West as a whole, was inevitably a party in these debates. Instead of a set of resolutely dualistic interactions between pairs of categories, each of which always holds the potential of being politicized into relations of enmity, what we see is a kind of triangle among lover, beloved, and rival, as in the tradition of courtly poetry. This triangle was not just a literary inheritance, however, but important because in colonial times there could be no relationship between Hindu and Muslim without the British constituting a third party to it. And much the same was feared of relations between men and women, since the latter's status had become a concern not only to missionaries, but to the colonial and later national state.

While Indian nationalists struggled to join Hindus and Muslims, along with men and women, in friendship against the British seen as their common foe, the triadic relation among them meant that any one party could befriend another against the remaining third. Two of the parties might even vie with one another for the third's friendship, with the Indian National Congress and the All-India Muslim League constantly accusing each other of consorting with the British in this way. And this posed the problem of deciding which was the genuine lover. Syed Ahmed Khan, for instance, could respond to the emergence of the Congress in the 1880s by seeing in its demands for majority rule little more than an effort to subordinate Muslims to Hindus and thus undo the very possibility of their friendship.[31] He advised the former to turn to the British for true friendship by pointing out that they not only shared a common religious tradition, but could also share each other's food and society much more freely than with upper-caste Hindus.

In responding to views like those of Syed Ahmed Khan's, the poet Akbar Illahabadi pointed out that for Muslims to desire friendship with the British was absurd, given their vastly unequal relationship: "You want to befriend him, what a strange desire! He's on the throne, you're in the dust, he's exalted, you're a pauper."[32] But this was also a question the British asked themselves. E. M. Forster's novel *A Passage to India* is all about the possibility of friendship as much as love between Indian and English. In trying to befriend Indian men, who were by definition unequal to them, his female characters, Adela Quested and Mrs. Moore, end up inadvertently reinforcing racial and gender distinctions in their most violent forms. At the close of the novel the possibility of friendship between men like Fielding and Dr. Aziz is explicitly posed and, despite their own desires, answered with a "No, not yet" and "No, not there."

The love triangle, however, was effectively a nineteenth-century theme, which in the twentieth was invoked only polemically to accuse one's friend, whether Hindu, Muslim, or British, of betrayal. The emergence of mass politics with Gandhi suddenly made the last of these figures seem irrelevant to India's future. Or rather, Britain's importance became purely instrumental, residing in its ability to help the Hindu or Muslim side in the struggle to define such a future. From possible partners or rivals in love and friendship, the British thus came to be seen as betraying their own claim to remain the neutral third party in India mediating between their various subjects understood in liberal and capitalist terms as interests. And having become partisan in this sense, without at the same time entering into any relationship of friendship with Hindus or Muslims, the colonial state's legitimacy collapsed, together with its ideology of disinterested governance.

For the purposes of my argument, of course, British rule serves to name colonial and Western dominance more generally. And it was the triangulation this made possible between men and women as well as between Muslims and non-Muslims that defined all these relations in nonbinary and erotic as much as in potentially political ways. To this day, it remains impossible to speak about gender in Muslim societies without bringing in the West, generally so as to discredit those who are seen as following Euro-American opinions as mentally colonized. I have tried to show in this chapter that at the same time as they were being shaped into distinctive subjects in their own right, Muslim women came to pose a threat to dualistic notions of sexual difference in part because it proved impossible to define them in purely biological ways. But this also meant that they were able to provide a model for other kinds of interactions in Muslim societies, if only at the risk of depoliticizing them. And the inability to sequester the language of gender relations from that of labor or interreligious ones only illustrates how women become generic Muslim subjects.

CHAPTER FIVE

Half in Love

B Y THE SECOND HALF of the nineteenth century, it had become not just possible but commonplace to imagine Islam's end in historical rather than metaphysical terms. Dismissing the rich apocalyptic tradition as a set of popular superstitions, Muslim writers began to search out precedents for what they thought was the threat facing Islam in the age of European imperialism. The Mongol conquest of medieval times, which had swallowed up the Abbasid caliphate and much of the Muslim world besides, provided an inevitable example. But since the Mongols had ended up converting to Islam, this turned out to be a more cheering than tragic illustration. The same was true of the Crusades, also an important moment in the genealogy of Western relations with Islam, but one that ended in the latter's victory. Crucial to the tragic understanding of Islam's history, however, was the loss of Spain and other European territories, such as Sicily, from which Muslims had been expelled.

All of these events were made into literary subjects among Muslims in many different parts of the world.[1] And they were often understood as instructive examples of earlier occasions when Islam had been threatened by Christian powers. They were also, of course, linked to the colonization of Muslims in contemporary times, with European depredations of the Ottoman Empire featuring as favored instances of this process from the end of the nineteenth century. Global in its tragic conception, this kind of historical imagination was not just a mirror image of European narratives about the Crusades or the Reconquista. It drew instead on a variety of indigenous sources to make for a quite distinctive sensibility in which Christians could be seen as friends and competitors as much as enemies. Indian history offers us a good example of the development of this sensibility, in which the *ummah*, or Muslim community, emerges as a global figure whose failure to represent Islam leads God to abandon it.

The first great lament for this nontheological vision of Islam's passing was Hali's epic poem of 1879, *The Flow and Ebb of Islam*, which we already encountered in the Introduction. It drew upon at least three literary genres. The first was the *shahr-ashob*, or lament for the city, whose Persian original had described the erotic attraction that low-born youths exercised upon well-born men.[2] It was a genre that celebrated the collapse of the city as the principal site of moral order in Muslim religious and political thought, for which not just sexual attraction but the promiscuous mixing of classes and the loss of self-control among men of rank had to be guarded against. Once poems of this kind started being composed in Urdu during the eighteenth century, their focus shifted from erotic attraction to the actual destruction of cities during the period. The seductive lower orders of the Persian lament became usurpers overturning the aristocratic dominance of urban life.

But it was the Indian Rebellion of 1857 that fundamentally transformed the genre. When the East India Company's troops mutinied against the British, they took the much-reduced Mughal emperor as their leader and received the support of many Indian noblemen. Once the rebellion was brutally put down, not only were these aristocrats destroyed, but their urban culture was also uprooted as Muslims were driven out of cities like Delhi. The laments written in the rebellion's aftermath continued to be realistic but soon abandoned the city as their sole site of action. Having been demolished as a model for thinking about virtuous as much as pleasurably sinful behavior, the city was sometimes replaced by the country, now absorbed into the colonial state, sometimes by the world itself as a figure of lament, and most importantly by Islam. Because the city had been so crucial in framing Islamic visions of moral order, both in the *shahr-ashob* and beyond, its disappearance from this and other literary genres left these ideas homeless. And Islam or its *ummah* was to provide them with a new home in the form of Muslim subjectivity rather than any geographical site of social or political order.

The other genre that defined Hali's lament was the *marsiya*, or elegy, for the martyred Imams of the Shia. Not coincidentally, his epic used the same meter as the elegy, as well as some of its mournful themes. The elegy, of course, represented the only really tragic rather than merely lovelorn or nostalgic genre of Muslim literature. And as such it didn't require the moral city as a framing device. Indeed, the caliph's capital and court were seen as sites of evildoing, while much of the elegy's action occurred in the desert bereft of human habitation. In this way, the elegy may have allowed Hali and those who followed him to imagine Islam and the community it had created as moral agents in their own right. Elegies for the martyred Imams, after all, took the Prophet's family and those faithful to them as moral agents without any reference to cities. And this meant that they disregarded urban life and so the state in which it was to be found as sites for the religious and political imagination.

While the elegy was nothing if not metaphysical, with its descriptions of angels, visitations, miracles, and divine succor, Hali's poem lacked all of these elements. Its final and most singular inspiration was a medieval Arabic genre of lament, and in particular a thirteenth-century poem, *Lament for the Fall of Seville*, by Abu al-Baqa al-Rundi.[3] It belonged to another genre about cities (the *ritha al-mudun*), whose defeat by infidels is lamented in order to prepare Muslims for jihad, thus adding an activist dimension to the different forms of mourning that characterized the *shahr-ashob* and the *marsiya*. For Hali, of course, it was the activism of reform and modernization that took the place of jihad. He had been asked to write in the style of the Arabic poem by the founding figure of Islamic modernism, Syed Ahmed Khan, who had published its original and an Urdu translation in 1878 during the Russo–Turkish War and after news of the fall of Plevna reached India.

Hali's poem, then, was truly global in both its derivation and its imaginative scope. In line with the post-1857 *shahr-ashob*, he abandoned the city as a moral and political model; or rather, he turned its historical ruins and fragments, as described in the tradition of Arabic lament, into signs of an altogether different subject. From Delhi to Cordoba, they had now come to represent not any kingdom or empire but Islam itself and the community to which it gave rise. As with the Shia elegy, therefore, the Muslim community came for Hali to represent Islam in its very defeat and deprivation of politics. Indeed, its globalization was premised upon the loss of a moral and political imagination like the one that had taken the city as its focus. While its ruins were spread across the world in the shape of texts and monuments, cultures and beliefs, Islam now had no place of its own and could live only in and through the *ummah*. Hali even calls this community the heir (*waris*) to Islam.[4]

But this way of thinking about Islam, as an inheritance, did not turn it from an acting subject into an object passed down for someone else's use. Instead, it became a kind of ghost haunting Muslims and asking them to be true to themselves in order to recover their past glory. This, of course, is the role of any inheritance, which represents the ancestor's need to live again through descendants. Like the ghost of Hamlet's father, Islam in Hali's epic and its many imitators was depicted as urging Muslims to avenge its decline. Another important writer, Shibli Numani, made this very clear in his own imitation of Hali's poem called the *Qawmi Musaddas* (Community Epic) of 1894. It was composed for a gathering at the Muhammadan Anglo-Oriental College in Aligarh, which was Syed Ahmed Khan's flagship institution. This gathering, called the *Tamasha-ye Ibrat* (Cautionary Spectacle), included the appearance onstage of Sir Syed and other luminaries dressed in historical garments to invoke Muslim heroes from the past.

Shibli's poem refers to India's Muslims but only as part of a global Muslim community, which he describes through its monumental relics: "The scenic beauty of Merv and Shiraz and Isfahan; the halls and walls and doors of the Alhambra; each stone of Egypt and Granada and Baghdad; and that beloved ruin of departed Delhi. In their fragments that spark still glints; they still remember all those stories by heart; someone should hear from them a tale of the homeland's friends; they who bring that same old dream before the eyes."[5] In addition to describing the Muslim community as a dream evoked by the ruins of empire, Shibli also sees it running like blood in the veins of the historical figures being represented onstage: "The stories of those men that affect you, the community; these were the same men in whose veins your blood flowed."[6] He refers to Syed Ahmed Khan and his associates by saying, "They are the interpreters of the community's scattered dream."[7]

The Muslim community, in other words, itself needed to come into existence before it could represent Islam. Hali describes the difficulty of this birth by writing that "the search for its wonders now proceeds with such fervor; as if it were a caravan lost in the desert with neither drum nor bell."[8] As its instrument, then, the *ummah* had to find itself and do all it could to keep Islam alive at the risk of betraying it. Unlike the Arabic lament's call for jihad against the infidel, in other words, Hali's set up a relationship of guilt and betrayal between Islam and its followers. Those followers had either to be reformed and so rendered capable of giving new life to Islam, or to be punished by history for being unable to do so. This was a project of remaking the Muslim self so as to represent Islam through its actions individually rather than in the collective life of cities or kingdoms.

Such a project, however, intersected with another, which had to do with the question of how to deal with those who had displaced and defeated Islam. Since Muslims themselves were to be blamed for betraying Islam and rendering it unable to act in history, the European powers that had subordinated them played a much more ambiguous role than the infidels against whom jihad was to be waged. Precisely because Islam was detached from any given political order or imagination to become an abstract and global phenomenon, it also escaped the control of Muslims who now sought to reclaim its universality and thus their own. This universality, as we saw in Chapter 1, was defined in terms of Islam's appeal to the human species by setting aside all divisions of race and civilization. Its egalitarianism, in other words, offered humanity a medium of self-expression for the first time in history. It was this kind of universality that Muslims had neglected, thus allowing Islam to fall into the hands of infidels who in this way became its true heirs to surpass their predecessors.

If Muslims had betrayed Islam's universal message, then, it found a congenial home in Christian minds. And Hali repeated a well-worn theme of Muslim apologetics by describing Europeans eagerly imbibing the learning of Muslim Spain. In order to reclaim their universality and make Islam live again through the *ummah*, in other words, Muslims had to recover it from their own European heirs. For in the meantime these rivals had developed what they learned from Islam much further than Muslims were able to do. Clearly an apologetic argument seeking to account for the power and knowledge of the West and enter into a productive relationship with it, this vision of Islam's history nevertheless made for a remarkably intimate if ambiguous relationship between Muslims and their European overlords. In some ways, we shall see, Europe took the place of the rival for a beloved's affection in the *ghazal* or lyric, itself the most popular poetic form in the Muslim world.

But because it was a rival for Islam's hand, the West also became a model for Muslims. As we saw in the Introduction, infidel practices had long offered attractive alternatives to Muslim piety. Whether it was the wine served by Zoroastrian or Christian youths in city taverns or the sensuous rites and philosophical depth of Hindu ephebes, unbelievers represented figures of seduction in the poetic canon. But then they were generally either minorities in Muslim societies or subordinated to them politically, serving therefore as subjects of reflection among Muslims themselves without becoming their interlocutors. With colonial rule, this way of thinking about non-Muslims started to undergo a change. In India, for example, the Hindu is replaced by the Englishwoman, European, or Christian in the lyric. This shift is clearly marked in the canon, with the celebrated mid-nineteenth-century poet Ghalib, for instance, writing, "Faith restrains me while infidelity pulls me on. The Kaaba is behind me, the church ahead."⁹

The decline of older visions of infidel seduction become even more clear by the end of the nineteenth century, with the famous satirical poet Akbar Illahabadi pronouncing, "They're becoming disappointed with their former glory. The idols that were in the temple are becoming church bells."¹⁰ The novelty of Christian attraction during colonial times, however, had to do with European power, which managed to break once and for all the old relationship of seduction with Hindus and other non-Muslim groups and for the most part expunge them as poetic subjects. Instead, Muslim

poets and their readers now expressed an obsessive desire to be like
the European while at the same time seeking to avenge the humili-
ation of conquest. The Christian here bears some resemblance to
the figure of the powerful Turk or the Mongol in classical Persian
poetry, though Indian writers rarely drew the comparison. This
new relationship between Christian and Muslim soon became the
subject of novels set in medieval Spain, France, Italy, and Palestine,
where Muslim men are depicted resisting the seductive power of
Christian maidens only to convert them eventually.[11]

The problem posed by European seduction had to do with the
fact that Muslims were no longer able to make it a subject merely
of some internal debate and were forced to take Christians as their
interlocutors as well. And this was difficult to do because it destroyed the literary tradition within which this seduction was made
thinkable. Akbar Illahabadi compares this process of interlocution
to the wooing of an English "Miss" by an eager young Muslim.
He writes: "My discourse has no effect on that Miss. Where guns
have effect, there magic fails."[12] In another poem he describes how
the Miss charmingly breaks down the structure of Muslim literary
understanding: "Such a coquette that if you call that idol 'infidel,' it
laughs, saying 'what a dear word, say it again.' Whatever you say
covers those eyes like intoxication. Call it disorder of the ages, call
it wine-bearer, call it wizard."[13] By mentioning wine-bearers and
wizards, Akbar references the Zoroastrian and Christian predecessors of the English Miss.

Old poetic and real-life narratives often had pious Muslims
falling in love with Hindu or Jewish as well as Muslim mystics to
forsake the path of religious austerity for ecstatic knowledge. Akbar
likewise has his Muslim suitor abandon Islam to attain his English
beloved, a story he sketches with great comic effect in his poem
Barq-e Kalisa (Lightning in the Cathedral). The young man in it, of
course, represents the Muslim liberal or modernist, who is suitably
chastened by his beloved's criticism of Islam's bloodthirstiness to
say: " 'Understand my Islam to be an old story.' She laughed, saying 'then understand that I'm yours.' "[14] In some ways, then, the seductive infidel here has returned to become a subject of internal
Muslim debate. But this time only because she is now capable of
destroying Islam itself from within, which the old pagan beloved

had never been able to do. How did the intimate if troubling relationship Islam came to develop with the West, as an object of desire as much as fear, play itself out in modernist, Islamist, and militant thinking?

Losing Islam to the Infidel

Islam's universality had to be recovered from those who had rightly or wrongly inherited it. Syed Ahmed Khan, who was Hali's patron and inspired the writing of his great poem, thought it should be done by reforming Islam so that it was in conformity with modern science. In a monumental effort of scriptural interpretation and exegesis, he contended that Islam, when cleansed of superstitious accretions, was both the most natural and the most universal of religions—this in the sense of being wholly in conformity with the laws of nature and so founded for the benefit of all humankind.[15] To make this argument, however, Syed Ahmed Khan had to separate humanity from all the other forms of life with which it was traditionally associated, including angels, animals, and spirits, together with their respective abodes, and have it stand alone on the hard earth as the unique recipient of divine favor. In his famous commentary on the Qur'an, this most eminent of India's Muslim modernizers had either to deny the reality of supernatural beings or at the very least to consign them to some ineffable and metaphorical place beyond the singular world of human interaction and morality.

Islam's universality thus was predicated upon its equivalence with nineteenth-century notions of nature and therefore with the human species, both of which stood outside the doctrinal sphere with its angels and miracles to provide the criteria of religion's veracity. But this did not entail subordinating religious truth to varying conceptions of science, only insisting that it be continually engaged with the times, whose forms of knowledge regulated scriptural interpretation while keeping Islam at the center of contemporary concerns. Syed Ahmed Khan saw as the only miraculous aspect of the Qur'an its ability to keep pace with scientific change, which in his own times meant its successful interpretation within the laws of nature, a notion that stood apart from earlier definitions of nature as an essence (*zat*), a disposition (*tabiat*), or an ingrained constitution (*fitrat*). Islam's conformity with nature conceived as law had to be demonstrated so that it might be presented as the universal religion of humankind.

One consequence of naturalizing religion in this way was to generalize its doctrinal vocabulary beyond the boundaries of Islam, so that it now became possible to think even of its central concepts as being universal to humanity. Of course, Muslim thinkers in the past had sought precedents and prognostications for Muhammad's revelation by linking it to religions predating Islam, well beyond the monotheistic coterie this latter formed with Judaism and Christianity. While the Muslim doctrines thus discovered in Hinduism, Buddhism, or Zoroastrianism might place all these religions within some universal history, however, there was no question about Islam representing its pinnacle. But the Victorian naturalization of religion meant that if Muslims could be said to have discovered the unity of humankind by way of Islam, they could not claim to possess it exclusively or forever. There was always the possibility that others might be able to lay claim to Islam itself, albeit under a different name, if Muslims were to abandon their duty to represent the human race.

Hali followed Syed Ahmed Khan's lead in focusing on the laws of nature as the secret of Islam's universality. His poem begins by describing the virtues that brought Muslims political power in times past and put them at the forefront of the arts and sciences. He then catalogues the decline of India's Muslims in particular and those of the world at large in practically every department of social life, attributing their decadence to the betrayal of Islamic virtues. Chief among these was fidelity to nature, seen as providing both the form and the content of human knowledge as a set of universal laws. The word that Syed Ahmed Khan and his followers used for "law" was *qanun*, which referred to royal rather than sacred order. By naturalizing this conception of law, then, Muslim liberals both dispensed with the king who had once defined it and legitimized sharia as a mere illustration of the laws of nature. And this is what allowed Europe's Christians, but also the poet's Hindu neighbors, to embrace the laws that Muslims had forsaken to move past the Prophet's followers in representing humanity.

Hali tells his readers that the nations of the West have succeeded Muslims at the head of the species by naturalizing religion
into the service of humankind: "This was the first lesson of the
Book of True Guidance: 'All creatures belong to God's family.' . . .
Those who act on the basis of this weighty utterance today flourish
upon the face of the earth. They are superior to all, high and low.
They are now the central axis of humanity. Those covenants of the
Holy Law which we have broken have all been firmly upheld by
the people of the West."[16] In order to make the argument that
Islam's role has been taken over by the Christian West, Hali had to
redefine the Muslim *ummah* in sociological terms. No longer a
juridical or theological category defined by ritual authority and
political practice, the *ummah* instead became a society that could
never again be contained within legal categories, and one whose
global character placed Islam outside the jurisdiction of any state.

While the loss of political power, therefore, was seen in the
poem as a sign of decline, its restoration did not serve as a condi-
tion for Muslim greatness, which was why Hali could take colonized populations like Hindus as models of virtue. About Islam's
loss of worldly dominion, and as yet unsuccessful quest to find
another way of representing the progress of the human race,
he says:

Government may have drawn aside from you, but you had
no monopoly over it. Who possesses a remedy against the
vicissitudes of fortune? Sometimes one is an Alexander
here, sometimes a Darius. After all, kingship is hardly divinity. What one owns today is someone else's tomorrow.
. . . Now that government has performed its proper function, Islam has no need for it left. But alas, oh community
of the Glory of Man, humanity departed together with it.
Government was like a gilt covering upon you. As soon as
it peeled off, your innate capacity emerged. There are
many nations in the world who do not possess the special
quality of empire. But nowhere can so great a calamity
have come as here, where each house is overshadowed by
abasement. The partridge and the falcon, all are high up in
the sky, it is only we who lack wing and pinion.[17]

Important about the new Muslim community was its elegiac character. And while this mournful vision of the *ummah* is often considered the consequence of colonial dispossession, I argue for a more complex reading of the trope. For the narrative of Muslim decline pioneered by Hali is related to another common in Europe at the same time. This is the story of European decadence conceived not in political or juridical terms, exemplified by the fall of kingdoms and dynasties, but in the vision of exhausted civilizations and depleted races.[18] Like the *ummah*, in other words, race and civilization are categories that may incorporate state power but continue to embody a people's greatness beyond the confines of the state. As a consequence, they have since the eighteenth century also been global categories, whose context is provided by other civilizations and races spread across the surface of the earth.

From the Comte de Gobineau's racial speculations in the nineteenth century to Oswald Spengler's best-selling *Decline of the West* in the twentieth, the modern history of this narrative coincides with that of Europe's greatest triumphs in domains ranging from the political to the scientific, so that it becomes impossible to see the story of Western decadence as a reflection of some general crisis there. Of course, the groups that subscribed to such accounts might well have been the losers of this history, which still tells us little about why they interpreted it in global terms. Could it be that Muslim ideas of community in the age of imperialism, as much as Christian ones of civilization and race, were attempts to imagine sociological formations at a planetary level well beyond the jurisdiction of states or empires?

By the nineteenth century, race, civilization, and religious community had become categories that took for their context the human race as such, though they could do so only by dividing it into a set of comparable and competitive sociological formations. And this meant that while humanity had abandoned its earlier and more philosophical roles of essence, abstraction, and regulative ideal to provide the demographic background for such global categories, it still did not exist as a subject in its own right. The narrative of decline characteristic of these new formations might well represent a degree of ambivalence about their lack of political reality as much as that of the species itself. For built into the categories of race, civilization, and religious community during this period was the fantasy of encompassing humanity as a whole, either by a process of assimilation or within some kind of hierarchical order.

Now the *ummah* imagined by writers like Hali dispensed with race and dealt with civilization only in a minor key, these categories existing uneasily in languages like Urdu merely as new glosses for older Arabic terms like "lineage" (*nasl*) or "pedigree" (*nasab*), "habitation" (*tamaddun*) or "refinement" (*tahzib*), none of which possessed a territorial character. Indeed, the Muslim community was celebrated precisely for its ethnic and cultural diversity and therefore was seen as being more natural to the species than race and civilization. But as an expression of Islam's fidelity to nature, this kind of universality surpassed the *ummah*, constituting a line of flight toward the horizon of humanity. It was only in this fleeting way that the Muslim community could represent a species still lacking subjectivity.

Catching Up with Oneself

Like some of the narratives dealing with the decadence of races or civilizations, the story of Islam's decline was predicated upon the inability of its adherents to keep pace with their own universality. In making this case, of course, Hali was invoking an old literary model, in which the fall of kingdoms was attributed to the moral corruption of their rulers, itself a consequence of worldly success. More than the ancient kingdoms that had in the past provided such cautionary tales, it was the career of Christianity that now offered Muslims warning about the perils of victory. At times Muslim writers saw in Christianity's very success a premonition of failure, with its religious spirit eclipsed by Europe's material glory in much the same way they thought had happened to Islam in the days of its imperial glory. It was not the reformers of the nineteenth century, however, but a writer from the twentieth who had the most to say on this issue. The poet and philosopher Muhammad Iqbal, whom we last encountered in Chapter 3, argued that when Christian virtues were universalized in Europe to become secular values, they ended up perverting both religious and profane life there.

Iqbal thought that the division of liberal societies into public and private realms had as its premise the metaphysical distinction of matter and spirit, which turned religion into a merely individual ideal and gave collective life over to exploitation of every kind, thus bifurcating humanity into master and slave classes, races, and even continents. As he put it in a speech from 1930: "Europe uncritically accepted the duality of spirit and matter probably from Manichaean thought. Her best thinkers are realizing this initial mistake to-day, but her statesmen are indirectly forcing the world to accept it as an unquestionable dogma. It is, then, this mistaken separation of spiritual and temporal which has largely influenced European religious and political thought and has resulted practically in the total exclusion of Christianity from the life of European states. The result is a set of mutually ill-adjusted states dominated by interests not human but national."[19]

Taking warning from the history of Christianity, Iqbal thought that Muslims should reclaim their lost universality by purifying Islam of the corruption wrought by its worldly success, which for him included ridding it of what he called "the stamp of Arabian imperialism." For like Hali before him, Iqbal was ambivalent about Islam's history of worldly success and thought that Muslims had the opportunity to rethink the universality of their mission in its aftermath. In a diary entry from 1910, he had this to say about Islam's postimperial mission: "As a political force we are perhaps no longer required; but we are, I believe, still indispensable to the world as the only testimony to the absolute unity of God. Our value among the nations, then, is purely evidential."[20]

Islam's postimperial mission, however, was not to be a quietist one, but instead an effort to represent the species against the false claims of states both colonial and national. Muslim universality, in other words, was now to be found in the idea of human solidarity alone and set against what Iqbal saw as the factional brutalities of nation-states in particular. He thought that nationality, or indeed any other form of collective identity, had to transcend territory if it was to coexist with other forms of self-definition within the human community. Islam's postimperial universality, then, was supposed to aim precisely at this goal, which, like that of communism or liberalism, had to be ideological in nature: "With us nationality is a pure *idea;* it has no material basis. Our only rallying point is a sort of mental agreement in a certain view of the world."[21]

While Muslim states might still exist and could even be cherished, Islam's abstract universality could no longer be grounded in them, being manifested rather in the adoption of a critical attitude to all politics. It was this purely human universality that Muslims had to recover, not simply from their own history but from the virtues of others as well. The many public figures who recommended such efforts of self-recovery often did so to draw attention to the virtues of Hindus or Christians and encourage Muslims to join them in some worthy enterprise. When after the First World War Gandhi launched his first great movement of noncooperation, bringing Hindus and Muslims together in support of the Ottoman caliphate, Akbar Illahabadi dedicated a laudatory mock-epic to him. In *Gandhinama* (The Epic of Gandhi), Akbar not only described the Mahatma's practice of nonviolent resistance as manifesting the Islamic virtue of *sabr*, or fortitude, which the poet considered to be more crucial than the ideals in vogue among Muslims themselves, but also represented the holy water that pilgrims bring back in bottles from Mecca finding its freedom by being poured into the sacred waters of the Ganges.[22]

Yet generalizing Islamic virtues beyond the Muslim community was an ambivalent process, since it could serve to promote cohabitation as much as competition with unbelievers. Two of Iqbal's poems, probably the most popular Urdu compositions of the twentieth century, provide good examples of this. Among the many imitations of Hali's epic on the *ummah*'s decline, and composed in the same meter, this pair of laments is regularly recited on Pakistani radio and television, with the country's most celebrated performers recording their own versions of it as a rite of passage. But perhaps the most famous, if summary, rendition of these works is by the Egyptian singer Umm Kulthum. She sang Iqbal's verses in Arabic translation just before and after the 1967 Arab–Israeli War, when they were taken as an instruction to Muslims on managing their defeat. Called *Hadith al-Ruh* (The Spirit's Converse), the song is played on Egyptian radio every evening, just before the call to prayer, thus turning Iqbal into an essential part of Arabic popular culture.[23]

Published in 1909 and called *Shikwa* (Complaint), the first work accuses God of abandoning Muslims for unbelievers by showering upon them the good things of the earth and leaving the former with a merely imaginary world.[24] This dereliction was all the more unjust given that Muslims had by means of great sacrifices freed human beings from slavery and spread the doctrine of human equality among them. Iqbal pictures idols rejoicing at the sight of Muslims departing the world with Qur'ans tucked under their arms, thus providing us with one of the first posthumous descriptions of Islam, a vision standing apart from earlier apocalyptic narratives concerned with the coming of the messiah and the end of time. He even goes so far as to call God a woman dispensing favors, now to her Muslim lover and now to his infidel rivals. Deploying the erotic vocabulary of the traditional lyric to great effect, Iqbal turns the stock figure of the rival for a mistress's affection into that of the strangers who would replace Muslims as God's elect and the representatives of their race.

A few years after the publication of this acclaimed and controversial work, Iqbal wrote *Jawab-e Shikwa* (The Complaint's Answer), in which he had God respond to the first poem, thus claiming for his composition the status of divine speech.[25] In this heavenly monologue of 1913, Muslims are blamed for abandoning their duty to represent humankind not only by taking leave of world-making activities like science and industry, but more importantly by forsaking the quest for freedom and equality to live upon past glories, described as the worship of so many idols. If infidels adopt the ways of Muslims, says the poem's divine interlocutor, then it is only right that they should receive the damsels and palaces promised to believers. But Muslim decline is finally blamed on the modern age itself, likened to a fire that feeds on traditional communities, though its flames can purify religions as well as destroy them. To find, like Abraham did in Nimrod's torments, a garden in the midst of modernity's fire, Muslims must take charge of the stylus and tablet God resigns to them and write out their own destiny, forsaking Islam's political and doctrinal inheritance if they must as long as they remain loyal to the Prophet.

Iqbal made it clear in this poem and elsewhere that the only thing keeping Muslims true to their religion's legacy was fidelity to the Prophet, who represented the historical origins of its universality. For as we saw in Chapter 2, Iqbal saw in Muhammad's claim to be God's final messenger the emergence of humanity as an actor in its own right, one cut off from the leading strings of divine guidance and put in charge of its own destiny. The founding of Islam thus signaled the coming to maturity of the human race, with the Prophet renouncing divine authority to humankind by putting an end to God's action in the world and marking the beginning of human history.[26] Iqbal went so far as to make human beings into God's partners if not successors by attributing divine creativity to them. Paradoxically, it was the very particularity of this origin that served as a link to the lost universality of Islam, whose other virtues had all escaped the grasp of religion to be generalized across the human race. Once Islam had ceased to provide a conceptual matrix for humankind's unity, therefore, it could represent the species only by such fragmentary acts as fidelity to Muhammad.

This turn to the Prophet as someone who provided by his very lack of miracles and other supernatural qualities a demonstration of Islam's call to humanity had for Syed Ahmed Khan, his associates, and his followers merely illustrated Islam's fidelity to nature. Iqbal, however, cited the work of medieval Sufis and contemporary philosophers like Henri Bergson in putting forward a theory of time as crucial for the self-realization of the species. His reference to Muhammad's promulgation of humanity as an actor in its own right meant that history had now replaced nature as the criterion of Muslim universality.

Iqbal frequently criticized the world conceived of as an external reality, claiming that Islam set itself against the particularity of what he called nature's race-making work. In an open letter to Jawaharlal Nehru in 1936, Iqbal wrote: "The student of history knows very well that Islam was born at a time when the old principles of human unification, such as blood relationship and throne-culture, were failing. It, therefore, finds the principle of human unification not in the blood and bones but in the mind of man. Indeed its social message to mankind is: 'Deracialise yourself or perish by internecine war.' It is no exaggeration to say that Islam looks askance at nature's race-building plans and creates by means of its peculiar institutions, an outlook which would counteract the race-building forces of nature."[27]

History had, of course, been a major preoccupation among Muslim writers from the nineteenth century, and Hali devoted a whole section of *The Flow and Ebb of Islam* to its writing, though he judged such texts by their fidelity to nature, which was supposed to provide rational and objective criteria for historians. For Iqbal, however, history not only housed the origin of Islam's universality, but formed the substance of its character as well, since he thought that the human race had to achieve self-consciousness by setting itself against nature. In this way the *ummah* abandoned its relations with race and civilization to join ranks with twentieth-century ideologies, which meant that Islam was now set against liberalism or communism, whose politics of class conflict was to be rendered meaningless within its universal embrace.

Yet this purely ideological foundation for human unity was by that very token remarkably vulnerable to attack, with Iqbal attributing Muslim conservatism, misplaced though it might be, to a glimmering recognition among the Prophet's followers that their religion and its universal mission was based upon nothing but a set of ideas: "Islam repudiates the race idea altogether and founds itself on the religious idea alone. Since Islam bases itself on the religious idea alone, a basis which is wholly spiritual and consequently far more ethereal than blood relationship, Muslim society is naturally much more sensitive to forces which it considers harmful to its integrity."[28]

The very strength of Islam's universality, therefore, was paradoxically also its weakness, necessitating what might be called a fanatical attachment to the religious idea insofar as it cannot be naturalized or taken for granted by being identified with any particular place or political order. Iqbal's view of Islam here comes close to that of Hegel, who defined Islam's modernity precisely by its attachment to an abstract idea of universality. While Hegel paired Islam with the Enlightenment in his admiring criticism of its universal ideal, in our own times such an analysis has been directed more against twentieth-century ideologies like communism, also regarded as the Enlightenment's progeny. It is no accident that for Iqbal communism was Islam's greatest rival because it possessed a comparably universal mission. All of which only went to show that if the history of such ideas might be claimed by Islam, only the immense effort required to instantiate them could prevent the disintegration and theft of their universality.

Once Islamic concepts and categories are universalized in the language of humanity, moving outside the field of religious doctrine and practice, the Muslim community risks sinking into a particularity from which it must constantly be rescued. Lost within the universality of humankind, this community can reclaim greatness only by being faithful to the history of its founding. What allows such loyalty to grasp at the universal is precisely its fragmentary character, whose devotion to the past is conceived as a practice of withdrawal from the inevitable partialities of the present. And the present, of course, belongs to democracy, where people jostle to represent the interests of the greatest number, and Islam's universality takes on a new countenance. Instead of embarking upon the futile task of representing the interests of all human beings, or even all Muslims, a number of thinkers following Iqbal argued that such political forms were both morally suspect and appropriate to states alone. Since the species cannot be represented politically, it is only the absence and indeed the sacrifice of particular interests, and therefore of politics itself in its conventional sense, that might capture its unity.

After all, Iqbal himself had written: "I am opposed to nationalism as it is understood in Europe, not because, if it is allowed to develop in India, it is likely to bring less material gain to Muslims. I am opposed to it because I see in it the germs of an atheistic materialism which I look upon as the greatest danger to modern humanity."[29] The kind of fidelity to Islam broached by Muhammad Iqbal was thus sacrificial in form, claiming to abandon the self-interest that defines politics by pointing to the disinterestedness of its practices. It is no longer the contested claim to some common interest that defines humanity, therefore, but rather its negation for a set of ideals and historical peculiarities that appear meaningless in the calculus of interests defining political representation.

Islam had come to represent humankind by sacrificing the very possibility of interest in the supposedly archaic demands it makes upon Muslims, for instance regarding forms of dress or comportment, whose antiquated provenance and incomprehensibility to modern minds only guaranteed their impartial character. The turn to history, in other words, had little to do with the romance and nostalgia that are characteristic of nationalist approaches to the past, and was certainly not an effort to return to the past, as many critics of modern Islam assert. For it is precisely because the culture of Islam's origin is dead that its habits can be universalized into a kind of technical routine freed of particularity and therefore political interest. Indeed, this form of Muslim devotion rejects the very idea of culture to focus on abstract and dislocated practices that make religion into something fully portable and universally convertible, as the sociologist Olivier Roy suggests.[30]

Such at least was the argument put forward by the Islamist thinker Abul Ala Maududi, who supplemented the older naturalization of Islam's universality with a new faith in the resources of history. He contended that the more resistant Muslim practices were to the rationality of interest-based political representation, the less likely would their misuse be in the politics of class or ethnic particularity. Taking up Iqbal's concern with the finality of prophethood, Maududi and his party, the Jamaat-e Islami, criticized the Sufis, the Shia, and most particularly the Ahmadis, whose reverence for spiritual leaders coming after the Prophet was held to compromise the latter's role in barring all access to divine authority.

It was only by putting a stop to God's intervention in the present that humanity could become an historical actor. And it was to safeguard humanity's freedom that Maududi made neutrality and disinterestedness into touchstones of Islam's universality, focusing on a life lived for the sake of Islam alone. But these attitudes are possible only once the deity has been expelled from history and his apostle's injunctions have assumed the form of so much detritus, whose functionality or beneficial consequences cannot overshadow their pointlessness as the remains of a past long dead. This is perhaps why God makes such few appearances in Maududi's prose, having been supplanted by Islam as the real or potential subject of Muslim and so human history.

In a speech he delivered in Karachi in 1951, Maududi argued that decolonization had not yet been achieved with Pakistan's independence, since the country and its people still conducted themselves according to Western modes of thinking.[31] For Maududi these ways of understanding were unacceptable not because they happened to be foreign, but because they made human solidarity impossible by holding all action to be motivated by specific and rival interests. These could be individual or collective, defined by

identities like tribe and territory or race and religion. All this he attributed to the medieval church, which, having based itself on the
false principles of Greek philosophy, was unable to tolerate the ad-
vancement of scientific knowledge but repressed it from the Re-
naissance down to the nineteenth century. The intellectual life of
modern Europe, therefore, was founded upon the cleavage between an increasingly irrelevant Christianity confined to private
life and an explicitly antireligious and materialistic understanding
of the world in all public endeavors where interests defined actions.

Lacking any transcendent ideals and thus a real commitment to
universality and human solidarity, Europe's power was based not
on any religious or philosophical values but on pure self-interest.
And Maududi described Hegel, Darwin, and Marx as the three
great theorists of such partiality seen as the motors of history, evolution, and class struggle, respectively. Dissatisfied with the violence entailed in the teleologies these men proffered, Maududi also
dismissed the moral thought of European scholars and clergy as
something purely academic in character. In reality, he claimed,
people in the West lived according to a mixture of epicureanism
and utilitarianism alone and were thus unconstrained by scruples
when dealing oppressively with people from other races or religions, countries or classes. Simply propagating religion, he said,
was useless in addressing this situation, as such faith would only be
appropriated and marginalized in any modern society as a merely
personal peculiarity.

Maududi thought that to succeed, Islam had to imitate the
West in one way at least, and that was by planning and accomplishing the complete takeover of every social, political, and economic
institution to transform them from within. He argued that what allowed Europe to succeed was the systematicity of its thought,
which he contrasted to the accidental and arbitrary Muslim attitude to conquest and conversion. Yet he could think of imitating
the West only by identifying and training good men and women
within a revolutionary organization, a rather too familiar strategy
drawn from communism and fascism in particular. His focus on
changing individuals betrayed Maududi's moralistic vision and rendered him unable to think about the human solidarity he desired
either in its own right or in its own name. Crucial as it was to him

and other Muslims, in other words, humanity remained an imponderable figure for them, as did the *ummah* that was meant to represent it. The individual therefore had to bear both the responsibility of bringing humanity to life through the Muslim community and the guilt of being unable to do so in betraying Islam as a religion founded for humanity.

The Guilt of Still Being Alive

Maududi had thought that Muslims could represent the human race by sacrificing their particular interests and living according to the disinterested because archaic precepts of Islam. Muslim militants in the new millennium, however, concentrated on death in God's name as the only kind of sacrifice capable of representing the *ummah* and so the human race. The line connecting Islamism and militancy, however, is not a straight one, just as Maududi cannot be seen as a direct descendant of Syed Ahmed Khan. The latter would not have approved of Maududi, just as Maududi in turn would not have approved of Al-Qaeda. What connects all these figures, instead, is a line of argument that each developed in very different directions. And this does nothing more than illustrate how disconnected the argument itself is from any specific political or indeed theological position. Nevertheless, each subsequent movement did inherit something from its predecessors, as we shall soon see when considering how nature and history were both made into criteria defining Islam's universality and its recovery.

One of Al-Qaeda's chief spokesmen, though in hiding somewhere between Pakistan and Afghanistan, was able to answer a series of questions from friends and foes around the world in April 2008. Submitted to Ayman al-Zawahiri through the internet and responded to in the same fashion, these queries included many expostulating with Osama bin Laden's lieutenant about the indiscriminate violence resorted to by those fighting in the name of Islam. Typical was this condemnation of militant methods: "How do you reconcile the values of your medical training—to help people and prolong their lives—with the fact that you killed Anwar al-Sadat and that you shape the minds of bombers and suicide commandos?"[32]

Zawahiri responded by stating: "During my medical studies, I learned that life is Allah's miracle and his gift. Thus, one must be careful to obey him. I have learned from surgery about how to save the body by amputating failing organs and removing cancers, and how to cure illness-inducing bacteria. Medicine, when practiced as a sacrifice to Allah and to help the oppressed, will grant the soul happiness and joy, which will never be experienced by those who have twisted it into a tool for greed, robbing others and exploiting their pain for their own benefit."[33]

This justification of violence illustrates the crucial role that the language of humanity plays in the narrative of militancy. Rather than being dedicated solely to the cause of Islam, in other words, militancy stakes claim to humanity itself as an ideal. Expanding upon the rhetoric of modern racism, for which threatened groups had to be purified from miscegenation and other forms of contamination by medical means, Zawahiri describes terrorism as a form of surgery whose aim is to save the human race itself from the cancers and other ailments that threaten its global body. Identified with medicine practiced according to the Hippocratic oath, this vision of militancy as a form of sacrifice for the sake of humanity is opposed to humanitarianism in its conventional and commercially organized forms, which Zawahiri argues are founded upon exploitation and profit. By representing the species as an individual, or rather by making the two interchangeable, Zawahiri treats it as a potential subject, one that requires the healing touch of jihad to speak in its own name.

Militant Islam's attempt to represent humanity as an historical actor comes to the fore in Zawahiri's response to another question put to him over the internet: "Can you clear up the confusion that many Westerns [sic] have about technology—on one hand, you shun modern values, but on the other hand you accept modern Western technology such as the Internet?"[34] Hastening to brush aside any account of terrorism that would confine it to some contradiction between Muslim tradition and Western modernity, Zawahiri makes it clear that even the greatest enemies must share a common history and partake of each other's achievements as members of the same species. In other words, he moves beyond the narratives of race or civilization from which the distinction of traditional and modern is often derived to focus on the human race as history's true subject.

Zawahiri responded:

> This question is based on two false premises. The fact that I accept or shun a certain value is not based on whether it is ancient or modern. But I am opposed to polytheism; scorning the religion; establishing relations based on material benefit and achieving sensory pleasures; lying, deceiving; acting on self-interest; alcoholism; gambling; vices; taking over other people's countries and oppressing them; stealing the riches of others; double standards; immunity against being held accountable for crimes for which others will be punished; spreading killing, abuse, destruction, and the destruction of the environment and climate merely to master the land, rob, and plunder.[35]

Let us pause here to note that apart from the ritual invocation of polytheism and blasphemy at the beginning of his response, there is nothing particularly Islamic about this assortment of crimes. Zawahiri is eager to prove that he opposes the very things that all human beings do.

He then goes on to say that the West has betrayed its kinship with the rest of the species by oppressing and plundering it:

> Scientific knowledge is neither Eastern nor Western—it is the property of mankind which circulates among us equally in various times and places. The scientific progress of the West was originally based on our riches, which they are still plundering to this day. Where is our stolen share? Secondly, the West tried to cover up its crimes against us and against the rest of mankind by priding itself in its scientific supremacy. Under the cover of this progress, they have attempted to convince occupied and weaker nations that they [the West] are superior to them, and more deserving to manage the world and to plunder its riches—and to demean other people. Neither the Muslims, nor anyone else, will be fooled by this trick any longer.[36]

The focus on a shared humanity in "militant" as much as "Islamist" and "liberal" thought brings Muslims and infidels together in such a way as to make possible relations of both amity and enmity among them. I am concerned here with the ambivalence that marks this relationship of would-be friends and foes, a quality evident in the passage from Zawahiri cited above. For at the same moment that he claims the achievements of his enemies as a properly human inheritance, Bin Laden's most eminent follower also suggests that some of the credit for amassing this legacy was stolen from Muslims and needs recovering. In other words, the relationship between Islam and its enemies is conceived as one of rivalry and theft, with Muslims having to recover their mission of representing humanity from the West's imposture.

. Militant argumentation is marked by the familiarity and even intimacy with which it approaches those seen as the enemies of Islam. Al-Qaeda's foes are considered to be people of the same kind as its friends, their supposed persecution of Muslims being reciprocated by the latter in procedures of mirroring that make it difficult to tell one from the other. Instead of dehumanizing their enemies, or even condemning them to subhuman status in the name of race or civilization, militants routinely aspire to compete with such foes in virtue as well as vice, something we see in Zawahiri's utterances quoted above.

But without defining humanity by means of a hierarchy, Bin Laden's acolytes were unable to establish any firm distinction between friends and enemies. Refusing to take responsibility for acts of violence by describing these merely as responses to infidel provocation does more than excuse such crimes. It serves to account for the dispersal of responsibility in a global arena where all are complicit in crimes against humanity, whether these are concerned with environmental degradation or genocide. Not accidentally, the only act militants claim full responsibility for is the minimal yet excessive one of martyrdom. Sacrifice therefore becomes the only distinctive element in Al-Qaeda's rhetoric, which otherwise shares everything with its foes. I return to this point in the next chapter.

Not the common virtues and vices of human beings, therefore, but the claim to martyrdom is what demonstrates Islam's universality in militant circles, though even such practices of sacrifice can be stolen from Muslims and so must be repeated in the most egregious of ways. And martyrdom is crucial because humanity cannot be represented in any positive fashion, lacking as it does a political or juridical form despite being invoked by lawyers and political leaders at every turn. As the supposed abnegation of all particularity and interest, sacrifice constitutes a kind of negative embodiment of the race. It provides in fact the most appropriate manifestation of this mysterious being, which exists without having become a subject in the global arena.

But such an embodiment of the species is not peculiar to Muslim terrorists and may be found in the sacrificial practices of many who dedicate themselves to humanitarian causes, from pacifists and environmentalists to those engaged in aid and relief work. Indeed, the idea of sacrificing oneself for humanity has a long and explicitly Christian history, having become common sense in the story of Jesus as a martyr not for the sake of God but of humankind. Representing as they do the most excessive forms of sacrifice, militant acts of martyrdom may be said to have placed themselves at the vanguard of all such procedures of embodiment.

The philosopher Karl Jaspers was perhaps the first to see varieties of sacrifice such as martyrdom as efforts to trace the lineaments of a species that could not otherwise be represented. In a lecture of 1945 subsequently published under the title "The Question of German Guilt," Jaspers distinguished traditional forms of guilt, such as the moral, political, and criminal, from something he called metaphysical guilt. This latter, he said, was felt by those who were innocent of wrongdoing in all its conventional senses but continued, nevertheless, to accuse themselves of living while others had died under Nazi rule. Though he took Germany as his example of a place in which metaphysical guilt had come to the fore, Jaspers was clear that fascism and the war it occasioned provided only the origins of this widespread phenomenon, which arose out of the fact that responsibility could no longer be confined to particular individuals or groups in events like the Second World War and belonged instead to the history of humanity.

"It is only now," Jaspers writes, "that history has finally become world history—the global history of mankind. So our own situation can be grasped only together with the world-historical one.

What has happened today has its causes in general human events and conditions, and only secondarily in special intra-national relations and the decisions of single groups of men."[37] The problem, of course, is that humanity has no political or juridical status and thus does not exist as a subject of history. Yet it cannot be said to be a fiction either, and Jaspers tells us that metaphysical guilt is a sign of the race's otherwise invisible solidarity, betraying as it does a consciousness of shared responsibilities in the global arena brought to light by the war: "Metaphysical guilt is the lack of absolute solidarity with the human being as such—an indelible claim beyond morally meaningful duty. This solidarity is violated by my presence at a wrong or a crime. It is not enough that I cautiously risk my life to prevent it; if it happens, and if I was there, and if I survive where the other is killed, I know from a voice within myself: I am guilty of being still alive."[38]

Going beyond all moral, legal, and political determinations of responsibility, metaphysical guilt invokes the species as a potential subject of history, if only by the desire to die in its name. For dying alone provides access to its negative being. Jaspers points out that such examples of unconditioned sacrifice are to be found, and are indeed celebrated, at the level of the family or between lovers, the source of metaphysical guilt being that they are not available, or very rarely so, at a purely human level: "That somewhere among men the unconditioned prevails—the capacity to live only together or not at all, if crimes are committed against the one or the other, or if physical living requirements have to be shared—therein consists the substance of their being. But that this does not extend to the solidarity of all men, nor to that of fellow-citizens or even of smaller groups, but remains confined to the closest human ties— therein lies this guilt of us all."[39]

Jaspers's friend Hannah Arendt would go on to interpret his argument by writing about what she called the shame of being human, which was the only thing that remained of the confidence with which prewar Europeans had thought about humanity as a moral and juridical category. Paradoxically, then, humanity assumed some kind of existential reality only in the shame ordinary people felt at its disappearance. "This elemental shame," she wrote, "which many people of the most various nationalities share with one another today, is what finally is left of our sense of international solidarity; and it has not yet found an adequate political expression."⁴⁰ Now by confining their analyses to the guilt of being alive or the shame of being human, Jaspers and Arendt are able to deal with death in the form of desire alone. I suggest, however, that the contemporary practice of Muslim martyrdom acts upon this desire to answer the call of an invisible humanity. For whatever the political calculations of Al-Qaeda and other movements that value sacrifice, their rhetoric of dedication to the species is founded upon shame or metaphysical guilt alone.

How else did Osama bin Laden's minions justify their acts of violence if not by invoking the guilt of living while others die? These others are not the terrorist's relatives, friends, or even compatriots, but unknown people in unknown lands, who by their suffering represent the race's victimization and lack of historical subjectivity. Indeed, the global Muslim community serves as a kind of model of humanity insofar as it, too, possesses neither political nor juridical reality and exists for militants only in the spectacle of its apparent victimization. Dying for Islam, therefore, means acknowledging the existence of Muslim solidarity around the world, and in the same moment the solidarity of the species as well. For in the end, it is militants' unfettered hold over the language and practice of sacrifice that allows them to represent their own community together with the human race itself as historical subjects, both of which enjoy the curious distinction of existing without existing in the global arena that came into being after the Cold War.

Through the Looking Glass

I have been looking so far in this chapter at the ways in which Muslims have responded to the West as friend, enemy, and rival since the nineteenth century, but this does not mean that modern Islam was shaped by outside forces that themselves remained unaltered by the contact. And so, I close this discussion by looking at the way in which the United States has also been changed by its interactions with militant Islam in strangely similar ways, as illustrated by one of Barack Obama's most significant speeches as president. Delivered to a full house at Cairo University on June 4,

2009, Obama's much heralded address to the Muslim world received the kind of global exposure that was matched only by his first inaugural speech as president. Indeed, it is difficult to think of any other occasion when the words of a US president have received such close attention around the world.

The only precedent that comes to mind is John F. Kennedy's famous speech of June 26, 1963, in West Berlin, given at the height of the Cold War on the very threshold of the Soviet Union. Like Berlin in its day, Cairo was a city divided between powerful rivals; that is, it had a repressive government enjoying Western support set against a religious opposition with worldwide connections. Also, like Berlin, it stood on the edge of a great precipice between global rivals that Obama identified by the names "Islam" and "America." But here the similarity ends, for while Kennedy's words were about the hemispheric struggle between a pair of superpowers, his successor spoke about the hostility of two very different actors that are by no means equivalents. How can a global religion like Islam, lacking any representative authority or institution, be related to a country like the United States, which operates within the framework of international politics?

I suggest that by forcing these incommensurable entities into a conversation, President Obama broke with the language of institutional politics altogether to conceive of global interactions among actors of many different and even indeterminate kinds. For if his invocations of dialogue and respect were treated by many in the press as an exercise in public relations, their massive audience tells us that it was precisely such a move away from the grammar of international politics that men and women around the world found interesting. But what, after all, was so novel about the speech? Certainly not the oft-repeated stereotypes about the entwined histories of "Abrahamic religions," the tolerance of Muslim Spain, or the Arab transmission of Greek learning to Christian Europe. Radical instead was Obama's effort to be true to the following statement made early in his speech: "I am convinced that in order to move forward, we must say openly to each other the things we hold in our hearts, and that too often are said only behind closed doors."[41] With this sentence the president not only opened the door to a remarkable confession of America's history of wrongful deeds in the Muslim world,

but abandoned the circumscribed categories of statecraft to deal
with the kind of popular prejudices and theories that proliferate in
blogs, web forums, talk radio, and everyday conversations.

At the same time, therefore, as he spoke about laying to rest
the "crude stereotypes" that some Americans and Muslims have of
one another, Obama took much greater ones onboard.[42] Such, for
example, was the anthropomorphic conception of Islam as one
kind of political agent that could be set against the West as another. However much the president tried to qualify this view by rejecting notions like that of a clash of civilizations, his whole speech
depended upon the possibility of their truth. And since so many
people take these conceptions seriously, Obama's engagement with
them cannot be dismissed as ignorant, particularly in light of the
fact that he departed the language and therefore the criteria of
conventional politics by entertaining them. After all, Islam does
not fit into the structure of international politics because in its incarnation as a threat animating terrorists dedicated to an undefined
global cause, it could not be confined to states or even would-be
states, which happen to be the only legitimate actors in the world's
political order as presently constituted. Indeed, Islam was seen as a
threat precisely because the terrorists who used its name were not
for the most part likely to take over states or even to be supported
by them.

Yet by appealing to Islam in a way that brought the limits of
conventional politics to light, Obama was only following the lead
of political leaders who had in the past done much the same. From
Napoleon to Kaiser Wilhelm II, to say nothing of Ronald Reagan,
European and North American heads of state have quite regularly
appealed to Islam in order to bring about world-historical changes
that moved outside the bounds of normative politics. Such, at least,
was the fantasy that allowed the Emperor of All the French to
spread rumors about his conversion to Islam while conquering
Egypt, or the German emperor to rely upon similar stories while
attempting to rouse an anti-British jihad during the First World
War. And then of course there was the US president who did in
fact promote a jihad against the Soviets in Afghanistan by encouraging Muslims from around the world to support it. Naturally,
these projects can all be seen as attempts to use Muslim passions

for the purposes of realpolitik, though I would argue that the fantasy underlying them had long outstripped such aims, depending as it did on the vision of a worldwide uprising motivated by a specifically religious sensibility that Christianity could no longer muster. Whatever accounts for the relative absence of Christian movements in the West, it is certain that Islam has for some time now provided an important model for imagining the limits of international politics there.

Obama's appeal to Islam, however, unlike that of his predecessors, was not meant to encourage a holy war in order to go beyond the limits of conventional politics. Its function was in fact more analytical than political or even rhetorical in character. For once he had interrupted the institutional narrative of everyday statecraft by pairing the United States with Islam, the president was able to acknowledge the impossibility of such a politics in the global arena from which the religion of Muhammad takes its meaning. As a supposedly global actor, after all, Islam could not be confined to any particular place or interest, thus forcing Obama to describe any engagement with it only in the terms of a common humanity. From there he went on to speak about other issues, including pandemics, financial crises, and nuclear war, that also affected the whole of the human race and so could not be engaged in the name of any political interest but only that of humanity itself: "This is a difficult responsibility to embrace. For human history has often been a record of nations and tribes—and yes, religions—subjugating one another to serve their own interests. Yet in this new age, such attitudes are self-defeating. Given our interdependence, any world order that elevates one nation or group of people over another will inevitably fail."[43]

As if to mitigate the radical implications of this statement, the president smuggled political interest in by the back door, appealing to Americans and Muslims to deal with each other on the basis of "mutual interest and mutual respect."[44] But in doing so he fell in with the reasoning, down to their very words, of Al-Qaeda's founders, who routinely spoke of humanity's interdependence and the consequent impossibility of interest-driven politics, recommending instead an ethics of sacrifice in which global problems are dealt with precisely by mutual interest and respect. And indeed, Obama's

speech marked the first time that the United States had engaged
Al-Qaeda in a conversation. Not only did he cross any number of
red lines by acknowledging US mistakes in places like Iraq or Iran,
but more importantly he put aside the principles of statecraft to invoke the world outside. And this was all made possible by the president's reference to Islam as a global agent. Despite the language of
partnership and mutual benefit, then, at issue in the speech was the
decay of political realism in the face of humanity as a new kind of
interconnected reality, one threatened by the actions of both state
and nonstate actors in a way that was never before possible. Unlike
his immediate predecessor, George W. Bush, who spoke the language of traditional politics while rejecting a number of its accepted practices having to do with torture, indefinite detention,
and the like, Obama had restored these practices but spoke a different language, as if realizing that the political authority of the
past can never be reinstated.

While it is clear that Islam is not a category amenable to the
tradition of political realism, the absence of a nonrealist political
order meant that Obama, like his alter ego Osama bin Laden, was
able to deploy it only by drawing upon his own background and
offering himself up as the model of a global leader. His audience
was thus treated to well-known and even trite references to his
parents, race, childhood, and the like, quite unlike the attitude of
previous American presidents who had aimed for a kind of generic
universality. Yet the naming of his particularity by no means prevented Obama from laying claim to the universal, because exactly
these particularities were what connected him to the rest of the
globe, whether as a product of mixture and migration, or as a
Christian with a Muslim family background. Whereas presidents in
the past had seen their universality in national terms, Obama situated his within a global arena.

And in fact, the president did nothing more than represent in
his person the global influence that his country exercised. If Ken-
yans, for example, claimed Obama as if he were their representative
in the United States, it is because they realized how much of their
destiny was determined by that country. With Obama's election
many of them might have felt as if they, too, had some role in
bringing someone to power in the state that decided their future.

And by representing this obscure vision of a global democracy, in which people from everywhere can claim to be represented by an American president, Barack Obama transformed the language of international politics more than Kennedy had done as his country's first Irish and Catholic head of state. For with him the old feminist slogan of "the personal is the political" had moved from the particularity of gender and race to a global universality, but only by leaving behind the lexicon of states, institutions, and interests to adopt the language of the bazaar in which stereotypes serve as the chief actors of a global politics.

In the bazaars of the Middle East as much as in that of the internet, Islam and the West it has brought to life function as the agents of a global politics that possesses as yet no institutional space of its own. Like Frankenstein's monster, these entities are made up from historically recognizable pieces, but neither has a world to call its own. Yet it is this that makes them truly global, as Obama himself pointed out by pairing religious extremism with the dangers of pandemics, nuclear proliferation, and, he might also have added, as Osama bin Laden often did, climate change. By speaking in Cairo of America's seven million Muslims, for example, the president was pointing out that Islam was a domestic as much as an international fact and therefore had no geographical center, something that he emphasized again when mentioning widely dispersed countries like Indonesia, Egypt, Morocco, Iraq, Afghanistan, and Pakistan in the same breath. Moreover, by stressing the higher-than-average economic and educational status of Muslims in the United States, Obama also made it evident that this minority could on no account be viewed as posing a problem for the state on old-fashioned socio-economic grounds. In such ways as this, Islam has managed to undo the inherited categories of American as much as international politics, since it refuses to be confined to the discourse of immigration, discrimination, and deprivation, not least because Muslims in the United States include a large proportion of local converts, mostly Black, as much as immigrants from every part of the world.

Whether it is the struggle with radical Islam that is at issue or the struggle against global warming and nuclear war, the international order's inability to deal with such threats was both highlighted and hidden by the president of the United States, who could speak to these issues only in his personal capacity, which is to say as the product of a mixed-race marriage, the son of an African immigrant with a childhood spent in Indonesia, etc. And despite the entirely predictable statements of policy scattered in his Cairo speech, crumbs eagerly swept up by the press as providing the only recognizably "political" elements in an address that was otherwise puzzling in the inordinate length of its rhetorical flourishes, Obama's only solution to these problems was also purely personal in nature. But this is where he was truly radical, as his statement on abjuring violence demonstrated:

> Resistance through violence and killing is wrong and does not succeed. For centuries, black people in America suffered the lash of the whip as slaves and the humiliation of segregation. But it was not violence that won full and equal rights. It was a peaceful and determined insistence upon the ideals at the center of America's founding. This same story can be told by people from South Africa to South Asia; from Eastern Europe to Indonesia. It's a story with a simple truth: violence is a dead end. It is a sign of neither courage nor power to shoot rockets at sleeping children, or to blow up old women on a bus. That is not how moral authority is claimed; that is how it is surrendered.[45]

Invoking the great movements against colonialism, segregation, and apartheid led by Mahatma Gandhi, Martin Luther King, Jr., and Nelson Mandela, as well as the color revolutions of Eastern Europe and the rejection of dictatorship in Southeast Asia, the president not only redrew the map of our political geography by putting together Asian, African, American, and European struggles; he did so by foregoing the institutional jargon of our political tradition. For in all these cases nonviolence meant breaking the law while being willing to take the consequences of it in acts of sacrifice, suffering, and martyrdom. Furthermore, nonviolence here was conceived of in purely moral and individual terms, and precisely not political ones having to do with states. Indeed, such movements have always appealed to ordinary people rather than to institutions. As among its great representatives in the past, this kind of nonviolence was also meant to foster a certain kind of moral subject instead of simply achieving some predetermined goal. And in all these ways it served as the mirror image of Osama bin Laden's theory of violent sacrifice and martyrdom, addressing and refuting it on its own terms. This the Bush Administration had never been able to do, because despite its rhetoric of ideological purity, it was deeply mired in the language of instrumental action and social engineering that has come to constitute the substance of realpolitik in a way that was previously true of Soviet communism. But this is not the first time that a movement, neoconservatism in this case, has ended up hijacked by the very opponent it has fought for so long.

When Barack Obama ended his speech saying that he had come to Cairo because he had faith in other people, he was doing nothing more than acknowledging the limits of political realism in the global arena where we all live. Since these limits were brought to light by Islamic militancy as a global movement divested of traditional institutional forms, the president could address them only by speaking from a standpoint that was set, as it were, outside his own office—thus the constant references to his race and background as entirely nonpolitical factors. But by turning in the end to the language of faith, Obama proved himself to be the most Christian of American presidents, certainly more faithful to the possibility of human virtue than George W. Bush with all his religious supporters. Is it possible, then, that the appeal to Islam is at the same time a call to Christianity or any other faith in the new world that confronts us today, the global dimension of whose problems have rendered so much of our interest-based politics obsolete?

CHAPTER SIX

Hollow Men

I
N AN ENGLISH-LANGUAGE VIDEO released soon after the Islamic State proclaimed its caliphate in 2014, a Chilean convert is shown kicking over and trampling a sign demarcating the border between Iraq and Syria.[1] By its title, "The End of Sykes–Picot," this video refers to the famous and initially secret agreement between Britain and France to carve up the Middle East between them once the Ottoman Empire had been defeated in the First World War. Jumping back and forth across the now invisible line dividing these former Ottoman provinces, the Chilean seems to be announcing the return of a caliphate lost during the Great War. Yet we shall see that the political claims made in the video, as well as by the emergence of the Islamic State itself, were everywhere belied by the rhetoric and practices of the Islamic State itself. This prompts me to ask the following question: What if the brutality of ISIS emerged not from its claim to politics but the reverse, by the fact that it was unable to assume a political identity?

Speaking directly to the camera, the narrator proceeds to take us on a tour of a captured military base. A number of bound prisoners, soldiers from the Syrian army, are shown inside the facility. The narrator chats amiably with a few of them, each identified by his sectarian identity. We then leave the building with the Chilean, who continues his smiling, TV-presenter's patter inside an SUV, out of which he eventually climbs to get a good view of the prison in the distance. As he burbles on, we see the place blown up with all those inside. What is important about this video is its refusal to define anything it depicts in a recognizably political way. Unlike the ostentatiously statelike conventions of terrorist propaganda, such as a militant's communiqué and list of demands or a captive's confession and execution, this video takes the form of a documentary whose presenter finds everything interesting and even amusing, but never the subject of indignation or an occasion to express regret for the "unfortunate necessity" that tends to accompany traditional terrorist attacks modeled on the procedures of states at war.

Portrayed in the most detached fashion, the events of the video are also treated as if they were quite banal in character, and thus lacking in the distinction from everyday life that usually accompanies important political statements. The prisoners are killed without any ceremonial, while neither the narrator nor his car and driver are seen to possess any official status. Even the initial scene, in which the Iraqi–Syrian border is erased, may thus be interpreted as an elimination of the state and so politics as such. One reason why such a situation might not be so puzzling has to do with the history of a number of Islamist movements upon whose thought ISIS intermittently drew. At least in the Sunni tradition, these movements of the mid-twentieth century, dominated by the Pakistani Abul Ala Maududi and the Egyptian Sayyid Qutb, have tended to be suspicious of both politics and the state, as we saw in Chapter 3. For emerging as they did either under colonial rule or in the sometimes secular but authoritarian nation-states that succeeded it, such movements sought to limit the inroads of modern politics into Muslim societies. The modernity of such a politics, after all, consisted in its autonomy from the sacred law, even when it recognized and honored the latter. And it was this autonomous logic that Muslim thinkers sought to subordinate if not destroy in visions of an Islamic state lacking sovereignty and run according to the sacred law.

These paradoxical visions of an Islamic state were in vogue until the end of the Cold War, when such ways of thinking about Islam in terms of the ideological state were put at risk with the collapse of the Soviet Union, the decline of its Third World clients, and the emergence of a global arena for what came to be called new social movements. While in some places neoliberal ideas about nonstatist forms of Islamic governance took the place of older narratives about revolutions and constitutions, in others a new kind of militancy emerged out of authoritarian or lawless contexts. Of these the chief one was, of course, Al-Qaeda, a global movement that had always refused to adopt the model of a state. As such, its dealings with sovereignty were vested not in territories and institutions but in individuals, and in particular the iconic figure of the suicide bomber who both kills and dies to embody power in all its purity, with nothing left over from the act of violence.[2]

This fragmentation and dispersal of sovereignty had a long history in anticolonial thought. Gandhi, too, had vested sovereignty in the individual, who exhibited it in nonviolent acts like fasting, celibacy, noncooperation, civil disobedience, and finally martyrdom, all forms of sacrifice set against the protection and flourishing of life that legitimized colonial rule.[3] These sacrificial acts were meant, in other words, to negate the positive and supposedly life-enhancing sovereignty of imperialism so as to claim India's freedom by its rejection. Al-Qaeda's sacrificial acts, however, rhetorically addressed themselves to the West's refusal to extend life and security to those under its power but beyond its domains. This explains its common refrain: if we can't enjoy life and security, neither will you. As such, militant forms of sacrifice served to universalize the insecurity and death to which the West was seen as consigning its enemies. And it is to the profoundly nihilistic character of this sacrifice that I now turn.

The Logic of Mirrors

Like every other form it takes, the individualization of sovereignty has to be disavowed, since it, too, threatens to usurp that which belongs to God alone. And this might be one reason why Al-Qaeda's acts were justified not simply by the sacred law they were meant to uphold, but as the mirror images of Western attacks on Islam. This logic has indeed become gruesomely familiar: we kill your civilians, including women and children, as you do ours. Beyond trying to disclaim responsibility for violence, Al-Qaeda's ubiquitous logic of mirroring was important because it deferred and displaced the sovereignty of its own actions onto those of its enemies. Militant actions were seen as being negative in character and so deprived of ontological weight, with any positive identity they happened to possess derived from the deeds of Al-Qaeda's enemies. Only in this indirect way, it seems, were militants capable of partaking in a sovereignty that had otherwise to be repudiated. But this by the same token entailed militants' paradoxical experience as well as recognition of intimacy with an enemy from whom they derived their subjectivity. And indeed, compared to the vocabulary of radical incomprehension that characterized Western views of Al-Qaeda, its members never spoke of their rivals in anything but the most familiar of ways.[4]

Al-Qaeda's de-territorialized or global arena of operations, however, marked by individualized if indirect and disavowed forms of sovereignty, was put at risk by the Global War on Terror. Although this war is often seen as being unprecedented in its scale of operations, what it in fact did was to re-territorialize Islamic militancy by attacking Afghanistan and Iraq and so defining its enemy in conventional ways as rivals for the control of territory. Out of this emerged not only insurgencies of a more or less familiar kind in both countries, as well as in places like Mali, Nigeria, and Pakistan, but also a movement such as the Islamic State, which rejected Al-Qaeda's unfixed position in the global arena, founding instead a new state to which it gave the hoary title of "caliphate." While ISIS continued to draw upon the repertoire of its predecessors, making use of communiqués and confessions as much as suicide bombers and practices that mirrored those of its enemies, these had all taken on a novel meaning, if not lost one altogether.[5]

The American journalist Jim Foley was dressed in an orange jumpsuit and repeatedly waterboarded before his execution by the group in 2014, but for no other reason than to imitate what Americans do with their jihadi suspects—as his waterboarding was merely a form of torture that didn't seek to extract any information, and the tracksuit did not have the function of marking him out as a prisoner easily spotted in the event of an attempted escape. This truncated form of mimicry suggests that the Islamic State no longer derived ontological meaning from the West, not least because its great enemy was now internal to Islam, represented by the

Shia in particular but by many other groups similarly defined in sectarian rather than civilizational terms.

Al-Qaeda had famously distinguished between the "near enemy," that is to say dictatorial regimes in the Muslim world, and the "far enemy," comprising the Western powers that propped them up.[6] By attacking the United States and Western European countries, then, Al-Qaeda's spokesmen sought to force them either to reconsider their support of such client regimes or to enter the field of battle in their own right and so dispense with them in another way. A vastly expanded battlefield such as this, argued its theorists, men like Osama bin Laden and Ayman al-Zawahiri, would compel the timorous or undecided Muslims who collaborated with one or the other kind of enemy to take a stand against them both. By recognizing that the West supported and depended upon violent despotisms in their own countries, in other words, Muslims would no longer be able to appeal to one against the other. They would instead be forced to abandon as false both the nostrums of democracy hawked by the far enemy and the appeals to nationalism made by the near.

The Islamic State, however, turned its attention back to the near enemy, understood now to include not just local dictatorships but more importantly all those who unknowingly or even unwillingly supported them out of ignorance, fear, or bad faith. Since Al-Qaeda was seen as having failed to shift these ordinary Muslims from collaborating with such enemies, ISIS made them foes in their own right as social groups and individuals. Dictatorial states and their functionaries were therefore displaced by sectarian and minority groups as the Islamic State's chief targets. On the one hand, of course, this allowed for the militant mobilization of Sunnis in places like Syria and Iraq in particular, though also in Pakistan and Afghanistan where significant Shia populations also resided. But more interesting is the possibility that these sectarian communities represented the new social, civilian, and individualized character of enmity, one that we shall see Sunnis could also embody or be seduced by.

All of this meant that the West had merely become a site of global publicity and recruitment for ISIS. While still acknowledged as an enemy, though by now a rather obvious and even banal one, it no longer played a conceptually important part in the language of militancy. Instead, terrorist attacks in Europe and the United States were meant to foreground Islam as the only real challenge to the existing global order dominated by them and draw new converts as well as second- or third-generation Muslim immigrants to join an alternative utopia in the Levant. But this led to a transformation in the ritual and rhetorical practices of militancy. Al-Qaeda's mimicry of the West was thus overshadowed by other forms of violence. The burning alive of a captured Jordanian pilot in a cage or the casting of homosexuals from rooftops became exemplary acts of violence for ISIS, neither one invoking Al-Qaeda's logic of mirroring.

Of course, by setting alight the caged Jordanian pilot in 2015, ISIS was staging the death he would have suffered had he remained in his stricken fighter plane, which after all had become nothing more than a burning metal cage. Yet this punishment no longer represented a form of mimicry or imitation lacking ontological gravity, but instead a form of analogical thinking or judgment, perhaps modeled on the classical juridical principle of *qiyas* or reasoning by analogy. But such reasoning was detached from any given school of law or tradition of jurisprudence, since it drew upon Islamic texts and practices almost at random and without much consideration for their historical and intellectual contexts. Whatever else the legal debates among ISIS authorities indicate, I suggest that this freewheeling approach to the law had as its immediate predecessor the nineteenth-century liberal attempts to modernize it. And before this there was the eighteenth-century Wahhabi and Salafi vision of Islam, which would abandon the received Muslim legal tradition and claim the freedom to return to original sources.[7] Despite Muslim modernists' disagreeing with the illiberal conclusions of these earlier thinkers, it is interesting to note that well into the twentieth century the same modernists acknowledged an intellectual kinship with them.

Unlike the Wahhabis or Salafis, however, the Islamic State's legal practice appeared to be far more liberal in its reasoning if not results. For by ranging across the jurisprudential tradition without regard to its distinctive schools of thought, ISIS had in effect adopted something like the Anglo-Saxon model of case law—though without the inherited custom upon which that case law depends. Its highly original legal decisions became precedents in the making of a new tradition no longer based on the old principles of jurisprudence. Far more than Al-Qaeda, which at most sought legal justification for its practices from several disparate authorities generally beyond its control, the Islamic State produced its own law but was for this very reason animated by a concern with disavowing sovereignty when doing so. This concern was manifested in its increasingly fragmented if not desperate recourse to scripture, whose efforts at legitimization went well beyond any juridical tradition, to say nothing of mere propaganda. Its effective adoption of a case law model lacking sovereign status did nothing more than define this legal order in purely social terms, so that what exists or is visible becomes identical with what is lawful. It was the absolute dominance of jurisprudence in militant actions that prevented them from becoming political ones. For politics requires some degree of autonomy and integrity outside or even within the parameters of the law, an arena of action that was given no conceptual ground in the Islamic State. ISIS was obsessed with defining all human relations in legal terms because it identified law with a social realm outside of which nothing could be allowed to exist.

If Al-Qaeda's logic of mirrors was shattered by the Islamic State, which had gone on to elaborate a new and analogically defined vision of legal practice and punishment, militants' subjectivity, too, was transformed in similar ways from one movement to the other. For example, suicide bombers ceased to be iconic figures drawing an indirect sovereignty from their enemies, but were now workaday martyrs who enjoyed no particular celebrity. The militant subjectivity of Al-Qaeda's suicide bombers was largely posthumous, coming into view only in their martyrdom videos, whose virtual immortality was achieved just as their real selves and messier, more complex, or contradictory lives came to an end. The subjectivity of ISIS fighters, by contrast, was no longer posthumous in nature and disdained the webcam or reality TV model of Al-Qaeda's martyrs. Indeed, they almost entirely discarded the martyrdom video as a form of self-expression. Instead, their elaborately staged spectacles of violence, achieved by the use of multiple camera angles, clever editing, and special effects, created two different kinds of subjects.[8]

On the one hand there was the coherent and uniform virtual self, as produced in the studio and archived on the internet, and on the other an increasingly fragmented original more and more dependent for meaning on its studio-produced doppelganger. It might even be the case that the making of a virtual militant allowed the original to behave more freely or, as was increasingly common among ISIS fighters, in a less Islamic fashion than otherwise.

For Al-Qaeda, Islam was represented by the medieval flummery on view in militant forms of dress, speech, and habit, which rehearsed the sovereign gestures of an imagined past in a kind of fancy dress. But there was nothing homogeneous about this sartorial repertoire, with militants both named for their national origins, as for instance "Al-Britani" or "the Britisher," and dressed in some combination of national costumes, generally linked to important sites of contemporary jihad like Afghanistan or Chechnya. This gave them a highly diverse and even multicultural appearance. But such habits were always mixed up with other traditions of sovereign action, from the military fatigues of regular and would-be armies to the Kalashnikovs of earlier terrorist movements. ISIS retained much of this repertoire, to which it added objects like the white trainers or running shoes common to American and European gang culture, as popularized in rap music videos, and ninja-style black costumes from Hollywood films. Both these forms of dress were legitimized by its founder, Abu Musab al-Zarqawi, during the American occupation of Iraq.[9] In other words, the evolution of militant symbolism seems to proceed in two directions simultaneously: on the one hand the conventionally political language of the state or indeed the formal international order, and on the other an informal or social rhetoric of popular culture and crime.

The criminal actions of so many ISIS members, who in Europe often tended to have a background in petty theft and drug dealing, together with a lifestyle that included religiously proscribed habits like consuming alcohol or extramarital sex, has been much remarked upon, with the philosopher Alain Badiou dedicating the better part of a book to their analysis.[10] But more important than its nonideological or nonpolitical nature might be the way in which such criminality represents one of the last haunts of old-fashioned sovereignty, which has now been confined to social rather than political life.

Another French philosopher, Jean-Paul Sartre, in his book on the criminal-turned-writer Jean Genet, argued that crime was one of the few social phenomena that still retained what he called feudal forms of sovereignty.[11] By this he meant the sacrificial and, to our eyes, excessive acts of killing and dying that had once defined the ideals of the aristocrat as much as the saint. Unlike the ethic of production that characterized capitalist societies, Sartre wrote, criminals not only extricated the desire for possession from the necessity of productive work, but also structured their social relations on medieval codes of honor. These were famously represented in popular culture as well as in reality by the Italian Mafia, to whose example Badiou also refers in his book.

For Sartre, then, modern-day criminals, often even in their own imaginations, took on the dual or alternative roles of aristocrat and saint. One might add that all three roles were available to ISIS members, but rather than simply harking back to a medieval past, which of course they also and explicitly did, these forms of sovereign power tell us less about the survival within society of precapitalist sovereignty than the contradictions of a capitalist and especially neoliberal order. Yet another philosopher, Wendy Brown, for instance, argues that financial and other forms of globalization have fragmented the kind of sovereignty that once defined the modern nation-state as having absolute control over an enclosed territory and everything in it.[12] It is precisely when such states no longer possess national economies, can control migration, or can even secure their territories from terrorist attack, she contends, that ostensibly medieval patterns of sovereignty reemerge.

In the contemporary state, Brown claims, these patterns include the truly premodern fashion of building walls on national territory to create internal or international borders in places like Israel or between the United States and Mexico. There is also the increasing appeal to religious and royal forms of sovereign authority, to which we may add the revival of the "just war" tradition from medieval Christianity and the public acknowledgment and approbation of torture in the West after 9/11. For Brown such practices illustrate the coming apart of modern sovereignty into its constituent parts, with its economic, theological, aristocratic, and even territorial dimensions floating free of one another and no longer subordinated to a strongly national vision of the polity as the welfare state had once done. If this is true, then we might say that ISIS militants, too, exhibited the fragmentation of sovereignty in their behavior, recalling its older, medieval forms in a manner not so dissimilar from that of their enemies housed in apparently more stable nation-states. A good example of this was provided by the Islamic State's minting of gold coins in 2015. While they were supposedly meant to break "capitalist enslavement," it is also clear that these coins harked back to a much older notion of sovereignty and its embodiment in precious metal.

I suggest that despite its establishment of a state, though one possessing neither actual nor proclaimed borders, ISIS was still characterized by the old Islamist obsession with society or social order and self-regulation. But then this is not so unlike the neoliberal state of either Muslim or Western vintage. This might be why its claims to sovereignty were so ambiguous, from a largely silent caliph attributed with little or no command and charisma, to violence exercised in ways that did not distinguish between the social and the political and indeed refused to lend the latter any autonomy. If anything, the Islamic State derived its own indirect and disavowed sovereignty from its Shia enemies, represented as they were by the Islamic Republic of Iran. In the heavily sectarian rather than anti-Western narrative that defined ISIS, therefore, the caliph served as an antithesis to Iran's supreme leader, while the *sahaba*, or companions of the Prophet, were made counterparts to the sinless Imams of the Shia. For it was only after the Islamic Revolution in Iran that the caliphate, as well as the sacred status of Muhammad's companions, became an important part of Sunni thought following decades of oblivion.[13] Of course these institutions weren't always anti-Shia, and in the immediate aftermath of Iran's revolution they often represented little more than a Sunni effort to imitate Shia political thought, and that too among radicals and moderates alike.

The sectarian narrative that defined ISIS had emerged soon after the Iranian Revolution in countries like Pakistan and tied the Islamic State to its Shia alter ego, the Islamic republic, in a parasitical relationship of violent intimacy. After all, the task of Sunni sectarianism is to inveigh against what it considers Iran's attempt to usurp God's sovereignty by associating partners like the Imams or supreme leader with it. And yet it can do so only by imitating the very innovations that such sectarianism abhors, with ISIS deploying its own anti-Imams and anti–supreme leaders against Shia Iran, which for a number of reasons having to do with its institutionaliza-tion of a clerical establishment and belief in the continuity of divine authority within a line of Imams is the only country to have defined an Islamic politics in fully sovereign terms. Like the mirroring rhet-oric of Al-Qaeda, the Islamic State's process of negative imitation imbibed a disavowed sovereignty from the world of its enemies, but in a way that constantly threatened to collapse one into the other. This may be why the Shia were characterized in ISIS narratives pri-marily by their powers of seduction.[14]

A Secret Sovereignty

If the Islamic State's rhetoric was so consumed by the threat of Shia deception, this is surely because it recognized the latter's seductive power. Traditionally linked to the Shia doctrine of dissimulation or *taqiyya*, which obliged its followers to assume Sunni attitudes when they were in a minority or under threat, this emphasis on secrecy has in the past lent support to an esoteric view of religion, and in more recent times has been considered a gesture of courtesy to-ward dominant social norms. But sectarian polemics have tended to paint it in the colors of hypocrisy, if not treachery, and the idea of deception in ISIS rhetoric has in fact come to represent the most important threat the group faces, as well as the chief accusation it makes against enemies of all kinds. While the Shia might constitute its most depraved form, in other words, deception and the hypoc-risy that attended it assumed a more general salience in the demon-ology of the Islamic State. But why should this be the case?

The Islamic State's fear of all that is concealed and its concomi-tant desire to render everything transparent suggested, I think, a deep anxiety about the sovereignty it disavowed. The social visibility ISIS demanded was always placed under the name of the law, inso-far as every one of its actions, however bizarre and repugnant, had to be justified and indeed glorified by invoking scriptural and juridi-cal precedent. What remained invisible, therefore, was not only out-side or against the law, but, by that very fact, was something that transcended its purely social realm. Included in this transcendence was of course God as the sovereign power who founds the law and exists beyond it, as also the political sovereignty that Islamists have always suspected of usurping God's place. If the Islamic State was therefore obsessed with transparency, to the degree of publicizing even its most revolting acts, this had to do not simply with the requirements of propaganda, but rather with a will to reduce everything to the social or at least its juridical form.

As a form of social rather than political life, the divine law played the role of a second nature, in both the idiomatic and literal sense of that term, for Islamists as much as for militants of all kinds. In other words, it not only represented a reality located firmly outside the state in the hands of experts and the hearts of believers, but was also meant to displace pre-Islamic, heretical, profane, and even the merely inherited culture of the Muslim past as society's true or second nature. Culture seen as inherited custom was the dark matter that had to be destroyed and substituted by a divine law that, like the ideologies of the Cold War, was to be naturalized to become a new social reality.

But if the insistent visibility of this new nature presupposed the evisceration of all inner life, seen as a redoubt for the secret and seductive falsehood best represented by the Shia, it did not for its part require the presence of some alternative reality behind the strictures of the law. For in tune with the media images that defined them, such militant subjects were quite flat or even superficial, with their brutality perhaps meant to destroy rather than build an inner life. The superficiality of the new terrorist subject was manifested in the unprecedented rapidity of militant radicalization, which no longer required the kind of indoctrination that once characterized ideological movements during the Cold War, whose aim was precisely to build a new kind of inner life. But while the destruction of such a life, by its subordination to the avatar or virtual identity of social and digital media, might speed up radicalization, it was also likely to produce remarkably brittle subjects.

Like Al-Qaeda's game of mirrors that I described earlier, the Islamic State's juridical forms were appearances without a reality lurking somewhere in the background. What they appeared calculated to do was turn the men and women under their sway into nothing more than subjects of law, giving existential reality to the legal person otherwise invoked only when we act as signatories to a contract or are made responsible for some duty as much as infraction. By rejecting inner life for outward appearance, and depriving the latter of its traditional antonym, which is to say reality, the Islamic State's obsession with the law as social visibility transformed militant acts into gestures and rituals. For as Sartre comments in his book on Genet, many of the threatening habits of criminals are meant to reveal and even constitute those criminals as figures inspiring fear, loathing, or admiration. The habits are not merely instrumental acts but gestures that belong to the realm of aesthetics. The world of ISIS, as seen through its mediatized spectacles of violence, was also defined by aesthetics rather than by its cunning deployment of propaganda behind which some other reality lurks.

Sartre recognized that Genet's paradoxical desire to embody evil ended up bringing him even closer to goodness, if only because his philosophy of betrayal eventually led him to sacrifice evil as well and thus assume the mien of a saint and even a martyr, the two roles, along with that of actor, that his book's title used for Genet. Sartre thought Genet's life and literary career were dedicated to the impossible task of embodying evil understood as the negation of being, a category whose positivity represented all that was good since it defined every object of desire. And because evil is always imagined as something other than the being of which God is the highest manifestation, Genet was determined not to be a subject who desired it but rather an object for others and therefore a dead externality. We might compare this effort with Islamic militants' wish to renounce sovereignty and thus subjectivity itself so as to become echoes of their enemies' evil. And like Genet, these militants are already dead, having chosen their own martyrdom while still living.

But it turns out that becoming nothing or nobody is an extraordinarily difficult enterprise, one full of hidden dangers that risk catapulting the devotee of evil into the domain of goodness, as in Genet's case. Similarly, Muslim militants' effort to avoid God's sovereignty risks becoming a sacrilegious identification with it. To do evil for pleasure or profit, for example, was for Genet to turn it into a version of the goodness of being by making evil merely an instrument by which to achieve the kind of happiness that everyone desired. Evil could be experienced, therefore, only by suffering it oneself, for unlike the happiness derived from other people or things, suffering was the evildoer's alone and so free of being because it was experienced as deprivation. And if Genet experienced evil in this kind of self-imposed suffering by deliberately betraying his friends and lovers, militants did so by voluntarily choosing sacrifice and death to avoid the pleasure of a sovereignty that should belong to God alone. But in both cases this kind of suffering freely chosen represents an experience that is singular and lacking transcendence, because unlike happiness, it requires, in Sartre's words, only the evildoer and not God or any other being for its existence.

In Sartre's argument, Genet was unable to resist the seduction of being, and could at most caricature and rob it of reality by deploying it as an appearance, something whose deception has always been understood as satanic in nature. Appearance brings together being and nonbeing, and Sartre tells us that it represents both the being of nonbeing and the nonbeing of being. Genet therefore treasured the idea of a senseless crime, one that was either inexplicable in terms of motive or out of proportion to anything the criminal intended. Such a crime put being and therefore God and goodness into question by shaking people's faith in all the conventional narratives that defined reality. Such narratives, about the dominance of law as much as the criminal's desire for the same goods that others wanted, served only to confirm the hegemony of being and so goodness. But the kind of criminality that exceeded such desires forced people to confront the nothingness at its heart by showing it to be an appearance. Such actions could never take on a positive character. For if it was not to accede to the goodness of being, evil had to remain in its shadow, just like the sovereignty disavowed in Al-Qaeda's logic of mirroring.

A Life on the Surface

We tend to ignore the importance of militancy's world of appearances, or what we might call its injunction to have life exist on the surface of things. This turns militancy into a mere instrument of

divine command without any substance of its own. Instead, our accounts of movements like Al-Qaeda, and later ISIS, tend to be
structured as attempts to plumb the militant's depths. These efforts
can be defined historically, as when we trace militant Islam to recent or far-off events, such as the invasion of Iraq or the Ottoman
Empire's defeat and dismemberment after the First World War. Or
they may be described sociologically, by looking at the age, class,
and social prospects of ISIS supporters. Most commonly, of course,
this search for hidden depths is conducted as an inquiry into militant ideology, which in some cases can reach back as far as the
founding of Islam. Yet what if it isn't depth but surface that proves
the more important factor in understanding the militancy of a
group like ISIS?

The unparalleled rapidity of ISIS fighters' radicalization, especially when it emerges out of largely stable personal or social back-
grounds and outside the Middle East, seems to give the lie to
sociological narratives about ISIS, as it had for Al-Qaeda before.
After all, the followers of neither group appeared to fit any demographic profile, except perhaps in terms of age. But then the same
is true for all forms of militant activism on the left and the right.
The equally rapid reversion of some among these radicals to non-
militant forms of belief, the unprecedented number of new converts to Islam who were involved, and the ignorance of Muslim
tradition and theology among many fighters (illustrated by the two
British men who purchased *Islam for Dummies* and *The Koran for
Dummies* on Amazon before setting off to fight for the Islamic
State in Syria) also appear to cast doubt on accounts relying upon
the historical and ideological depth of such militancy.

This might be one reason why the Cold War term "indoctrination," which had been used to describe the lengthy and arduous process of remaking an individual's inner life, has been replaced in our
own day with "radicalization." If "indoctrination" was used to describe the reprogramming (another favorite term of the time) of individuals under communist rule, "brainwashing" could also refer to a
similar operation carried out in capitalist countries by religious and
other cults as much as the deep state. Whether deliberately or not,
the replacement of "indoctrination," "reprogramming," and "brainwashing" by "radicalization" suggests that at issue in new forms of

militancy is not ideological fervor or religious fanaticism in the old-fashioned sense of a fully reasoned explanation of the world. Instead, we are faced with a form of belief and attachment that neither amounts to an ideology nor requires an inner life carefully built up by sequestering its subjects from the society around them. Quite unlike such methods of creating alternative selves, the militants of our day revel in the culture they attack while at the same time rejecting some of it. And they do not need to separate themselves from their unaware families or friends until the time for violence comes.

Olivier Roy has argued that these surprising and unprecedented forms of mobilization suggest that the militancy of Al-Qaeda and ISIS should be understood not as the radicalization of Islam but the Islamization of radicalism. That Islam, in other words, has come to represent one of the only remaining forms of resistance and counterculture available to young people around the world in the aftermath of the Cold War and the destruction of a revolutionary left.[15] It is possible, of course, to identify any number of personal and particular motives that go into the making of ISIS. But as a globally dispersed movement, it surely possesses its own integrity and can't simply be understood as the sum total of such motivations. It might be the movement's very globalization that allows its followers to discard deeper and more located forms of identity to live instead on the screens and surfaces of social media. Becoming shallow, we might say, is a difficult task, for only by refusing any kind of anchored subjectivity are militants given over to their cruelties. Many of these cruelties, such as concubinage, slavery, or some of the Islamic State's more peculiar forms of execution, have no precedent that goes back much more than a decade even in the history of radical Islam and therefore possess no intellectual or political genealogy.[16]

Now to focus on the surface of militancy is not to suggest that it is superficial. For terms like "surface" and "depth" do not describe some physical reality but permit us to recognize how the brutal rhetoric and practices of the Islamic State, for instance, occur as the detached and impersonal fulfillment of a purely external duty. This is why ISIS propaganda films depart from the impassioned denunciations of earlier terrorists, to showcase figures unperturbed and even laughing at the violence they unleash—and from which they appear to be entirely disconnected. ISIS was in fact dominated by a hatred of all historical, sociological, and ideological depth, which, after all, justified its destruction not only of pre-Islamic monuments, but also of all "traditional," "heretical," or "infidel" persons, practices, and sites, including mosques and the shrines of Sufi saints.

Our impulse to look for the secret wellsprings of ISIS violence constitutes a rhetorical gesture, in which such acts of terror are seen as possessing a certain kind of authenticity and so a deeply subjective truth, whether of a sociological, historical, or ideological kind. But this way of thinking about violence is a relatively recent and even literary one, as the critic Lionel Trilling made clear in his book *Sincerity and Authenticity*.[17] Authenticity, Trilling argued, was a category that emerged in the second half of the nineteenth century and named an existential truth coming from deep within society to break its moral, aesthetic, or political norms. For these were now seen as a set of conventions and hypocrisies that merely obscured the profound truths of society. This is what allowed the criminal to become a literary subject, with Trilling identifying Kurtz, in Joseph Conrad's *Heart of Darkness*, as its most extreme example.

Like Kipling's tale of the Himalayas, *The Man Who Would Be King*, published ten years before Conrad's novella in 1888, *Heart of Darkness* described an adventurer who sought to brush aside the hypocritical humanitarian claims of colonization by founding a society that honestly acknowledged the brutal necessity of its ideal, which had only to be carried to its logical conclusion. The subsequent influence of this "honest" and therefore "authentic" fidelity to a principle has been remarkable, with *Heart of Darkness* being transposed to the Vietnam War in Francis Ford Coppola's 1979 film *Apocalypse Now*, which dealt with the period of decolonization that put an end to the process Kipling and Conrad had written about. Also published in 1979 was V. S. Naipaul's *A Bend in the River*, which returned to Conrad's Congo and restaged *Heart of Darkness* in the newly independent state, as if to show the authenticity of its vision. We might place the ISIS capital of Raqqa in this dystopian genealogy, marking, as its founding does, the postcolonial state's violent coming apart.

Sincerity, on the other hand, had become an important moral category in the seventeenth century, naming the overwhelming and sometimes even violent desire to bring one's inner life into harmony with its outward norms or surface appearance. Of this Trilling offers Goethe's *The Sorrows of Young Werther* as an illustration. Published in 1774 to immediately become a European sensation, this novel describes the way in which its young hero's failure to live sincerely leads eventually to his suicide. Disgusted by the hypocrisy of a society that refuses to abide by its own ideals, Werther decides that he can't exist in it with any degree of sincerity and so has to die by a logical as much as an existential necessity. Although it plays a much less important role in our culture than the narrative of authenticity, I suggest that sincerity, as Trilling represents it, allows us to think about militancy more productively.

Even if only by way of analogy, then, the suicide bomber might be recognized as Werther's descendant. For with its sacrificial imperative to have one's life conform to a vision of the sacred law as a set of outward observances imposed by God, rather than drawn from some profoundly existential truth, the martyr's Islam is far more congruent with sincerity and its focus on the surface of social life than with authenticity and its language of depth. And if I have deployed these categories here, it is not so much to claim them for militancy as to attempt the latter's translation into another kind of language, one that might allow us to attend more seriously to its world of ideas. It is to this world that I now turn, looking at the way in which Al-Qaeda and ISIS, each in its own way, have grappled with the problem of living sincerely, by identifying militancy with a fidelity to the sacred law seen as a wholly external demand.

Hypocrisy at Bay

The Muslim radicalism of our day is obsessed with the loss of sincerity in its repeated condemnations of hypocrisy. But why should this "ordinary vice," as the philosopher Judith Shklar describes it, play a role so important among militants as to represent their chief term of opprobrium for enemies of all kinds?[18] These include Muslims who deny the need for jihad, as well as Europeans and Americans who claim to be acting in the name of freedom or human rights. Such an attitude toward hypocrisy is, however, a commonplace one and had played an important role among anticolonial activists in the past.

Today it can be recognized in the accusation of double standards that has become a mainstay of the reasoning not only of militants, but of many others, whether Muslim or not. The double standards of the West in upholding ideals like democracy, then, receive more attention from the critics of hypocrisy than any analysis of the principles it betrays.

It is not the content of the West's principles that is put into question, or even seriously considered in such accusations, but the hypocrisy revealed in their affirmation. And while this position is a natural one for those who would defend the fulfillment of such ideals, it can be found even among those who explicitly reject them. For militants this sometimes amounts to an oddly pluralistic desire, that the West be true to itself rather than being judged by other principles, as communists, fascists, or fundamentalists had once done. An example of such anarchist criticism is provided by 9/11 "mastermind" Khalid Sheikh Mohammed's testimony at Guantánamo Bay.[19] Instead of making an argument based on Islamic law as a universally valid set of principles, Mohammed turned his tribunal into a trial of the US justice system, by arguing that its officials had betrayed their own ideals. Such an inversion, of course, was not unfamiliar to anticolonial activism in the past, its most famous example being Gandhi's "confession" during his trial for sedition in 1930.

While Mohammed certainly believed in the sharia's universality, he knew that it offered no common ground for a conversation with his captors, who thus had to be engaged in what I am calling an anarchist way and judged by their own ideals. But this meant that the content of Mohammed's own principles, too, was not as important as his lack of hypocrisy in living by them. His approach to the sacred law in which these principles were embodied was therefore existential rather than merely social or indeed juridical in character. He demonstrated Islam's truth by having it compete with its rivals, if only to see whose supporters remained faithful to the principles they professed. This competition was about being true to a set of external prescriptions, with Mohammed demanding the sacrifice of an inner life whose very autonomy from the law was taken as a sign of deception and hypocrisy.

This concern with a life on the surface is taken to another level in the Islamic State's obsession with transparency, visibility, and sincerity, which demonstrates a fear of all that is secret, hidden, and profound. Remarkable about the ISIS lexicon of blame is its domination by sins like hypocrisy, dissimulation, and even sorcery, all examples of hiddenness. Such an anxiety about depth was never part of Al-Qaeda's project, which had to do with distinguishing militants' sovereignty from that of their enemies in a global arena where responsibility had become dispersed and universalized. In an address from September 2014 called "Indeed Your Lord Is Ever Watchful," the Islamic State's chief propagandist, Shaykh Abu Muhammad al-Adnani ash-Shami, described his Western enemies by saying, "They argue in their favour, falsify the events and realities, fool people and endeavour to mobilise them against the rightful while portraying the people of falsehood with every aspect of rightfulness and power in desperate attempts to falsify at all times the truth and to scare and defeat its followers."[20]

His description of the Shia "heretics" (rafidah) deploys the same reasoning. Because of their esoteric forms of religion, especially the doctrine of taqiyya or "protective dissimulation," the Shia have traditionally been accused of dissembling in Sunni polemics, but with ISIS they simply represented hypocrisy's purest form and were not otherwise distinguished from the Islamic State's other enemies. Indeed, the language of hypocrisy has become so universalized that it even characterizes the views of anti-Muslim movements in the West, which routinely accuse so-called moderates of doublespeak. Adnani warns Sunnis of Shia hypocrisy, saying, "O Sunnis of Iraq, it is time for you to learn from the lessons of the past, and that nothing works with the Rafidah but the slicing of their throats and the striking of their necks; they pretend to be helpless until they get strong; they hide their hatred, anger and enmity towards the people and conspire against them; they show false affection towards them and flatter them as long as the Sunnis are strong, while they try to keep in step with them, compete with them and try their hardest to weaken them when they are equal in power."[21]

Naturally, the deception identified in the enemy can also be found in oneself, which is why it might need to be so ferociously externalized in the first place. So Adnani warns the Islamic State's troops: "Know that from time to time a trial, purification, and selection are necessary since some people, who are not of you, as well as pretenders have entered your ranks and disorder has taken place. A trial is therefore necessary to drive out the dirt and purify the ranks."[22] How did an apparently minor vice like hypocrisy become the Islamic State's chief object of fear? The hypocrite (*munafiq*) was of course an important figure in the Qur'an, serving as the name for those who only pretended to follow Muhammad. But even there—to say nothing about later Muslim texts and societies—the hypocrite by no means represented Islam's greatest enemy. In Europe's more recent history, however, and for apparently the first time since the early modern hermeneutics of suspicion that was deployed against Iberian *conversos* and *moriscos* following the Reconquista, or by Catholics and Protestants against one another during and after the Reformation, hypocrisy did become a significant political category with the French Revolution.

In her book *On Revolution* the political philosopher Hannah Arendt writes about how men like Robespierre sought to unmask the hidden motives of those he considered France's enemies.[23] This he did to destroy the hypocrisy, now increasingly secretive, upon which the old regime's decadent and corrupt society had been founded. In her consideration of hypocrisy's twentieth-century afterlife, Arendt went on to argue that in fascist and communist states its unmasking took on a teleological character, where the race or class enemy appeared according to the logic of history and had to be periodically unmasked. She suggests that show trials and forced confessions in these states were used by those who held power not simply to dispose of defeated rivals, but because such unmasking was required and so legitimized by the laws of history.

Arendt drew on the work of another philosopher, Maurice Merleau-Ponty, who showed in great detail how even the victims of such show trials managed to believe somehow in the betrayal of which they were accused and so came to accept the accusation. His example was the Soviet politician Bukharin, who disagreed with Stalin while at the same time acknowledging his own treachery and going to his death without protest even though it was clear that his confession would not gain him any reprieve.[24] Here, too, in other words, we see the operation of a sacrificial logic that has nothing to do with irrationality or religious fanaticism. If anything, Bukharin's behavior was more reasoned out than that of ordinary politicians.

And in holding himself responsible for treason, he ended up both claiming and paying for an illegitimate sovereignty outside that which belonged by right to the Communist Party or the Soviet state even when they did wrong, as he continued to believe was the case.

Given the Islamic State's rejection of history and ideology, however, it seems unlikely that its anxiety about hypocrisy and its desire for sincerity can be identified with any of the cases Arendt or Merleau-Ponty considered. Instead, its obsession with transparency and the will to live entirely on the surface was manifested in ISIS by the requirement that all action be rendered visible as law. And the law itself was conceived in an unsystematic and merely arithmetical rather than ideological way, whereas the Islamists had understood it as a system with a set of recognizable social functions. Unlike Al-Qaeda, then, which didn't have to justify its acts legally if they were simply mirroring those of an enemy, ISIS had to give all its practices the name of law. This included even those bizarre forms of murder, such as throwing people off buildings, setting them alight, or drowning them, for which it was difficult to find textual or traditional justification.

The Absent Sovereign

By exposing even their most brutal acts to public scrutiny, ISIS meant them not only to inspire fear or attract recruits, but as a consequence to refuse what we may call the open secret of sovereign power. In conventional states, this open secret, by which sovereignty is manifested outside the very law it institutes, tends to occur in the routine of extralegal practices in the police, army, or intelligence services. And these do nothing more than extend into everyday life the formal or public exception that defines sovereignty at the highest reaches of the state, when regular laws are suspended in times of emergency like war.[25]

The Islamic State lacked the kind of extralegal force that defines sovereignty as a form of transcendence, which is to say the ability to act outside or above the law even if only temporarily. Its most horrific acts were performed neither by a formal declaration of emergency nor as an open secret, but publicly and even on film

by agents who murdered with smiles on their faces as if to repudiate the pretended exceptionality of the sovereign act. Even Al-
Qaeda, in this respect following its terrorist predecessors in different parts of the world, used to accompany its violence with expressions of regret, justifying them as an unfortunate necessity. But the
way in which ISIS conducted itself demonstrates that by subordinating all action to the law, it was unable to behave in a sovereign
or transcendent manner. The suicide bomber was no longer its
iconic representative.

If ISIS had no sense of political transcendence, it curiously
didn't possess one of a religious kind either. Its caliph was not endowed with any special power or charisma, and was indeed rarely
heard from, representing a quite different figure from Osama bin
Laden in this respect. Even the apocalyptic visions for which the
Islamic State was known appear to have been of a banal and ritualistic kind. Its online magazine, *Dabiq*, named for the Syrian town in
which the messiah was meant to appear, was full of the most quotidian and even anodyne stories about the opening of schools or
regulation of trade in the marketplace. Here, too, the language of
the law triumphed over any belief or practice that would serve as a
form of exception to it, with apocalypse providing the only way to
imagine sovereignty as a kind of transcendence—but only as one
that is yet to come.[26]

If a genuinely apocalyptic element existed in the Islamic State's
rhetoric, it was a parochial one having to do with the caliphate
conceived of as Islam's last stand. By announcing the institution's
reappearance, something no other Islamic movement had done
since its abolition by the new Turkish republic in 1924, the Islamic
State in the same movement resigned its own room for maneuver
as well. Having fallen, therefore, the caliphate should never rise
again, since all attempts to institute it subsequently would have to
account for its ISIS version. In this way the movement seemed deliberately to be claiming Islamic categories so as to institute them
in the form it preferred, and if not, then allow them to be destroyed forever. The Islamic State may thus represent a point of no
return for Muslim militancy in general, which could also explain
the sheer brutality of its violence—upon which it would be difficult
for any successor to improve.

The apocalypse, in other words, is in some sense peculiar to Islam, with ISIS propagandists drawing upon a theme made popular in the late nineteenth century, when Muslims were warned that if they didn't remain true to the faith, God would reject them for their enemies—at that time Europe's colonial powers. As we have seen, such relations with the enemy were politically ambiguous, so this threat was deployed both by those who urged Muslims to draw closer to the West and by those who counseled the opposite. Here is how the ISIS spokesman Adnani describes this last stand, in the now familiar vocabulary of anxiety about the threat of deception and the corresponding desire (expressed by a quotation from the Qur'an) for truth made visible so that life can be lived on the surface:

> O soldiers of the Islamic State, be ready for the final campaign of the crusaders. Yes, by Allah's will, it will be the final one. Thereafter, we will raid them by Allah's permission and they will not raid us. Be ready, for by Allah's permission you are befitting for it. The crusaders have returned with a new campaign. They have come so that the dust clears, the fog disappears, and the masks fall, and thereby the hoax of falsehood is exposed and the truth becomes clearly visible, and so that those who were to perish (for their rejecting the faith) might perish upon clear evidence, and those that were to live (i.e., believers) might live upon clear evidence (Sura 8, Spoils of War, 42).[27]

Hannah Arendt, we have seen, argued that the politics of sincerity, in its twentieth-century versions, like forced confessions and show trials, had sought to unmask hypocrisy in a mechanical way. Hypocrites needed to be unmasked in order to fulfill the laws of history that predicted and so called for their appearance. And this meant that ideology in communist and fascist states worked as a kind of infernal machine, requiring the periodic revelation of treachery for its justification. Of course, liberal democracies, too, rely upon the periodic occurrence of scandals that serve to correct and so legitimize the social and political order they represent. Such revelations, however, are personal in nature and made by the private media, with the secrets exposed being those of financial or sexual impropriety. It is this that makes liberal hypocrisy an ordinary vice.

In the case of ISIS, unmasking hypocrisy was no longer crucial, since its supporters already knew who these sectarian, religious, and other enemies were and so needed only to guard against their own susceptibility to being deceived by them. By destroying these enemies, then, they were in some sense externalizing and eliminating their own inner selves in the effort to live entirely on the surface— not least in the ability to endure their own violence without any apparent effect. And this required that all their actions had to be rendered visible in the form of law, even those whose brutality was earlier seen as breaking all legal convention. It is not the laws of history that made ISIS rhetoric into an infernal machine, but the attempt to bring all action under the authority of God's law by eliminating the hypocrisy that would conceal any extralegal or sovereign desire.

It is as if the militant subject had been reduced to the virtual self in video games like *Assassin's Creed*, itself gesturing toward a medieval Muslim history and, perhaps not accidentally, popular among some of the Islamic State's European and American followers. Like ISIS propaganda, *Assassin's Creed* is also filled with apocalyptic references that point to a sovereignty and transcendence yet to come, and of whose mystical reality the gamer is only vaguely aware. The video game's virtual players, of course, are placed within a received narrative where all enemies and obstacles are known, and their task is to surmount and defeat them by the use of skill alone. More interesting than its virtual reality, however, is the possibility that this militant figure is meant to instantiate a legal subject, hitherto simply an abstraction or mask—or a persona, as Arendt would say. She thought that figures like Robespierre and his communist or fascist successors wanted to destroy the legal persona and expose the inner depths of the individual underneath its mask to public view, an impossible desire that would end by eliminating that individual's integrity and autonomy. My argument is that ISIS wants to destroy this interiority altogether and reduce the subject to its mask or legal persona.

On the one hand, ISIS was dominated by the desire to destroy all religious, institutional, and other forms of mediation between the believer and God as the embodiment of sovereignty and transcendence—thus the now familiar gesture used by its fighters, who pointed to the skies as if to justify their acts by direct reference to the deity's singularity. Or the archaic-looking image of the Prophet's seal taken from the medieval imagery of the Abbasid caliphate that was impressed upon the ISIS flag, as if Muhammad himself had validated its followers. But on the other hand, this transcendent power was made to disappear within the law. Eliminating sovereignty in this way, by repeatedly absorbing it and making it visible within the law, can even be said to represent the Islamic State's principle of movement—by which the law devours everything, including its own limits and therefore its very possibility.

The Islamist vision of sharia over the course of the twentieth century, we might say, was ideological because it rationalized the law as an instrument of social justice and so gave it a secular function as the modernists had done before them. And yet the sharia continued to bear a largely negative character, as it was meant to prevent the exercise either of democratic or of dictatorial sovereignty. For the power to constitute and abrogate law was reserved for God alone, with only minor details being left for religious specialists to decide upon. In this sense Islamism was antipolitical, despite its project to found an Islamic state, and if not anarchist its engagement with politics was correspondingly opportunistic and therefore often violent.

Al-Qaeda dispensed with the law as an instrument of ideology understood as a system whose function was to create a just society. It was instead seen as a set of prescriptions by which one could live without hypocrisy in a sacrificial and therefore transparent way. For spectacular acts like suicide bombing were meant to demonstrate the law's truth in their very sincerity, best enunciated in the braggadocio about militants loving death more than their enemies did life. But sacrifice as a form of sovereignty, one that exceeded the law by destroying its subject, remained a negative and even nihilistic act incapable of proposing any kind of alternative order or reality to the West that Al-Qaeda's practices tended self-consciously to mirror.

For ISIS the law continued to exist without ideological rationalization, but its practices had now lost much of their excessive or sacrificial aspect, and therefore the possibility of sovereign action as well. Instead, it was concerned with forms of pleasure that were more mundane than heroic, as befits "ordinary" life in a state. From its earliest days, even before it had achieved a state or official name, ISIS had advertised its project as one in which fighters could enjoy not only the rule of sharia, but also money, goods, and sex in addition to power. Early advertising for the jihad in Syria was dominated not by the language of sacrifice so much as Instagram images of "conquered" villas and swimming pools for fighters to enjoy.[28] The law here seems to have abandoned its repressive form altogether, to make permissible all manner of hitherto outrageous desires, from elaborately imagined executions to sexual slavery.

More than forsaking its repressive function, the law had actually become an instrument to compel its subject's enjoyment, as if in a perverse homage to the Western "decadence" against which its leaders routinely inveighed. Here, then, was one place in which the mirror that Al-Qaeda held up to the West continued to play its role. But to compel enjoyment is also to destroy its freedom and even, perhaps, its substance in the process. The fantasies of desire played out by men as well as women in ISIS territory became ever more excessive as if in order to reclaim their sovereignty, which nevertheless had to be continuously exorcised so as to end up in the law's embrace. Such pleasures, in other words, had become duties without an inner or existential source, obliging their militant agents to live on the surface of things in a perpetual performance of themselves.

Invisible Enemy

Although they were both global movements, Al-Qaeda and ISIS demonstrated the difficulty of conducting a global politics. This was due not to their own peculiarities as much as to the absence of such a politics in the post–Cold War world. For a global politics would require some kind of territorial as much as maritime and even aerial division of space between friends and enemies. But it was precisely this kind of division that proved so problematic to make during the Global War on Terror. It was a conflict that not only brought every state in the world into an alliance against terrorism, however fraught this might have been, but also exceeded the domain of international law to enter an effectively borderless world in procedures of surveillance and rendition. In these circumstances it was almost impossible to draw clean and clear distinctions between friend and enemy, not least when they couldn't be geographically placed. And we can see this inability to achieve a political grasp of the war not only for militant Islam but for its American foe as well. This became evident with the killing of Osama bin Laden in 2011.

Released by the Pentagon following the US assassination of Osama bin Laden in Pakistan, an already "iconic" image showing Al-Qaeda's frail leader watching footage of himself on an antiquated television set inadvertently reveals some truths about the War on Terror. For one thing, it is difficult to imagine this setting as part of a command center for global terrorism, thus giving the lie to US claims about taking out an active terrorist. And for another, the international reaction to Bin Laden's assassination cast doubt on the US narrative of war and victory on a global scale. Crucial about this reaction, after all, was the fact that people around the world seemed interested in the event primarily because of the extraordinary public response it generated in the United States. Even in countries like Britain and Spain, which had themselves been the victims of Al-Qaeda's militancy, there was little if any public demonstration of satisfaction at Bin Laden's death. Yet it continued to be the subject of massive media coverage precisely as an element in US domestic politics.

In the Muslim world, too, those who mourned the "Sheikh's" death did so for a variety of reasons, many of which had more to do with local politics than anything so grand as a global war against the West. Indeed, there was something curious about the endlessly replayed shots, in the American and European press, that attempted to demonstrate Osama bin Laden's popularity among Muslims by showing his photograph being sold in Pakistani shops. For these images often had as their context pictures of other celebrities, like unveiled and heavily made-up starlets from Lollywood, as the Punjabi film industry based in Lahore is known. The popularity of Bin Laden's photograph, sold as a commodity alongside posters of film stars and boxes of Barbie dolls, says nothing at all about that of the jihad he advocated. His celebrity status had more to do with the fact that Bin Laden was dignified by the United States as its greatest enemy and thus had gained a degree of infamy with little connection to Pakistani concerns. He had become just another celebrity.

Al-Qaeda's spectacular attacks, notably those of 9/11, were impressive enough to win it a certain admiration, sometimes for aesthetic as much as religious or political reasons. But it is not clear how much of this translated into material support. By the time of Bin Laden's assassination, even anti-American sentiment among Muslims appeared to have abandoned him as an Islamic hero and moved in other directions. It was only the US public that continued to be mesmerized by Bin Laden, which was appropriate enough given that he had always been a factor of US domestic politics. The political use to which President Obama put Bin Laden's killing, therefore, was a continuation of his predecessor's strategy, which consisted of using fears about security to consolidate his power at the national level. I am not saying that the Bush Administration used the 9/11 attacks in a cynical exercise to bolster its support, nor that the United States used them as an excuse to remake the world in its own image. I think, rather, that the United States has been unable to conduct a global politics.

During the Cold War, US administrations were interested in securing America's economic and political dominance in the context of a hemispheric conflict. But the collapse of the Soviet Union meant that US geopolitics suddenly shrank to become merely an aspect of the country's domestic concerns. Its global victory, in other words, domesticated US politics, so the nation's greatest enemies could now be only internal ones. Surely the escalating tension between liberals and conservatives in the United States, whose mutual hatreds had their origin in the culture wars of the 1980s, demonstrates the truth of this situation. Neoconservative thinkers had recognized the novelty of this withdrawal from geopolitics very soon after the Soviet collapse, though they saw it as a sign of America's victorious domination of the global arena. Francis Fukuyama's celebrated "end of history" thesis, as elucidated in his 1992 book *The End of History and the Last Man*, was the first important statement about America's inability to engage in a global politics, now seen as an extension of its domestic conflicts and interests.[29]

While ostensibly disagreeing with Fukuyama's thesis, Samuel Huntington's equally influential "clash of civilizations" argument, as elaborated in his 1996 book *The Clash of Civilizations and the Remaking of World Order,* also recognized the end of a traditional geopolitics based on states and sought to redefine worldwide conflict in cultural and nonstatist terms.[30] In their own ways both thinkers saw that with the Soviet collapse, a global arena had come into view that was no longer circumscribed by states or even the international system, and thus did not possess a politics proper to itself. And it was in such an arena that a phenomenon like Al-Qaeda's nonstate militancy could arise and seek to give political substance to an entity like the global Muslim *ummah* or community, which itself had no historical precedent or institutional life. An admirer of Huntington's book, Osama bin Laden put into action its idea of a geopolitics determined by nonstate actors. In doing so he sought to occupy a global arena that had remained politically vacant since the Cold War's division of the globe into rival hemispheres.

By launching the Global War on Terror, the United States was, among other things, trying to reclaim a global politics for itself. But this was an effort doomed to failure since Al-Qaeda was unable to present it any kind of military challenge, becoming instead a factor of US domestic politics in the aftermath of 9/11. Despite the exotic appearance and terminology of its militants, moreover, Al-Qaeda operated not as an external enemy but rather internally, by turning the logic and instruments of the West against itself. This viral form of attack was in full evidence with the 9/11 attacks, whose perpetrators trained at US flight schools and used US aircraft to strike their targets from inside the country. And this lack of externality was only augmented by the militants' exaltation of martyrdom, which robbed Al-Qaeda of its very ontology as a foe that death might defeat. Even the war's economic and other spoils were reserved primarily for the United States, whose allies had to fall in line for crumbs that might enrich individuals but had little bearing for an international system that had been subordinated to American designs.

In waging what it considered a global war, in other words, the United States did nothing more than hollow out if not demolish an international system whose binding of enemies within a single order had already been weakened by the Soviet collapse.[31] This new global arena was therefore recognized and supported by the United States, which dismissed and even violated the legal and other formulae of the international order to occupy it in policies like rendition, torture, and preemptive war. America's great power, in other words, has robbed it of geopolitics as a distinct field of action, confining its practices to the kind of self-interest that is incapable of distinguishing domestic from international arenas. As a consequence, the United States operated internationally only by seeing and reproducing itself everywhere in an impossible gesture of narcissism. And this meant that the more it acted in the world, the more the United States actually withdrew from the world's reality by refusing to acknowledge any rival within it.

Osama bin Laden's assassination and disposal at sea provided a good example of this, representing a squandered opportunity for the procedures of international ethics as much as justice, sacrificed as both of these were in favor of a purely domestic politics. But the risk of such behavior is very high indeed since it entails the turning inward of all conflict. So quite apart from the mutual recriminations of Republicans and Democrats, there is the increasing use of War on Terror procedures within the United States itself for purposes like crime prevention that restrict the civil liberties of US as well as British and European citizens, to say nothing of those in other parts of the world, with countries like India, China, and Russia all taking up the American model of antiterrorism for use against all kinds of people who had nothing to do with it. Also indicative of this turn inward is that Muslims today are seen by many Americans more as an internal threat than an external one, with their coreligionists abroad still free to become clients and allies of the United States.

The early years of the War on Terror had seen nothing like this rise in what is often called Islamophobia, which has gained ground in the United States only after years of uninterrupted security and the absence of any major terrorist attacks. Like these domestic concerns, Bin Laden's killing, together with the reactions it elicited, offers us the clearest possible example of America's loss of geopolitics and its withdrawal from the world. Is this why the Ukraine war came as such a godsend to US policymakers and some of their

European allies? For it seemed to offer a return to the kind of geopolitics last seen during the Cold War.[32] And, indeed, this war was
discussed on all sides in the terminology of a dead past. On the
Russian side we had a narrative of Western expansionism, from
Latin Christendom to NATO; and on the American one, the story
of Russian expansion, from its nineteenth-century empire to the
Warsaw Pact. All this suggests the war was part of a deeply nostalgic
enterprise.

From Ukraine to Gaza

If the Ukraine war had to be understood in such nostalgic terms,
this is because it was never able to match up to them. The war illustrated not the return of global politics but its breakdown, since the
non-Western world in particular refused to participate in the conflict by taking sides in it. Instead, it revived the principle of neutrality that had been done away with during the Global War on Terror.
A repudiation of that war's effort to revive Western hegemony on a
global scale, the return of neutrality signaled both the political maturity of the so-called Global South and its recognition that Russia
posed at most a regional threat rather than vying for superpower
status. Non-Western attitudes toward China were for the most part
similar and indicated the move from a global to a regional politics
in which the superpower competition of the Cold War had no
place, whether in its unipolar, bipolar, or even multipolar variants.[33]

A similar failure of political imagination was evident in the
Gaza war, also regionalized by the Global South opting for neutrality in calls for a ceasefire. By refusing the global narratives promoted by Israel and its Western allies as much as by the Palestinians
and theirs, this approach condemned such visions to analytical irrelevance and reinforced the West's loss of geopolitics. For like Al-
Qaeda and ISIS, Ukraine and Gaza were as much a part of the
West's domestic politics as they were about international affairs.
The Gaza war did unite Muslims globally, but we shall see that it
did so by the diminution of Islamic terminology. Instead, and remi-
niscent of Muslims organizing for the Bosnians or Rohingya in
other genocidal conflicts after the Cold War, those backing the
Palestinians resorted to a hollowed-out international order and its

humanitarian principles. Rather than supporting this order, however, their approach only accentuated its crisis in the War on Terror's wake. For given their predictable rejection by the West, such appeals were meant to demonstrate the failure of international law as much as to gain its succor. Yet for most Muslims around the world there was no alternative to this repeated rehearsal of failure. This has been particularly true of Palestinians who have, after all, long sought to join the Cold War's international order rather than to challenge it.[34]

By invoking sanctions before the war and resorting to international courts during it, Palestinians and their supporters sought either to redeem the UN system or show it to be a farce. Apart from its propagandistic purpose, after all, turning to the International Criminal Court and the International Court of Justice represented a political failure.[35] For these courts were being asked to hand down decisions and penalties as if they were adjudicating on behalf of a sovereign state in its domestic jurisdiction. But that is not how international law works. It rather operates by the mutual agreement of the parties to any dispute. States agree to be bound by it to the same degree as their enemies in a kind of honor system. Only in cases where a country has been defeated in war and its government dissolved do courts dispense decisions as they would in domestic law, for those brought before such tribunals no longer represent a party to any convention. A judicial determination that crimes like genocide had been committed by Israel, therefore, might serve to deter some of its supporters in the West for fear of eventual lawsuits and arrests, while restricting the movement of some Israeli leaders, soldiers, and settlers. But it wouldn't propose a political solution nor even be capable of stopping the war.

As with Ukraine, then, the crisis of the international order and so of global politics was manifested not just in the inability to stop the war in Gaza, but in the failure of the political imagination to grasp its novelty. On the Israeli side we had invocations of "anti-Semitism," a term from nineteenth-century Europe, as well as "terrorism" from the vocabulary of early twentieth-century colonialism and "genocide" from the period following the Second World War. These may have been accurate categories to describe some of the ideas and aims of Palestinian movements like Hamas, but they were

also too broad and deployed too transhistorically to have much analytical purchase in understanding the specificity of events like the
attack of October 2023 that set off the Gaza war. When used in unchanging ways, such terms gave rise to conspiratorial narratives, as
with "anti-Semitism," in which history was defined by timeless motives and ends that foreclosed any political settlement.

This was also true of the terms favored by Palestinians, such as
"settler colonialism," dating to the Americas in early modern times;
"apartheid," from twentieth-century South Africa; and now "genocide" as well.[36] But settler colonies give rise to nationalism, of which
Zionism and the Palestinian movement are examples. These categories are open-ended and cannot tell us much about recent events
without considering their historical development. In their own day,
after all, the Algerian war of independence and the Vietnam War
were not seen by those who supported the freedom of these countries
merely as iterations of decolonization. They were instead theorized as
representing new forms of both repression and revolution linked to
the global capitalist economy. This has not yet happened with Gaza,
on both sides of whose war trivial invocations of the past dominate.
Punishing Israel by way of boycotts, sanctions, and divestment, for
example, is often linked to the dismantling of apartheid.[37] But sanctions emerged from colonial blockades to enter international law
after the First World War, as punitive measures short of armed conflict that target civilians.[38] Their success has been ambivalent at best
and cannot account for the end of apartheid. The West abandoned
white South Africa only once it was no longer needed as an ally after
the Cold War.

The narratives deployed by both sides in the Gaza war also had
much in common, with Palestinians following the precedent of
Zionism. The Holocaust as the trauma of Jewish nationhood was
matched by the Nakba. The Jewish ghetto of Europe's past was
paired with the besieged Gaza Strip as well as Palestinian villages divided by Israeli walls and roads in the West Bank. The Jewish right
of return was countered by demands for the return of Palestinian
refugees. The Temple Mount as a religious symbol had its equivalent in Al-Aqsa. Each side laid claim to prior occupation of the land,
in a global context where indigeneity characterizes far right and
anti-immigrant parties. Indigenous peoples have received symbolic

restitution in some settler societies, where they are too insignificant to possess political power. But neither Palestinians nor Israelis fit into such models of indigeneity. Muslims instead have come to be the chief targets of indigenist politics from Europe and North America to India, Myanmar, and beyond, where they are seen not just as aliens but inassimilable due to the strength of their religion.

While Hamas's attack on Israel in October 2023 was routinely compared to Al-Qaeda's on the United States in September 2001, they have been understood in strikingly different ways. The 2001 attacks were seen as being unprecedented not only in their scale, but as heralding a new political future for the globe. This is not true of the 2023 attack and the war that followed it in Gaza, both viewed as continuations of the past, however unprecedented in scale. For Israelis this was the past of Palestinian or Islamic terrorism, and for their opponents of colonialism and apartheid. The victimology of one was matched by that of the other in an intimacy that showed up the failure of a political imagination, which requires a real opposition and not claims to represent the same ideals. But this is because they both continue to be drawn from the humanitarian principles of the post–Cold War period despite the evisceration of these principles during the Global War on Terror, which provides the only historical precedent for Gaza.

No one disagreed that anti-Semitism, terrorism, genocide, colonialism, or apartheid were bad things. They had therefore to be disavowed and attributed to the enemy in mutual accusations of hypocrisy. It is only when we look at the narratives and actions of the so-called Axis of Resistance, which brought together Hamas with Hezbollah, the Shia militias of Iraq, the Houthis in Yemen, and Iran, that we see a recognition of novelty that goes beyond the terminology of the international order. It represented the real politics of Palestine, enabling the pressure and propaganda exercised by others though rarely acknowledged by them. In this vision Israel had lost its war, and the international order was being remade.[39] Victimology was displaced by martyrdom as death in a worthy and victorious cause. Yet Hamas's attack and the Israeli response that followed it appears to have shifted the former's rhetoric back into the register of victimology and humanitarianism in tune with the global protests to which the war soon gave rise.

Given the violence of its incursion, the humanitarian principles invoked by Hamas may seem at least as disingenuous as Israel's claims to them. But its attack also destroyed Hamas as one of the last of the Cold War's Islamist movements. For it had until then focused on an ideological program to secure and defend Gaza and its people from Israel, whether by fighting or creating a working relationship with it.[40] This long-standing program collapsed during the attack, which, whether deliberately or not, exposed Gaza and its civilian population to massive Israeli retribution without leading to a more general uprising among Palestinians either in Israel or in the West Bank, to say nothing of military or even much diplomatic support from Arab countries. It increasingly looks like the attacks of October 2023 were part of an effort by Hamas's military wing in Gaza to take command of the movement as a whole both from its political wing in Doha and from its sponsors in Tehran. Compelled to support this unforeseen initiative despite realizing how ill-advised it was, the self-proclaimed Axis of Resistance had to face its severest test, thanks to the naïveté of men like Yahya Sinwar and Mohammed Deif. Hamas did not return to the suicide missions that had defined its struggle before it took Gaza over in 2006, but instead protected its fighters in tunnels while leaving ordinary Palestinians defenseless in a reversal of the sacrificial thinking characteristic of militant groups.

While Hamas abandoned its religious vocabulary and ideological reasoning, many Israelis invoked biblical precedents for anti-Palestinian violence. Hamas's founding covenant of 1988 had treated Islam as a Cold War ideology encompassing every part of life.[41] The Palestinian struggle was placed within this larger context, and the covenant even quoted from Muhammad Iqbal's poetry. But by the time it issued a statement in January 2024 accounting for the attacks of the previous October, Hamas had shifted to the international order's humanitarian narrative. Like Israel, it justified its actions as defensive ones aimed at combatants.[42] Also like Israel it raised the threat of genocide to justify violence as a form of humanitarianism, in the kind of reasoning that has always been part of international human rights law. Because the life of a people comprised the ultimate value, anything was permissible to protect it. The slogan "never again," intoned after the Holocaust, came in this way to be paired with "by any means necessary," the anticolonial phrase used by Frantz Fanon and Malcolm X.

But perhaps the greatest failure of the political imagination on display in the Gaza war had to do with the fact that it was primarily waged between Israel and Hamas. Yet, the West Bank and parts of Lebanon, Syria, Iraq, Yemen, and Iran were also on the war's front lines, along with societies in many Western countries that were wracked by protests, violence, and arrests. If we were to link it to some genealogy, the conflict might best belong to the history of US counterinsurgency and proxy war meant to assert hegemony globally. The Global War on Terror had been the culmination of this enterprise, with its failure returning us to a more regionalized and even less successful working of its principle. For hegemony cannot be achieved by force alone, which is what the United States and its allies were reduced to in supporting the Gaza war. Pretending that the United States was or could be neutral in such a war created a false and personalized narrative about what might be possible if the White House only listened to reason. From its support of Saddam Hussein's war against Iran in the 1980s to Saudi Arabia's against Yemen in the 2000s, the United States has regularly engaged in such conflicts across the region. Israel could not fight its war in Gaza or Lebanon without US arms, diplomatic backing, logistical support, and coordinated military planning. Instead of analyzing it as a US war, however, many commentators have tended to condemn the United States for supporting Israel due to the influence of factors like Jewish monetary interests and in this way returned to the traditionally economic or rather antipolitical themes of anti-Semitism.

Like the Ukraine war before it, that in Gaza represented the crisis of the Cold War international order and the collapse of global politics. Each conflict was prolonged because of the United Nations' incapacity to deal with it. Both proxy wars, whether to preserve Western hegemony or achieve strategic autonomy for its rivals, these conflicts transformed their actors. Ukraine lost its integrity and autonomy while Russia was pushed out of Europe. Israel lost its legal and moral standing in the world and came to depend completely on its Western backers in a betrayal of Zionism's promise, while Hamas abandoned Cold War ideology for a broken-down humanitarianism. Rather than portending the revival of Zionism or Islamism, the war in Gaza signaled their defeat along with the Cold War order that had given both meaning. It is possible to argue that these proxy wars in Eastern Europe and the Middle East represented not just the regional heirs of the Global War on Terror, but even more importantly the self-destruction of global politics and, as a consequence, the delayed collapse of Cold War Islamism.

Having emerged as a movement of Muslim laymen directed against their religious as much as political authorities, Islamism today survives only under the leadership of its old clerical rivals. Its most successful exemplars, after all, are the Islamic Republic of Iran, the Taliban's Islamic Emirate in Afghanistan, Hezbollah in Lebanon, and now-dispersed groupings like Somalia's Islamic Courts Union. Islamism's appropriation by old clerical establishments requires a study of its own but suggests at least two important developments. One has to do with Islamism's loss of influence and integrity more generally, and the other with the fact that its global narrative has allowed the clerical classes to broaden their own vision and claims beyond the inevitably local contexts of the law. For despite the universalistic language of jurisprudence, the sacred law has traditionally been focused on very specific issues. The remaking of Islam as a protagonist of history, however, allowed these men to speak in the name of a global subject for the first time. But this happened only at the cost of Islamism's anticlericalism, signaled among other things by the simultaneous dependence of Hamas on Hezbollah and Iran and its increasing distance from their aims and narrative. The Gaza war may therefore illustrate not the revival but the further breakdown of Islamism in a situation where the international order and its political imagination have come apart.

Like the Muslim Brotherhood in Egypt, which briefly ruled the country during the Arab Spring, Hamas was thrown out of power by both the violence of the state it contested and the indifference of the people it sought to represent. Seeking to avoid this fate, Tunisia's Islamist party, Ennahda, had already shed its Cold War ideology to achieve power by renouncing Islam's global mission. But that did not prevent it from being ousted by the state whose dictatorial features it had sought to diminish. Similarly, the Hayat Tahrir al-Sham, a militant outfit once associated with Al-Qaeda and ISIS, renounced this past to take power in Syria with Turkish support at the end of 2024, just before the inauguration of a second Trump presidency in the United States. While its future and that of Syria is not yet clear, the group's transformation offers yet another example of the fact that neither Islamism nor globalized forms of militancy are going concerns. If anything, Hayat Tahrir al-Sham's victory confirms the increasing power of regional rather than global politics in the Middle East, signaled as it was by the destruction of the region's last Cold War regime. All of which suggests that the global arena remains vacant and deprived of politics, the very situation that had allowed Al-Qaeda and ISIS to emerge in the first place.

Conclusion

I N THIS BOOK I have looked at how Islam became an actor in modern history. Its emergence as a subject of this kind, I argued, was prompted by the crisis of Muslim sovereignty in the age of European empire. But its emergence as a subject also provided a way of thinking about agency in a global context, with Islam understood as having the potential to represent the human race itself as a newly empirical rather than simply moral reality. And having become the privileged representatives of Islam in this way, Muslims were, in addition, freed from traditional forms of Islamic authority to make different kinds of claims in its name. The problem with conceiving of Islam as an impersonal actor in history, however, was that it could not be defined in either religious or political terms. More than this, its very existence as initially a civilizational and then an ideological subject ended up depriving figures like God and his Prophet of their theological subjectivities. By the same token, Islam's role as an historical actor robbed the Muslim community and its authorities of their political agency.

This did not, of course, mean that religion or politics vanished, only that they became increasingly unthinkable in Islamic terms. What, then, did it mean for Islam to act in history, and how did Muslims experience and understand its novel subjectivity? I have sought to explore these questions in chapters on historical thinking and human agency, on the Prophet's drift into narratives about identity or property, on God's disappearance and the idolatrous

claims to his sovereignty, on gender and the making of an antibio-
logical Muslim subject, on how the West came to be Islam's lover
as much as rival, and on the hollowing out of Muslim agency in
twenty-first-century militancy. Arising out of specific political, economic, and other contexts, such debates nevertheless tell us something about the global arena as a site of thought and action more
generally. Instead of seeing modern Islam as representing the irre-
ducibility of theological ideas and their link to politics, in other
words, many of the debates defining it have been marked by the
impossibility of forging such a link.

As an historical subject largely defined in sociological terms by
its demography and cartography, Islam puts categories like religion
and politics into question for its adherents. But in doing so it also
gestures toward their declining relevance in other global contexts
as well. Yet as a figure representing the deferral and displacement
of religious as much as political agency in a global arena, Islam is as
vulnerable as they are to irrelevance. I conclude by exploring some
of the ways in which it has already ceased to play a role in many if
not all the most important Muslim movements of our day. I am interested particularly in the massive mobilizations that have characterized the Green Movement in Iran protesting alleged electoral
irregularities in 2009–2010, the protests against dictatorship of the
so-called Arab Spring in 2011–2012, those led by Muslims in India
to protest changes in citizenship law in 2020, and finally, again in
Iran, the civil unrest of 2022 following the death in custody of a
young woman who had infringed the Islamic Republic's dress code.

With the mid-twentieth century's independence and revolutionary movements as their only precedents in terms of scale and
extent, these mobilizations were nevertheless not throwbacks to
earlier forms of secular, nationalist, or democratic politics. On the
contrary, such protests inherited more from the very Islamic movements they otherwise abjured. While none of them foregrounded
Islam, for example, neither did they call for a secular state or seek
to police boundaries between religious practice and political activity. Only in India, where Muslims are a minority and secularism
has long been part of national identity, did the term enjoy some
visibility. Just as the debate on secularism had been meaningless for
Islam as a global subject, so, too, did it recede from view in these

mobilizations, which brought together Muslims and non-Muslims, believers and unbelievers, as equal participants in projects that did not require it. Also unlike the national movements of the past, these mobilizations were not organized in the name of any political party, with the Green Movement's support of opposition politicians an exception corrected by Iranian protests against the enforcement of female dress codes a decade later.

Politics Without a People

As they spread rapidly across North Africa and the Middle East in 2011, the hugely popular mobilizations against corrupt and dictatorial governments presented a conceptual difficulty for participants and observers alike. How were they to be named, and what did they signify historically? In the West these demonstrations came to be known by a seasonal metaphor familiar from the Cold War, as an Arab Spring comparable to the Prague Spring representing Eastern Europe's apparently natural repudiation of communism. But in the Middle East they were called revolutions and thus belonged more to a Soviet world of reference than a Euro-American one. These opposed naming practices signaled the fundamental ambiguity of the events they sought to define. And yet they both gestured toward the same Cold War context, with its vocabulary of states and peoples, reforms and revolutions, to make these mobilizations meaningful. I suggest, however, that such a genealogy is fundamentally mistaken.

More important as precedents might be post–Cold War mobilizations like the color revolutions that swept a number of ex-Soviet states in Eastern Europe, the Caucasus, and Central Asia during the early years of the century. Named after colors or flowers, these movements, like the revolutions of the Arab Spring, also refused any conventionally political designation. Perhaps their setting aside of familiar terms like "socialist" or "democratic" indicated that such terms had been discredited in the course of the Cold War. The color revolutions emerged, as the Green Movement later would, in response to disputed elections. But like it they sought to do without political parties and ideologies and took on the appearance of vague or single-issue demands against corruption. As with the short-lived success stories of the Arab Spring in Tunisia and Egypt, similarly, the color revolutions were sometimes able to unseat governments but never to capture and transform the state itself, since they remained social rather than conventionally political movements.

Then there is the model provided by globalized forms of Islamic mobilization. After all, the sudden and organizationally unlinked spread of protests across the region during the Arab Spring shared a great deal with the way in which demonstrations against insults to the Prophet had been occurring since the end of the Cold War. In this case the suicide of a Tunisian street vendor protesting the humiliations meted out by a corrupt state provoked uprisings from Morocco all the way to Bahrain that mirrored each other by way of media reports but without possessing any real interconnections. The Islamist parties they brought to power in Tunisia and Egypt, moreover, were quickly challenged and removed by the protestors themselves, who thus occupied a place outside institutional politics. Both the color and Arab revolutions eventually ended as failures because they were unable either to prevail against the regimes they opposed or to prevent even worse governments from emerging in the wake of their few successes. But they still represented the struggle of the new against the old and thus, unlike their enemies, belong to the future.

While they were occurring, the protests of the Arab Spring managed to displace Al-Qaeda's militancy from the forefront of Muslim mobilization globally. And it is only with their failure after 2012 that ISIS was able to capture public attention and gain recruits. The relationship between these varied forms of mobilization, therefore, is marked by both their intimacy and their opposition. And it was perhaps to avoid acknowledging such a relationship that so much commentary on the Arab revolutions then and now continues to be fixated on their radically unforeseen character, while nevertheless gesturing toward precedents and models that might make them historically comprehensible. If it isn't a regional history of Arab rebellion against authority that is invoked, then we are offered an international one having to do with antimonarchism, anticolonialism, or anticapitalism. And in all this our initial surprise at these remarkable events is shunted aside as indicating nothing more than a deficit of knowledge about the societies and peoples involved in such uprisings.

However accurate the genealogies proffered to make sense of these revolts, I think that the surprise they caused was not due to a lack of knowledge as much as its irrelevance. For the events were revolutionary not in any conventional sense, involving political parties, ideologies, and historical utopias, but precisely because they lacked such traditional political forms. Indeed, those most surprised by this revolutionary wave appear to have been the very people who made it possible. And if there is one sentiment that these men and women voiced over and over again, it was wonder at their own transformation. Most revolutionary about these events, in other words, might have been the sudden fearlessness that took the Middle East's protestors aback. And this may have had something to do with the absence there of a revolutionary politics in its traditional form.[1] The enormous numbers involved on both sides of the internecine conflict that followed the protests in Egypt and Syria, after all, show that no singular people and so revolution can be said to exist in either country.

Commentary on the left as much as the right tends to be dominated by the supposed logic of history, whose narrative of precedents and genealogies makes events calculable after the fact. And yet this appeal to history often ends up denying the change that is its essence. The Arab revolutions, for instance, were marked by efforts to take back the state and reappropriate its symbols. This was particularly the case in Egypt, with flags, anthems, and slogans abundantly deployed by the protestors. But in the process these symbols of the people, nation, and state were also evacuated of their conventionally political content and joined up with explicitly civilian forms of celebration. Thus, the sloganeering and revelry in Cairo's Tahrir Square borrowed freely from the chants and other practices of football fans, including dancing and face painting. Even the solicitude for the nation displayed by Egyptians eager to do things like clean the streets of Cairo absorbed such categories of the state into everyday practices in newly democratic forms.[2]

Similar was the creation of new relations between rich and poor, Christians and Muslims, or the people and the army, which was after all seduced from its duty to the state by the protestors in Tahrir Square. Of course, many of these extraordinary phenomena have not survived the Arab Spring, but even so they illustrate both the power and the possibilities of action beyond the limits of inherited politics. The relatively superficial use made of terms like "people" and "revolution" in these events, then, suggests their attenuation as political categories. By taking them over, the Arab Spring had in some ways given the old categories of Middle Eastern politics a new reality. So, for instance, the revolts imitating each other across the region made Pan-Arabism into a mass movement for the first time, but only in a negative way and without any ideology to match. Previously a statist ideology, Arab nationalism suddenly became a popular reality in the uprisings, though without ever constituting a political aim or even a subject of debate in its own right.

In their still ambiguous and unformed reality, the region's revolutions probably belonged to a number of possible genealogies, of which one is surely provided by global Islam and its militant form in particular. In the wake of Arab nationalism and Marxism, after all, what other movement has possessed such a pan-Arab dimension? Add to this a decentralized and media-informed politics, though one with neither a party nor ideology to back it, and the comparison is complete. The left in Europe and North America has always kept this comparison at bay, seeing it as being characteristic of a fear-mongering right. My point in drawing it is not to claim that Islamic militancy remained a possibility in these rebellions, but instead to demonstrate that it had been overcome within them. What else did the protestors' imitations of sacrificial and even suicidal practices across the region signify if not the occupation and indeed conquest of such militant forms?

Even the inability or unwillingness of Islamists to dominate protests wherever they occurred in the Middle East may be attributed to militancy more than to a resurgence of secular nationalism. For if Al-Qaeda had provided the revolutions with their individualistic modes of organization and dissemination, it also displaced the centralized parties and ideologies of the past. Like their socialist equivalents, after all, Islamist parties are Cold War organizations dominated by centralized and ideological visions of order. The unexpectedly popular resistance to long-established and apparently popular Islamist parties like the Muslim Brotherhood in Egypt or Ennahda in Tunisia cannot simply be attributed either to fears of an Islamist plot against democracy or to the desire for dominance by a liberal or secular elite supported by the army. Indeed, the emergence in both of these countries of Salafism, an individualistic version of Muslim piety that, unlike Islamism, is not defined by the desire for ideologies or revolutions, demonstrates that Islam in public life has moved beyond the Cold War.

These accounts of anti-Islamist feeling have proliferated since the violent removal of Egypt's first postrevolutionary government led by the Muslim Brotherhood. But they tell us nothing about the intellectual collapse of Islamism as a Cold War ideology dedicated to the promulgation of a revolutionary state and its drift to liberal and indeed neoliberal forms. This is exhibited most clearly by Turkey's ruling party, which struggled to win over other Islamists to its model of electoral politics during the Arab Spring.[3] Similarly, it is evident that the secular opposition is no longer confined to a narrow and militarized elite. In Egypt, the immense population whose vehement opposition to the Brotherhood drew from Islamophobic narratives in the West included any number of pious men and veiled women. This curious situation cannot simply be attributed to their capture by anti-Islamic propaganda but tells us that Islamism has been repudiated by many practicing Muslims. Might their criticism of the Brotherhood derive in some part from a sense of its historical decline and even irrelevance in the post–Cold War world?

In an essay on the way in which the Arab Spring played out in the blogosphere, the sociologist Armando Salvatore points out that Egyptian bloggers in particular had learned from their peers in Iran's Green Movement to disdain many of the inherited categories of political and ideological thought, from the "system" (*nizam*) that defined both the Islamists and the regime to the former's slogan "Islam is the solution."[4] Indeed, they conflated the otherwise opposed figures of the Muslim Brotherhood and the state, both relics of the Cold War in their institutional and ideological forms. Rather than seeing either one, and especially the latter, as a distinctively national or even regional entity, moreover, the Arab state in particular was understood as "the agent of a global system of corrupted, and already post-Westphalian, governance."[5] Instead of representing some inherited vision of an integrated people or *demos*, therefore, the protestors constituted a "disfigured social body" whose "fragmented yet

powerful type of agency bypasses conventional notions of either democratization or authoritarian repression."[6]

The notable absence of Islam as a subject in the events of the
Arab uprisings did not entail the emergence of some new and more
clearly political actor in its place. Instead, it suggested the evanes-
cence of every other kind of political agent as well, from the people
and party to the revolution. The Arab Spring did not signal a return to secular, liberal, or even socialist politics but put the political
subject into question across the board. And yet the ghostly presence of these former subjects continued to be called up in uprisings
from the Atlantic Ocean to the Persian Gulf. All except Islam,
which nevertheless provided the protests with many of their net-
worked and media-inspired practices. In this sense, we might
argue, the waning of Islam meant the end of the very possibility of
some old-fashioned historical as much as political or religious subject. Just as Islam in its modern incarnation had displaced politics
and religion together with their subjective forms, so, too, did the
Arab Spring decenter Islam as a new kind of global actor to leave
the site of agency ambiguous if not empty.

A Nation of Women

While the demonstrations of the Arab Spring brought together
women and men as well as Muslims and non-Muslims, among
other social identities, they were solidly masculine in their imagery
and practices. In Iran and India, however, women have been at the
forefront of protests and even gone on to define them. For example, in 2012 it was a young Tunisian man whose suicide inspired the
Arab uprisings as their symbol, but in Iran it was a young woman
killed by the police, Neda Agha Soltan, who became the face of the
Green Movement in 2009. And if the antigovernment protests of
2022 there were inspired by the death of another young woman,
Mahsa Amini, in India two years previously, the largest Muslim
demonstrations since independence took elderly grandmothers
protesting in Delhi as their icons while being led all over the country by women who could have been their granddaughters. In this
way Iran belongs with countries like India, Pakistan, and Bangladesh, where women have historically played a far more visible and

active political role than in the Arab world. But why were women so important to these movements, and how did they transform the political landscape in both India and Iran?

Its numbers and extent matched only by Gandhi's mobilizations against colonial rule more than eight decades ago, the protest movement led by Muslim women in 2020 emerged out of the passage of the Citizenship Amendment Act (CAA) that year. The CAA sought to offer immigration and eventually citizenship rights to non-Muslim religious minorities persecuted in the Muslim-majority countries around India. It was often paired with the National Register of Citizens (NRC), which seeks to determine the nationality of all those who reside in India, having been tried out in the border state of Assam to exclude Muslims understood as having come illegally from Bangladesh. Coinciding with the construction of large detention centers in various parts of the country, the CAA led to fears of Muslim disenfranchisement, and student protests against it had already been met by the use of police violence. This prompted a number of poor and elderly Muslim women to begin a sit-in at a square called Shaheen Bagh in Delhi, which turned out to be the spark that set off similar demonstrations and protests all over the country.

On the one hand, objections to the CAA had to do with universalization as a constitutional ideal, which refused to exclude a single community from the rights bestowed on others. Protestors often mentioned, for example, the case of Muslims persecuted in Burma and Sri Lanka, or specific Muslim groups like the Shia or Ahmadis who might be persecuted in Pakistan and Afghanistan, and asked why they weren't eligible for refugee status and eventual citizenship in India. On the other hand, some feared that the act would serve to disenfranchise Indian Muslims through the NRC by rendering them ineligible for citizenship once they were deemed to be nonnationals. But this was a supplementary argument, and it was the claim to universality that defined the protests, for which copies of the constitution were central together with portraits of Gandhi and his political rival, the low-caste leader Ambedkar in his role as one of the document's framers. The fact that Ambedkar had eventually repudiated the constitution and left formal politics was left unmentioned, though the protests can be seen as manifesting his abandonment of the state for a politics grounded in society. It is this that allows him to be paired with Gandhi.

Yet to think of these protests as a return to old-fashioned nationalism or secularism would be a mistake, since Muslim mobilization at the national level had taken on, for the first time since independence, a political and constitutional rather than cultural or religious character. After independence Muslims found themselves stripped of their politics. For the first time they were unable even to make any constitutional claims about their cause representing the needs of minority or caste groups more generally. Reduced to a special interest, Muslims came to focus on issues limited to defending their religion and protecting its personal law. These included several famous controversies: the Hazratbal incident of 1963, when a relic's disappearance from a Kashmiri shrine gave rise to mass protests; the Shahbano case of 1985, when a court's decision to grant alimony to a Muslim divorcee was seen as interfering in Muslim personal law; and the Babri Masjid dispute, which rose to national prominence in 1990 when Hindu nationalists laid claim to and eventually destroyed a sixteenth-century mosque allegedly built on the ruins of a temple.

These dramatic events occurred against the background of demands for the protection of Muslim lives and properties in communal riots, government support for their cultural and educational institutions, and calls for greater representation in government service. They were not helped by wars with Pakistan in 1948, 1965, 1971, and 1999, which led to greater suspicion of Muslim loyalties, as well as an insurgency in Kashmir beginning in the 1990s and followed by terrorist attacks in many parts of India. Whether voiced through Muslim mobilization or in arguments and petitions, in other words, such demands adopted a largely defensive posture and were justified by invoking the principle of secularism in order to protect Muslim religious institutions and practices. This was their sole reference to larger constitutional issues, though only in order to secure their own specifically religious rights under it rather than agitating for any larger political cause.

This postindependence history of Muslim mobilization culminated in countrywide protests over the destruction by Hindu nationalists of the Babri Masjid in 1992. For nearly thirty years after this event, which was followed by riots in various parts of the country, Muslims seem to have lost the capacity to mobilize. The mosque's destruction also spelled the destruction of Muslim politics as it had been practiced since independence. Muslim elites continued to mediate grievances about religious and cultural identity at the center, while clerics continued to privilege religious issues in the provinces. But they were no longer particularly successful in accomplishing either task, to say nothing of protecting their constituencies from threats to life and property. With the slow collapse of this clientelist politics based on defending elite Muslim identities and interests, there emerged another from the fragmentation of the 1990s, a period of coalition governments with no single party able to hold power at the center.

Setting aside the occasional resort to insurgency and terrorism, which only accentuated the failure of the clientelist model that had characterized Muslim politics since independence, we can discern the beginnings of another political genealogy in the new century. Muslims seemed to have been cowed by the violence they faced under the ruling Bharatiya Janata Party government, whose principal instances followed upon the Babri Masjid's destruction in 1992 and an attack on Hindu pilgrims in Godhra in 2002. Even major decisions taken by the government or its courts, such as the banning of divorce by repudiation under Muslim personal law or awarding to a Hindu temple the land on which the Babri Masjid had stood, gave rise to little or no protest. And neither did newly routinized acts of violence like lynching Muslims over their alleged seduction of Hindu girls or transport of cows for slaughter. We have to wait until their protests against the CAA in 2020 to see the return of Muslim mobilization countrywide.

But on this occasion Muslims adopted the constitution's own unitary ideal instead of asking for a separate accommodation within it. Now it was the Hindu nationalists who were calling for the differential treatment of citizens. Perhaps because it possessed no religious or cultural cause, the protest did not attract traditional Muslim leaders, and Islam was not an issue in it. Clerics and seminaries were both absent from and largely silent about the movement, as were politicians from most national and even regional parties. Students, however, were much in evidence, along with an array of ordinary people from various classes and a variety of religious and nonreligious dispositions. And they were joined by large numbers of Hindus and other non-Muslims all over the country, until the coronavirus pandemic allowed the government to shutter the movement by the use of violence and jail many of its activists (even following the Israeli model of bulldozing their houses without judicial process in the large and populous state of Uttar Pradesh).

Despite their very different context and genealogy, then, these Indian protests were remarkably similar to those in the Middle East and North Africa, as well as resembling the new wave of mobilizations globally, from the color revolutions to the Occupy movement and more. But let us attend to the role of gender in them. The anti-CAA protests not only represented the largest mobilization of women in Indian history, but for the first time were not dedicated to any cause specifically to do with gender.[7] Just as the movement, led though it was by Muslims, turned out not to be about them or Islam, in other words, so did the women who represented it agitate in a cause not about their gender. The protests cannot be understood as a form of identity politics. On the face of it, the Iranian demonstrations against dress codes were also about women and gender, and yet they not only were represented by the death of a young Kurdish woman belonging to a religious and ethnic minority, but also took their slogan, "woman, life, freedom," from Kurdish politics.

Did the Kurds, as one of the Middle East's most widespread and often persecuted minorities, come to represent a cause in Iran for which the nation, to say nothing of its dominant religion, was no longer a credible vehicle? Muslims in India, of course, are also that country's most important minority and subject to routine discrimination, and yet they were capable of representing the nation through its constitution in a situation where it had been captured by the state. Rather than being about or even inclusive of women or minorities in any simple sense, therefore, what we see in both Iran and India is a continual displacement of identities, which no longer represent any kind of authenticity. This is where the Kurdish references of Iran's protests are so interesting. For in addition to ignoring rather than excluding Islam, that variant of the Kurdish movement represented by its imprisoned leader, Abdullah Öcalan, is also critical of older ideas about peoples and nations as much as states and ideologies and dedicates itself to humanity instead.

Drawing upon anarchist themes, Öcalan, who is also the author of the slogan that defined Iran's women-led protests, condemns the state form itself as oppressive and imperialist. He calls for the freedom and equality of women, seen as representing history's first colony, and derides the xenophobic and homogenizing tendencies of nationalism, together with the environmentally destructive capitalism that underlies them.[8] Far more than influential ideas, Öcalan's writings have been put into effect in the leading role that women play in Kurdish politics and its military outfits. And while these ideas may well come out of Öcalan's reading of Western theorists on the left, it should be clear that they draw upon themes of long provenance in the region and, indeed, in the Muslim or former Third World as well. What does it mean to revive nationalism, or for that matter revolution and Arab solidarity, as empty or nonsovereign forms? Do they illustrate the difficulty of imagining a suitable politics for the new global arena, or simply the poverty of political imagination?

In one sense Kurdish nationalism bears some resemblance to its more settled and secure peers elsewhere. For globalization has deprived nation-states of a number of the foundations of old-fashioned sovereignty: the control of an economy, nationality, and borders. This leads to the increasing importance of cultural and religious rather than economic or political forms of national identity, of which the European Union with its single currency and lack of internal borders provides us with several instances. In addition to that continent's xenophobic parties, after all, there also exist Scottish and Catalan movements for independence, which no longer claim traditional forms of sovereignty but would instead rely upon the existence of the EU for their financial and security needs. While the Kurdish movement does not incline toward a vast, European-style bureaucracy, its effort to hold together local and global modes of belonging are familiar to new national movements more generally.

Unlike Öcalan's global version of Kurdish politics, the protests in India and Iran seemed to possess a conventionally nationalist context and point of reference. But a closer look reveals a quite different picture. Unlike the Green Movement, which was still invested in

Iran's electoral politics, as symbolized by its slogan "Give me back my vote," the women's movement, as pointed out by the scholar of Persian literature Fatemeh Shams, had rejected the political process altogether, along with its leaders and parties, to focus on the body and its liberties alone.[9] Unlike the Indian protests that preceded them, the Iranian ones were violent and sought to destroy state symbols. This meant they were also explicitly antireligious.[10] All this suggests not a turn to some alternative vision of the people or nation, but their total repudiation for a kind of solidarity without a traditionally political context. The class aspect of the Iranian movement is also notable, with the often poor and religious supporters of the Islamic Republic gratuitously attacked along with ordinary clerics by middle-class and upper-middle-class demonstrators. Indeed, workers remained conspicuous by their absence from the movement.[11]

By contrast, the Indian protests seem to have drawn fulsomely upon the history of the national movement. Yet here, too, things are more complicated than they seem. The movement's appeal to nationalism was in fact incoherent. On the one hand it foregrounded figures like Gandhi and Ambedkar, who are today more than ever seen as being opposed to one another, a pairing that I have suggested makes sense only if we see the latter joining the former in his rejection of statist political forms despite the movement's valorization of the constitution he had forsaken. On the other hand the protests made reference to slogans and songs from equally contradictory political visions. Muslim protestors, for example, participated in Hindu rituals and chanted slogans that had historically been understood as being either sacrilegious or anti-Muslim. These included "Victory to Mother India" and "I Salute You, Motherland." And if such displays demonstrated their tolerance in a way that Hindu nationalists in particular demanded, other practices did exactly the opposite. The slogan "What Do We Want? Freedom!" was taken from secessionist Kashmiri nationalism. Also popular was a famous poem by the Pakistani poet Faiz Ahmed Faiz about one day being able to see the dawn of freedom in his country.

Were the protestors comparing their struggle to that of Kashmir and Pakistan, or were they assimilating the latter to India's own travails? Did their amalgamation of hypernationalist and even

Hindu nationalist slogans and practices with antinational ones display a broad-minded inclusivity or render the nation incoherent? It is impossible to say. In either case, however, we can see that the absence of Islam from the movement indicates neither some return to a secular past nor even a decline in the religiosity of its participants. As in the Arab Spring, we might be dealing here with the dismantling of inherited political categories and identities more generally. The end of Islam, then, turns out to mean its fulfillment—this in the sense that the displacement of religion and politics it had made possible from the middle of the nineteenth century has finally in the twenty-first resulted in Islam's own disappearance as an agent of history.

Notes

Introduction

1. Mir Taqi Mir, *Kulliyat-e Mir*, vol. 1 (New Delhi: Taraqqi-ye Urdu Bureau, 1983), 108. The Urdu original reads: *Mir ke din-o mazhab ko ab puchhte kya ho unne to / Qashqa khincha, dayr men baytha, kab ka tark islam kiya.*

2. "Religion" and "school" are, of course, not exact equivalents of *din* and *mazhab*, which are themselves terms with changing histories. But for my purposes they are common and serviceable-enough translations.

3. The classic account is by Wilfred Cantwell Smith, "The Historical Development in Islam of the Concept of Islam as an Historical Development," in *On Understanding Islam: Selected Studies* (The Hague: Mouton, 1981), 41–77. For recent scholarship on the problem of defining Islam, see Shahab Ahmed, *What Is Islam? The Importance of Being Islamic* (Princeton: Princeton University Press, 2016); and Caner K. Dagli, *Metaphysical Institutions: Islam and the Modern Project* (Albany: State University of New York Press, 2024).

4. Altaf Husain Hali, *Hali's Musaddas: The Flow and Ebb of Islam*, trans. C. Shackle and J. Majeed (Delhi: Oxford University Press, 1997), 143. The Urdu original reads, *Raha din baqi na Islam baqi / Ik Islam ka rah gaya nam baqi.*

5. For recent scholarship on the early history of these terms, see Rushain Abbasi, "Islam and the Invention of Religion: A Study of Medieval Muslim Discourses on *din*," *Studia Islamica* 116 (2021): 1–106; Nicholas Boylston, "Islam from the Inside Out: 'Ayn al-Qudat Hamadani's Reconception of Islam as Vector," *Journal of Islamic Studies* 32, no. 2 (2021): 161–202; and Mohsen Goudarzi, "The Cultic Dimensions of *din, islam,* and *hanif* in the Quran," *Journal of Near Eastern History* 82, no. 1 (April 2023): 77–102.

6. See Marshall G. S. Hodgson, *The Venture of Islam: Conscience and History in a World Civilization*, 3 vols. (Chicago: University of Chicago Press, 1974).

7. Hodgson, *Venture of Islam*, 3:389.

8. Hodgson, *Venture of Islam*, 3:389.

9. Another example from the period is Wilfred Cantwell Smith, *The Meaning and End of Religion* (New York: Harper & Row, 1978). As the title of Smith's book suggests, scholars have been taken up with the idea of religion as a generic and so secular category. Yet however deprived of theological character Islam may be, it is not defined by the question of secularism. Whether Muslim thinkers accept or reject secularism as a general principle, after all, they have not been concerned with drawing distinctions between what is and is not religious. This is because such distinctions remain irrelevant to Islam considered as a subject in history.

10. Maxim Romanov, OpenITI NgramReader+, Version 2020.1, Zenodo, published March 24, 2020, http://doi.org/10.5281/zenodo.3725855; ADHFAIS APPE{ENDIX} 1:NgramReader, 2023 (OpenITI, Release ver. 2023.1.8), https://eis1600.aai.uni-hamburg.de/shiny/OpenITI_NgramReader/ ?fbclid=IwAR30aQ2-w8yTeROZCJ-kF1BsZkE_oyK-Wp4DxamMT-PqW4Bg8b6mtCPoiugI.

11. Sometimes, however, scholars did acknowledge Islam's quite different meaning in its early days. The Indian writer Muhammad Hamidullah, for example, who was the most important Muslim academic in mid-twentieth-century France, made this clear in his immensely popular and much-reprinted translation of the Qur'an first published in 1958. In it, he routinely translated the word "Islam" as "soumission," or the practice of surrender, in order to show that it had not yet become the proper name of a distinct religion. See *Le Coran: Traduction Intégrale et Notes de Muhammad Hamidullah* (Paris: Club Français du Livre, 1977).

12. For a stimulating criticism of the Western and more particularly imperial understanding of globalization, see Shruti Kapila, "Global Intellectual History and the Indian Political," in Darrin M. McMahon and Samuel Moyn, eds., *Rethinking Modern European Intellectual History* (New York: Oxford University Press, 2014), 253–274.

13. Smith, *Meaning and End of Religion*, 111.

14. Andrew March, in his book *The Caliphate of Man: Popular Sovereignty in Modern Islamic Thought* (Cambridge, MA: Belknap Press, 2019), correctly points out that by the twentieth century Islam could no longer be held in the guardianship of such authorities and is now seen by Muslims as a properly human inheritance. But "humanity" is a global category that does not easily translate into popular sovereignty within the nation-state. It is instead isomorphic with Islam as a global actor and thus unable to become a political agent in its own right.

15. The most recent and detailed representation of this argument is Noel Malcolm's *Useful Enemies: Islam and the Ottoman Empire in Western Political Thought, 1450–1750* (Oxford: Oxford University Press, 2019). See also Lucette Valensi, *The Birth of the Despot: Venice and the Sublime Porte*, trans. Arthur Denner (Ithaca, NY: Cornell University Press, 1993). The most sophisticated version of the argument is to be found in Alain Grosrichard, *The Sultan's Court: European Fantasies of the East*, trans. Liz Heron (London: Verso, 1998).

16. This is Olivier Roy's argument in *Globalised Islam: The Search for a New Ummah* (London: Hurst, 2004).

17. It was also Olivier Roy who was prescient enough to first point this out in *The Failure of Political Islam*, trans. Carol Volk (Cambridge, MA: Harvard University Press, 1998).

18. For this last movement, see Walaa Quisay, *Neo-traditionalism in Islam in the West: Orthodoxy, Spirituality and Politics* (Edinburgh: Edinburgh University Press, 2023).

Chapter One. The Proper Name

1. For an eccentric biography by his grandson, the art historian, Keeper of the Queen's Pictures, and sometime Soviet spy, Anthony Blunt, see Earl of Lytton, *Wilfrid Scawen Blunt* (London: Macdonald, 1961). For Blunt's relations with the Churchills, see Warren Dockter, "The Influence of a Poet: Wilfrid S. Blunt and the Churchills," *Journal of Historical Biography* 10 (Autumn 2011): 70–102.

2. Wilfrid Scawen Blunt, *The Future of Islam* (London: Kegan Paul, Trench, 1882), 38.

3. Blunt, *Future of Islam*, 45–46.

4. Blunt, *Future of Islam*, 56.

5. Blunt, *Future of Islam*, 46.

6. Wilfrid Scawen Blunt, *Tarjumah-e Future of Islam*, trans. Akbar Illahabadi (Delhi: Matbua Mahbub al-Matabeh Barqi Press, 1951).

7. See, for instance, Mohammad Barakatullah, *The Khilafet* (London: Luzac, 1924).

8. Blunt, *Future of Islam*, 38.

9. Blunt, *Future of Islam*, 23.

10. Juan Cole, *Napoleon's Egypt: Invading the Middle East* (New York: St. Martin's Press, 2007).

11. See Nikki R. Keddie, *An Islamic Response to Imperialism: Political and Religious Writings of Sayyid Jamal al-Din "al-Afghani"* (Berkeley: University of California Press, 1983).

12. Gemmal Eddine Afghan, "Au Directeur du Journal des Débats," *Journal de Débats*, May 18, 1883. Unless otherwise noted, all translations are mine.

13. Afghan, "Au Directeur."
14. See, for instance, Carl Schmitt, "The Turn to the Discriminating Concept of War," in *Writings on War*, trans. Timothy Nunan (London: Polity, 2011), 30–74.
15. Maeve Ryan, *Humanitarian Governance and the British Antislavery World System* (New Haven: Yale University Press, 2022).
16. Muhammad Iqbal, "Islam as a Moral and Political Idea," in *Thoughts and Reflections of Iqbal*, ed. Syed Abdul Vahid (Lahore: Sh. Muhammad Ashraf, 1992), 50–51.
17. Iqbal, "Islam as a Moral," 51–52.
18. Muhammad Iqbal, "Political Thought in Islam," in *Thoughts and Reflections*, 75.
19. Iqbal, "Political Thought," 60.
20. John Buchan, *Greenmantle* (Oxford: Oxford University Press, 1999), 182–183.
21. Buchan, *Greenmantle*, 183–184.
22. Buchan, *Greenmantle*, 272.
23. Syed Ameer Ali, *The Spirit of Islam: A History of the Evolution and Ideals of Islam* (London: Chatto & Windus, 1978), vii.
24. Ameer Ali, *Spirit of Islam*, 137.
25. Wilfred Cantwell Smith, "The Historical Development in Islam of the Concept of Islam as an Historical Development," in *On Understanding Islam: Selected Studies* (The Hague: Mouton, 1981), 41–77.
26. Ameer Ali, *Spirit of Islam*, 137–138.
27. See for this Sandria B. Freitag, *Collective Action and Community: Public Arenas and the Emergence of Communalism in North India* (Berkeley: University of California Press, 1990).
28. For the argument that caste came to define Hinduism as a social phenomenon with the truncation of kingship, see Ronald B. Inden, *Imagining India* (Oxford: Basil Blackwell, 1990).
29. Ameer Ali, *Spirit of Islam*, vii.
30. Ameer Ali, *Spirit of Islam*, 138.
31. See for this Shogo Suzuki, *Civilization and Empire: China and Japan's Encounter with European International Society* (New York: Routledge, 2009).
32. Cemil Aydin has explored Islam's emergence as a civilization in *The Idea of the Muslim World: A Global Intellectual History* (Cambridge, MA: Harvard University Press, 2017).
33. Aydin, *Idea of the Muslim World*.
34. Nazir Ahmad, *Banat un-Nash* (Lucknow: Munshi Nawal Kishor, 1967), 185–186.
35. The key text here is Abul Kalam Azad, *Maslah-e Khilafat-o Jazirat-ul Arab* (Calcutta: All-India Khilafat Committee, 1920). Azad was the most prominent theorist of the caliphate in India and went on to become president

of the Indian National Congress and a minister in Nehru's cabinet after independence.

36. The classic text here is by a distinguished civil servant in India. See W. W. Hunter, *The Indian Musalmans: Are They Bound in Conscience to Rebel Against the Queen?* (London: Trübner, 1871).

37. See, for example, John M. Willis, "Azad's Mecca: On the Limits of Indian Ocean Cosmopolitanism," *Comparative Studies of South Asia, Africa and the Middle East* 34, no. 3 (2014): 574–581.

38. See, for instance, Ahmed Dailami, "Militancy, Monarchy and the Struggle to Desacralize Kingship in Arabia," in *Islam After Liberalism*, ed. Faisal Devji and Zaheer Kazmi (New York: Oxford University Press, 2017), 203–218.

Chapter Two. A Prophet Disarmed

1. See, for this, Kecia Ali, *The Lives of Muhammad* (Cambridge, MA: Harvard University Press, 2016).

2. SherAli Tareen, *Defending Muhammad in Modernity* (Notre Dame, IN: University of Notre Dame Press, 2020).

3. See, for example, Avril Powell, *Muslims and Missionaries in Pre-Mutiny India* (Richmond: Curzon Press, 1993).

4. A Parsee, *The Mahomedan Riots of Bombay in the Year 1851* (Bombay: Bombay Summachar Press, 1856), 60.

5. A Parsee, *Mahomedan Riots*, 22.

6. A Parsee, *Mahomedan Riots*, 16.

7. A Parsee, *Mahomedan Riots*, 17.

8. J. Barton Scott, *Slandering the Sacred: Blasphemy Law and Religious Affect in Colonial India* (Chicago: University of Chicago Press, 2023), ch. 6.

9. *The Bombay Riots of February 1874: Re-printed from the Times of India* (Bombay: Times of India Printing Works, 1874), 1.

10. *Bombay Riots*, 1.

11. *Bombay Riots*, 2.

12. Angelo J. Lewis, ed., *The Indian Penal Code: Indian Law Manuals, no. 2* (London: Wm. H. Allen, 1870).

13. See Asad Ali Ahmed, "Specters of Macaulay: Blasphemy, the Indian Penal Code, and Pakistan's Postcolonial Predicament," in *Censorship in South Asia: Cultural Regulation from Sedition to Seduction*, ed. Ravinder Kaur and William Mazarella (Bloomington: University of Indiana Press, 2009), 172–205.

14. "Bombay Mahomedans Protest Against the Play of 'Mahomet,' " *Times of India*, November 10, 1890, 3.

15. "Bombay Mahomedans," 3.

16. Shabbir Akhtar, *Be Careful with Muhammad! The Salman Rushdie Affair* (London: Bellew, 1989), 55–56.

17. Akhtar, *Be Careful*, 93.
18. "Fatwa Against Salman Rushdie," *Iran Data Portal*, Syracuse University, last modified April 1, 2013, https://irandataportal.syr.edu/fatwa-against-salman-rushdie. For the Persian text, see https://irandataportal.syr.edu/wp-content/uploads/rushdie-fatwa-persian.pdf.
19. See Baqer Moin, *Khomeini: Life of the Ayatollah* (London: I. B. Tauris, 1999), 283.
20. The standard work on Ahmadi theology is by Yohanan Friedmann, *Prophecy Continuous: Aspects of Ahmadi Religious Thought and Its Medieval Background* (Berkeley: University of California Press, 1992). For the history of Ahmadi persecution in Pakistan, see Ali Usman Qasmi, *The Ahmadis and the Politics of Religious Exclusion in Pakistan* (London: Anthem Press, 2015).
21. Adeel Hussain, *Revenge, Politics and Blasphemy in Pakistan* (London: Hurst, 2022).
22. Zaki Rehman, a doctoral student in history at the University of Oxford, explores these and other themes in the political thought of the Ahmadis in what will be the first significant study of it.
23. Muhammad Iqbal, *The Reconstruction of Religious Thought in Islam* (New Delhi: Kitab Bhavan, 1990), 126.
24. "Full transcript of Prime Minister Imran Khan's speech at the UNGA," *Business Recorder*, September 27, 2019, https://www.brecorder.com/news/524851.
25. Imran Khan (@ImranKhanPTI), "My Letter to CEO Facebook Mark Zuckerberg to ban Islamophobia just as Facebook has banned questioning or criticising the Holocaust," X (formerly Twitter), October 25, 2020, https://x.com/ImranKhanPTI/status/1320440661385093121.
26. Asad Hashim, "Pakistan PM Calls for West to Criminalise Blasphemy Against Islam," *Al Jazeera*, April 19, 2021, https://www.aljazeera.com/news/2021/4/19/pakistan-pm-calls-for-west-to-criminalise-blasphemy-against-islam. For the official broadcast of the prime minister's address on the state television station, PTV, see "Prime Minister of Pakistan Imran Khan's Address to the Nation, 19 April 2021," https://www.youtube.com/watch?v=wPoRCRWDkzc.
27. Sayyid Ataullah Mohajerani, *Naqd-e Tuteyeh-e Ayat-e Shaytani* (Tehran: Entesharat-e Ettelaat, 1378).
28. For an account of the history of the controversy, see S. Gopal, ed., *Anatomy of a Confrontation: The Babri-Masjid-Ram Janmabhumi Issue* (New Delhi: Penguin, 1990).
29. For an account of this incident, see Juan Cole, *Sacred Space and Holy War: The Politics, Culture and History of Shi'ite Islam* (London: I. B. Tauris, 2002), 161–172.
30. See for this Göran Larsson, Iselin Frydenlund and Torkel Brekke, eds., "Special Issue: Burning of the Qur'an," *Temenos: Nordic Journal for the Study of Religion* 60, no. 1 (2024): 5–184.

31. Among the many reports on the Saudi state's destruction of Mecca, see Mustafa Hameed, "The Destruction of Mecca: How Saudi Arabia's Construction Rampage Is Threatening Islam's Holiest City," *Foreign Policy*, September 22, 2015, https://foreignpolicy.com/2015/09/22/the-destruction-of-mecca-saudi-arabia-construction/.

32. See, for instance, the section on "Mohametanism" in G. W. F. Hegel, *The Philosophy of History*, trans. J. Sibree (Buffalo: Prometheus Books, 1991), 355–360.

Chapter Three. The Idols Return

1. Shabbir Akhtar, *Be Careful with Muhammad! The Salman Rushdie Affair* (London: Bellew, 1989), 1.

2. "Allah Hafiz to Khuda Hafiz," *Dawn*, May 24, 2009, https://www.dawn.com/news/833553.

3. Rachel Leow, "Sticks and Stones in the Allah Controversy," *East Asia Forum*, June 19, 2010, https://www.eastasiaforum.org/2010/06/19/sticks-and-stones-in-the-allah-controversy/.

4. C. M. Naim, "Be Crazy with God . . .," *Outlook*, updated on December 27, 2012, https://www.outlookindia.com/website/story/be-crazy-with-god/283453. The Persian expression is *Ba khuda diwana bash-o ba Muhammad hoshyar*.

5. Abuzafar Sirajuddin Bahadur Shah, *Kulliyat-e Zafar*, vol. 3–4 (Lahore: Sang-e Meel, 1994), 461. The Urdu text reads: *Khuda ke waste zahid parda na uttha kabe ka/Kahin aysa na ho yan bhi vohi kaffar sanam nikle*.

6. SherAli Tareen, *Perilous Intimacies: Debating Hindu-Muslim Friendship After Empire* (New York: Columbia University Press, 2023).

7. Muhammad Iqbal, *Javid-Nama*, trans. A. J. Arberry (London: George Allen & Unwin, 1966), 75. For the Persian text, see Muhammad Iqbal, "Javid Nama," in *Kulliyat-e Iqbal Farsi* (Lahore: Iqbal Academy, 1990), 564.

8. M. K. Gandhi, *Hind Swaraj or Indian Home Rule* (Ahmedabad: Navajivan, 2008).

9. Sayyid Abul a'la Maududi, *Islamic Law and Constitution*, trans. Khurshid Ahmad (Lahore: Islamic Publications, 1992).

10. Maududi, *Islamic Law*, 132.

11. Maulana Sayyid Abul Ala Maududi, *Khilafat-o Mulukiyyat* (New Delhi: Markazi Maktaba Islami, 2006).

12. Carl Schmitt, *Political Theology: Four Chapters on the Concept of Sovereignty*, trans. George Schwab (Chicago: University of Chicago Press, 2006).

13. "Document: The Objectives Resolution," *Islamic Studies* 48, no. 1 (Spring 2009): 92.v.

14. Ministry of Law and Justice, *Constitution of the Islamic Republic of Pakistan*, https://pakistancode.gov.pk/english/UY2FqaJw1-apaUY2Fqa-apaUY2Fvbpw%3D-sg-jjjjjjjjjjjjj, 1.

15. Imam Khomeini, *Islam and Revolution I: Writings and Declarations of Imam Khomeini (1941–1980)*, trans. Hamid Algar (Berkeley: Mizan Press, 1982), 27–125. For the Persian text, see Imam Khomeini, *Vilayat-e Faqih* (Tehran: Muasisseh-e Tanzim-o Nasr-e Asar-e Imam Khomeini, 1999).

16. Khomeini, *Vilayat-e Faqih*, 61.

17. "Admonition to Ayatollah Khamenei on the Limits of the Valiye Faqih's Authority and the Course of Its Stages," *Iran Data Portal*, Syracuse University, last modified May 29, 2013, https://irandataportal.syr.edu/admonition-to-ayatollah-khamenei-on-the-limits-of-the-valiye-faqihs-authority-and-the-course-of-its-stages. For the Persian text, see *Iran Data Portal*, https://irandataportal.syr.edu/wp-content/uploads/memo-by-grand-ayatollah-khomeini.pdf.

18. "Admonition."

19. "Admonition."

20. "Admonition."

21. "Admonition."

22. See, for this, Alexander Nachman, "Outside the Law: Khomeini's Legacy of Commanding Right and Forbidding Wrong in the Islamic Republic," *Sociology of Islam* 7 (2019): 1–21.

23. For this nontheological or what he calls the supplementary vision of sovereignty, see Alexander Nachman, "To Loosen and Bind: Khomeini, Rafsanjani, and Supplementary Governance in the Islamic Republic," *British Journal of Middle Eastern Studies* 47, no. 3 (2020): 482–496.

24. Ruhallah al-Musavi Khomeini, *Akhirin Payam* (Tehran: Sazman-e Hajj-o Awqaf-o Umur-e Khayriyyat, 2003), 1–2.

25. Khomeini, *Akhirin Payam*, 42–43.

26. Khomeini, *Akhirin Payam*, 1–2.

27. Khomeini, *Akhirin Payam*, 21.

28. Khomeini, *Akhirin Payam*, 22.

29. H. Sherwood and P. Oltermann, "European Churches Say Growing Flock of Muslim Refugees Are Converting," *Guardian*, June 5, 2016, https://www.theguardian.com/world/2016/jun/05/european-churches-growing-flock-muslim-refugees-converting-christianity.

30. For a recent study of the ambiguity of conversion from Islam in Europe, see Maria Vilek, *Former Muslims in Europe: Between Secularity and Belonging* (London: Routledge, 2021).

31. There appears to be no academic study of the phenomenon, but for one of many newspaper accounts, see Rama Lakshmi, "Are Poor Indian Muslims Being Forced to Convert to Hinduism?" *Washington Post*, December 12, 2014, https://www.washingtonpost.com/news/worldviews/wp/2014/12/12/are-poor-indian-muslims-being-forced-to-convert-to-hinduism/.

32. For some of these stories, see Simon Cottee, *The Apostates: When Muslims Leave Islam* (London: Hurst, 2015).

33. WIN–Gallup International, "Global Index of Religiosity and Atheism," 2012, https://www.webpages.uidaho.edu/~stevel/251/Global_INDEX_of_Religiosity_and_Atheism_PR__6.pdf.

34. See, for instance, Associated Press, "Hostage Crisis Leaves 28 Dead in Bangladesh Diplomatic Zone," Boston.com, July 2, 2016, https://www.boston.com/news/national-news/2016/07/02/20-hostages-killed-13-saved-bangladesh-restaurant-attack/.

Chapter Four. Women on the Verge

1. For a biography, see Deborah Baker, *The Convert: A Tale of Exile and Extremism* (New York: Graywolf Press, 2011). For an analysis of Jewish conversion to save Islam from Judaism's fate, see Sadia Abbas, "Itineraries of Conversion: Judaic Paths to a Muslim Pakistan," in *Beyond Crisis: Reevaluating Pakistan*, ed. Naveeda Khan (New Delhi: Routledge, 2012), 344–369.

2. See Maryam Jameelah, "An Appraisal of Some Aspects of Maulana Sayyid Ala Maudoodi's Life and Thought," *Islamic Quarterly* 31, no. 2 (January 1987): 116–130.

3. For a classic discussion of visuality and its criticism as an epistemological form, see Martin Jay, *Downcast Eyes: The Denigration of Vision in Twentieth-Century French Thought* (Berkeley: University of California Press, 1993).

4. For a recent consideration of gender as a nonbinary category in Muslim legal thought, one that was interrupted and displaced by a number of other categorizations, see Saadia Yacoob, *Beyond the Binary: Gender and Legal Personhood in Islamic Law* (Berkeley: University of California Press, 2024).

5. See, for instance, Afsaneh Najmabadi, *Women with Mustaches and Men Without Beards: Gender and Sexual Anxieties of Iranian Modernity* (Berkeley: University of California Press, 2005).

6. For the Muslim tolerance of un-Islamic practices among women before the nineteenth-century reformers came along, one only has to look at their texts recommending female education. For an example of one of the most important such texts, see Barbara D. Metcalf, *Perfecting Women: Maulana Ashraf Ali Thanwi's* Bihishti Zewar (Berkeley: University of California Press, 1990).

7. Nazir Ahmad, *Tawbat un-Nasuh* (New Delhi: Maktaba Jamia, 1987), 146–147.

8. Ahmad, *Tawbat un-Nasuh*, 151.

9. Ahmad, *Tawbat un-Nasuh*, 97.

10. Ahmad, *Tawbat un-Nasuh*, 139.

11. Ahmad, *Tawbat un-Nasuh*, 157–158.

12. Ahmad, *Tawbat un-Nasuh*, 163–164.

13. Akbar Illahabadi, *Intikhab-e Akbar Illahabadi* (New Delhi: Maktaba Jamia, 1990), 134. The Urdu text reads: *Lekin zarur hai ke munasib ho tarbiyat / Jis se biradari men barhe qadr-o manzilat. Har chand ho ulum-e zaruri ki alima / Shohar ki ho murid to bacchon ki khadima. Talim khub ho to na ayegi dam men / Khaliq pe lo lagayegi voh apne kam men. Ghar ka hisab sikh le khud ap jodna / Achha nahin hai ghayr pe yeh kam chhorna. Khana pakana jab nahin aya to kya maza / Jawhar hai auraton ke liye yeh bahut bara. Sina parona auraton ka khas hai hunnar / Darzi ki choriyon se hifazat pe ho nazar.*

14. Metcalf, *Perfecting Women*, 26.

15. Gail Minault, "Shaikh Abdullah, Begam Abdullah, and Sharif Education for Girls at Aligarh," in *Modernization and Social Change Among Muslims in India*, ed. Imtiaz Ahmad (New Delhi: Manohar, 1983), 229.

16. Altaf Hussain Hali, *Voices of Silence*, trans. Gail Minault (Delhi: Chanakya Publications, 1986), 81.

17. Hali, *Voices of Silence*, 81.

18. Arsalan Khan, "Pious Masculinity, Ethical Reflexivity, and Moral Order in an Islamic Piety Movement in Pakistan," *Anthropological Quarterly* 91, no. 1 (2018): 53–78.

19. Ziba Mir-Hosseini, "When a Woman's Hurt Becomes an Injury: 'Hardship' as Grounds for Divorce in Iran," *Hawwa: Journal of Women of the Middle East and the Islamic World* 5, no. 1 (2007): 111–126.

20. Sayyid Abul Ala Maududi, *Parda* (Lahore: Islamic Publications, 2003).

21. For a classic discussion of ritual and juridical as opposed to biological identity, see Abdelwahab Bouhdiba, *Sexuality in Islam*, trans. Alan Sheridan (London: Routledge & Kegan Paul, 1985).

22. Arshad Yousafzai and Uswah Zahid, "Who Is Jamaat-e-Islami's Chandni Shah?" *Geo News*, May 27, 2023, https://www.geo.tv/latest/489530-who-is-jamaat-e-islamis-chandni-shah.

23. For a version of this argument, see Joseph A. Massad, *Desiring Arabs* (Chicago: University of Chicago Press, 2007).

24. Cited in M. Alipour, "Islamic Sharia Law, Neotraditionalist Muslim Scholars and Transgender Sex-Reassignment Surgery: A Case Study of Ayatollah Khomeini's and Sheikh al-Tantawi's Fatwas," *International Journal of Transgenderism* 18, no. 1 (2017): 96.

25. Alipour, "Islamic Sharia," 95.

26. Alipour, "Islamic Sharia," 96.

27. Afsaneh Najmabadi, *Professing Selves: Transsexuality and Same-Sex Desire in Contemporary Iran* (Durham, NC: Duke University Press, 2014).

28. Olivier Roy, *The Failure of Political Islam*, trans. Carol Volk (Cambridge, MA: Harvard University Press, 1994), 73.

29. SherAli Tareen, *Perilous Intimacies: Debating Hindu-Muslim Friendship After Empire* (New York: Columbia University Press, 2023).

30. See Shruti Kapila, *Violent Fraternity: Indian Political Thought in the Global Age* (Princeton: Princeton University Press, 2021).

31. Sayyid Ahmad Khan, "Political Umur awr Musalman," in *Khutbat-e Sir Sayyid*, vol. 2 (Lahore: Majlis-e Taraqqi-ye Adab, 1973), 13–16.
32. Illahabadi, *Intikhab-e Akbar Illahabadi*, 59. The Urdu text reads: *Tujhe unse hai sar-e dosti teri arzu bhi ajib hai / Voh hai takht par tu hai khak par voh amir hain tu gharib hai.*

Chapter Five. Half in Love

1. See, for example, Yaseen Noorani, "The Lost Garden of Al-Andalus: Islamic Spain and the Poetic Inversion of Colonialism," *International Journal of Middle East Studies* 31 (1999): 237–254.
2. The authoritative study of this genre and its poetic descendants is Eve Tignol, *Grief and the Shaping of Muslim Communities in North India, c1857–1940s* (Cambridge: Cambridge University Press, 2023).
3. This discovery was made by Eve Tignol, "A Note on the Origins of Hali's *Musaddas-e Madd-o Jazr-e Islam*," *Journal of the Royal Asiatic Society*, series 3 (May 2016): 1–5.
4. Altaf Husain Hali, *Hali's Musaddas: The Flow and Ebb of Islam*, trans. C. Shackle and J. Majeed (Delhi: Oxford University Press, 1997), 123.
5. Muhammad Shibli Numani, "Tamasha-ye Ibrat," in *Kulliyat-e Shibli* (Lahore: Data Publishers, 1971), 24. The Urdu text reads: *Marw-o Shiraz-o Safahan ke voh zeba manzar / Bayt-e haram ke voh aywan voh diwar voh dar / Misr-o Gharnatah-o Baghdad ka ek ek patthar / Awr voh Dihli marhum ke bosidah khandar / Un ke zarron men chamakte hain voh jawhar ab tak / Dastanen unhen sab yad hain az bar ab tak.*
6. Numani, "Tamasha-ye Ibrat," 24. The Urdu text reads: *Tujh pe ay qawm asar karta hai afson jin ka / Yeh vohi the ke ragon men hai tere khun jin ka.*
7. Numani, "Tamasha-ye Ibrat," 22. The Urdu text reads: *qawm ke khab-e pareshan ki yeh taabiren hain.*
8. Hali, *Hali's Musaddas.* The Urdu text reads: *Khoj un ke kamalat ka lagta hai ab itna / Gum dasht men ik qafilah-e be-tabl-o dara hai.*
9. Mirza Asadullah Khan Ghalib, *Divan-e Ghalib* (Aligarh: Maktabah-e Alfaz, 1990), 198. The Urdu original reads: *Iman mujhe roke hai jo khenche hai mujhe kufr / Kaba mere pichhe hai kalisa mere age.*
10. Akbar Illahabadi, *Intikhab-e Akbar Illahabadi* (New Delhi: Maktaba Jamia, 1990), 133. The Urdu original reads: *Shan-e sabiq se mayus huwe jate hain / But jo dayr men naqis huwe jate hain.*
11. The pioneering novelist in Urdu of this genre was undoubtedly Abdul Halim Sharar in the late nineteenth century. For the most extensive discussion of his work, see Christopher Ryan Perkins, "Partitioning History: The Creation of an *Islami Pablik* in Late Colonial India, c. 1880–1920" (PhD diss., University of Pennsylvania, 2011).
12. Illahabadi, *Intikhab*, 37. The Urdu original reads: *Meri taqrir ka us miss pe kuchh qabu nahin chalta / Jahan banduq chalti hai vahan jadu nahin chalta.*

13. Illahabadi, *Intikhab*, 43. The Urdu original reads: *Shawkh aysa hai ke us but ko agar kafir kaho / Hans ke kahta hai 'pyara lafz hai yeh phir kaho' / Jo kaho chha jaye un ankhon pe masti ki tarah / Fitnah-e dawran kaho, saqi kaho, sahir kaho.*

14. Illahabadi, *Intikhab*, 82. The Urdu original reads: *Mere islam ko ik qissa-e mazi samjho / Hans ke boli to phir mujh ko bhi razi samjho.*

15. Sayyid Ahmad Khan, *Muqaddimah-e Tafsir-e Sir Sayyid* (Patna: Khuda Bakhsh Oriental Public Library, 1995).

16. Hali, *Hali's Musaddas*, 163.

17. Hali, *Hali's Musaddas*, 145–146.

18. Michel Foucault, *Society Must Be Defended: Lectures at the College de France 1975–1976*, trans. D. Macey (New York: Picador, 2003).

19. Muhammad Iqbal, "Presidential Address Delivered at the Annual Session of the All-India Muslim League at Allahabad on the 29th of December, 1930," in *Thoughts and Reflections of Iqbal*, ed. S. A. Vahid (Lahore: Sh. Muhammad Ashraf, 1992), 163–164.

20. Muhammad Iqbal, *Stray Reflections* (Lahore: Sh. Ghulam Ali and Sons, 1961), 15.

21. Iqbal, *Stray Reflections*, 24.

22. Akbar Illahabadi, *Gandhinamah* (Allahabad: Kitabistan, 1948).

23. For Umm Kulthum's career, see Virginia Danielson, *The Voice of Egypt: Umm Kulthum, Arabic Song, and Egyptian Society in the Twentieth Century* (Chicago: University of Chicago Press, 1998).

24. Muhammad Iqbal, "Shikwa," in *Kulliyat-e Iqbal Urdu* (Delhi: Educational Publishing House, 2001), 163–169.

25. Muhammad Iqbal, "Jawab-e Shikwa," in *Kulliyat-e Iqbal Urdu*, 200–208.

26. Muhammad Iqbal, *The Reconstruction of Religious Thought in Islam* (New Delhi: Kitab Bhavan, 1990), 126.

27. Iqbal, "Reply to Questions Raised by Pandit Jawaharlal Nehru," in *Thoughts and Reflections*, 285.

28. Iqbal, "Qadianis and Orthodox Muslims," in *Thoughts and Reflections*, 248–249.

29. Iqbal, "Presidential Address Delivered at the Annual Session of the All-India Muslim Conference at Lahore on the 21st of March, 1932," in *Thoughts and Reflections*, 196–197.

30. Olivier Roy, *Globalised Islam* (London: Hurst, 2004).

31. Sayyid Abul Ala Maududi, "Musalmanon ka Mazi-o Hal awr Mustaqbal," in *Islami Nizam-e Zindagi* (Lahore: Islamic Publications, 1962), 247–293.

32. Ayman al-Zawahiri, "Selected Questions and Answers from Dr. Ayman al-Zawahiri—part 2 released on: April 17, 2008," NEFA Foundation, http://www.actforamericaeducation.com/downloads/All_Files_by_Type/nefazawahiri0508-2.pdf, 8.

33. Zawahiri, "Selected Questions," 8.

34. Zawahiri, "Selected Questions," 7.

35. Zawahiri, "Selected Questions," 7.
36. Zawahiri, "Selected Questions," 8.
37. Karl Jaspers, *The Question of German Guilt*, trans. E. B. Ashton (New York: Capricorn, 1961), 23–24.
38. Jaspers, *Question of German Guilt*, 71.
39. Jaspers, *Question of German Guilt*, 32.
40. Hannah Arendt, "Organised Guilt and Universal Responsibility," in *Essays in Understanding, 1930–1954* (New York: Schocken, 1994), 131.
41. "Text: Obama's Speech in Cairo," *New York Times*, June 4, 2009, https://www.nytimes.com/2009/06/04/us/politics/04obama.text.html.
42. "Text: Obama's Speech."
43. "Text: Obama's Speech."
44. "Text: Obama's Speech."
45. "Text: Obama's Speech."

Chapter Six. Hollow Men

1. "Video: Islamic State Media Branch Releases 'The End of Sykes-Picot,' " July 1, 2014, *Belfast Telegraph*, https://www.belfasttelegraph.co.uk/video-news/video-islamic-media-branch-releases-the-end-of-sykes-pi-cot-30397575.html. For a consideration of militant video, see Anne Stenerson, "A History of Jihadi Cinematography," in *Jihadi Culture: The Art and Social Practices of Militant Islamists*, ed. Thomas Hegghammer (Cambridge: Cambridge University Press, 2017), 108–127. For ISIS in particular, see Charlie Winter, *The Terrorist Image: De-Coding the Islamic State's Photo-Propaganda* (London: Hurst, 2021).
2. For Al-Qaeda's thought and practices, see Faisal Devji, *Landscapes of the Jihad: Militancy, Morality, Modernity* (Ithaca, NY: Cornell University Press, 2005), and *The Terrorist in Search of Humanity: Militant Islam and Global Politics* (New York: Columbia University Press, 2009).
3. See Faisal Devji, *The Impossible Indian: Gandhi and the Temptation of Violence* (Cambridge, MA: Harvard University Press, 2012).
4. For perhaps the most important work on the historical background and emergence of Al-Qaeda, see Thomas Hegghammer, *The Caravan: Abdallah Azam and the Rise of Global Jihad* (Cambridge: Cambridge University Press, 2020). For Osama bin Laden's thought, see Flagg Miller, *The Audacious Ascetic: What Osama bin Laden's Sound Archive Reveals About Al-Qa'ida* (London: Hurst, 2015).
5. For the shift from Al-Qaeda to ISIS, see Mohammad-Mahmoud Ould Mohamedou, *A Theory of ISIS: Political Violence and the Transformation of the Global Order* (London: Pluto, 2018). For a study of the movement's organization and operations, see Ahmed S. Hashim, *The Caliphate at War: The Ideological, Organisational, and Military Innovations of Islamic State* (London: Hurst, 2018).

6. For the emergence and meaning of these terms, see Fawaz A. Gerges, *The Far Enemy: Why Jihad Went Global* (Cambridge: Cambridge University Press, 2005).

7. See, for example, Ahmad S. Dallal, *Islam Without Europe: Traditions of Reform in Eighteenth-Century Islamic Thought* (Chapel Hill: University of North Carolina Press, 2018).

8. See David B. Cook, "Contemporary Martyrdom: Ideology and Material Culture," in *Jihadi Culture: The Art and Social Practices of Militant Islamists*, ed. Thomas Hegghammer (Cambridge: Cambridge University Press, 2017), 151–170.

9. See Afshon Ostovar, "The Visual Culture of Jihad," in *Jihadi Culture: The Art and Social Practices of Militant Islamists*, ed. Thomas Hegghammer (Cambridge: Cambridge University Press, 2017), 82–107.

10. Alain Badiou, *Notre mal vient de plus loin: Penser les tueries de 13 novembre* (Paris: Fayard, 2016).

11. Jean-Paul Sartre, *Saint Genet, comédien et martyr* (Paris: Gallimard, 2011).

12. Wendy Brown, *Walled States, Waning Sovereignty* (New York: Zone Books, 2010).

13. See for this Simon Wolfgang Fuchs, *In a Pure Muslim Land: Shi'ism Between Pakistan and the Middle East* (Chapel Hill: University of North Carolina Press, 2019).

14. See the September 2014 address by ISIS spokesman Abu Muhammad al-Adnani ash-Shami, "Indeed, Your Lord Is Ever Watchful," in *Al-Qaeda 2.0: A Critical Reader*, ed. Donald Holbrook (New York: Oxford University Press, 2017), 154–167. For a collection of ISIS texts and their interpretation, see Haroro J. Ingram, Craig Whiteside, and Charlie Winter, *The ISIS Reader: Milestone Texts of the Islamic State Movement* (London: Hurst, 2020).

15. Olivier Roy, "Le djihadisme est une révolte générationnelle et nihiliste," *Le Monde*, November 23, 2015, https://www.lemonde.fr/idees/article/2015/11/24/le-djihadisme-une-revolte-generationnelle-et-nihiliste_4815992_3232.html.

16. For the movement's lack of historical or ideological context, and its general inability to be understood in conventional ways, see the views of a highly placed US intelligence official: Anonymous, "The Mystery of ISIS," *New York Review of Books*, August 13, 2015, http://www.nybooks.com/articles/archives/2015/aug/13/mystery-isis/.

17. For a classic account, see Lionel Trilling, *Sincerity and Authenticity* (Cambridge, MA: Harvard University Press, 1973). See also Katherine Bergeron, "Melody and Monotone: Performing Sincerity in Republican France," in *The Rhetoric of Sincerity*, ed. Ernst van Alphen, Mieke Bal, and Carel E. Smith (Stanford, CA: Stanford University Press, 2009), 44–59. For hypocrisy and its opposite, sincerity, during the Counter-Reformation, see Jane Taylor, "Why Do You Tear Me from Myself? Torture, Truth and

the Arts of the Counter-Reformation," in *Rhetoric of Sincerity*, 19–43; and Frans-Willem Korsten, "The Irreconcilability of Sincerity and Hypocrisy," in *Rhetoric of Sincerity*, 60–77.

18. Judith N. Shklar, *Ordinary Vices* (Cambridge, MA: Belknap, 1985).

19. "Unclassified Verbatim Transcript of Combatant Status Review Tribunal Hearing for ISN 10024." I discuss this document in Devji, *Terrorist in Search*, 85–96.

20. Al-Adnani ash-Shami, "Indeed Your Lord," 154.

21. Al-Adnani ash-Shami, "Indeed Your Lord," 162.

22. Al-Adnani ash-Shami, "Indeed Your Lord," 156.

23. Hannah Arendt, *On Revolution* (New York: Penguin, 1977). For another account stressing conspiracy and the fear of secrecy in the French Revolution, see Francois Furet, *Penser la Révolution française* (Paris: Gallimard, 1978).

24. See Maurice Merleau-Ponty, *Humanism and Terror: An Essay on the Communist Problem*, trans. John O'Neill (Boston: Beacon, 1969), especially ch. 2, "Bukharin and the Ambiguity of History," 25–70.

25. For this, see Paul W. Kahn, *Political Theology: Four New Chapters on the Concept of Sovereignty* (New York: Columbia University Press, 2012).

26. See Jean-Pierre Filiu, *Apocalypse in Islam*, trans. M. B. DeBevoise (Berkeley: University of California Press, 2011).

27. Al-Adnani ash-Shami, "Indeed Your Lord," 156.

28. See Aris Roussinos, "Jihad Selfies: These British Extremists in Syria Love Social Media," *Vice*, December 5, 2013, https://www.vice.com/en/article/syrian-jihadist-selfies-tell-us-a-lot-about-their-war/.

29. Francis Fukuyama, *The End of History and the Last Man* (New York: Free Press, 1992).

30. Samuel P. Huntington, *The Clash of Civilizations and the Remaking of World Order* (New York: Simon & Schuster, 1996).

31. For the role of Cold War rivalry in creating and preserving the international order, see Sandrine Kott, *Organiser le monde: Une autre histoire de la guerre froide* (Paris: Broché, 2021).

32. For the dangers and delusions of the Cold War analogy, see Fred Kaplan, "Nostalgia for Cold War Diplomacy Is a Trap," *Slate*, January 5, 2024, https://slate.com/news-and-politics/2024/01/israel-ukraine-george-kennan-cold-war-diplomacy-trap.html.

33. For an elaboration of this argument, see Faisal Devji, "Ukraine, Gaza, and the International Order," Quincy Institute for Responsible Statecraft, February 6, 2024, https://quincyinst.org/research/ukraine-gaza-and-the-international-order/.

34. For the history of this rehearsal in the Palestinian case, see Lori Allen, *A History of False Hope: Investigative Commissions in Palestine* (Stanford, CA: Stanford University Press, 2020).

35. See, for instance, David Chandler, "International Law in the Shadow of the Silent Majorities," in Tor Krever et al., "On International Law and

Gaza: Critical Reflections," *London Review of International Law* 12, no. 2 (2024): 243–244, https://doi.org/10.1093/lril/lraeo12.

36. For the use of "genocide" to describe Israeli actions in Gaza, see A. Dirk Moses, "More than Genocide," *Boston Review*, November 14, 2023, https://www.bostonreview.net/articles/more-than-genocide/.

37. For a truly historical analysis of the comparison between apartheid South Africa and Israel, see Saul Dubow, "Apartheid in South Africa and Israel/Palestine: A Case of Convergent Evolution?" *Palestine/Israel Review* 1, no. 2 (June 2024): 257–288, https://doi.org/10.5325/pir.1.2.0001.

38. See, for example, Nicholas Mulder, *The Economic Weapon: The Rise of Sanctions as a Tool of Modern War* (New Haven: Yale University Press, 2022).

39. See, for example, the Iranian supreme leader's speech, "Zionists' Crimes Won't Be Forgotten Even After It Is Destroyed by the Grace of God," *Khamenei.ir*, January 9, 2024, https://english.khamenei.ir/news/10469/Zionists-crimes-won-t-be-forgotten-even-after-it-is-destroyed.

40. See Tareq Baconi, *Hamas Contained: A History of Palestinian Resistance* (Stanford, CA: Stanford University Press, 2022).

41. The Avalon Project, "Hamas Covenant 1988," Yale Law School, https://avalon.law.yale.edu/20th_century/hamas.asp.

42. See Palestine Chronicle Staff, "Hamas Document Reveals: Why We Carried Out Al-Aqsa Flood Operation—Summary & PDF," *Palestine Chronicle*, January 21, 2024, https://www.palestinechronicle.com/hamas-document-reveals-why-we-we-carried-out-al-aqsa-flood-operation-summary-pdf/.

Conclusion

1. Asef Bayat is the most original theorist of what we might call postpolitical movements in the Middle East. See, in particular, his book *Revolution Without Revolutionaries: Making Sense of the Arab Spring* (Stanford, CA: Stanford University Press, 2017).

2. For an ethnographic study of the Egyptian revolution, see Walter Armbrust, *Martyrs and Tricksters: An Ethnography of the Egyptian Revolution* (Princeton: Princeton University Press, 2019).

3. See, for this, Ezgi Basaran, *The New Spirit of Islamism: Interactions Between the AKP, Ennahda and the Muslim Brotherhood* (London: I. B. Tauris, 2024).

4. Armando Salvatore, "New Media, the 'Arab Spring' and the Metamorphosis of the Public Sphere: Beyond Western Assumptions on Collective Agency and Democratic Politics," *Constellations* 20, no. 2 (2013): 217–228.

5. Salvatore, "New Media," 221.

6. Salvatore, "New Media," 226.

7. See, for this, Zoya Hasan, "Occupying Streets: Women in the Vanguard of the Anti-CAA Struggle," in *Shaheen Bagh and the Idea of India: Writings on a Movement for Justice, Liberty and Equality*, ed. Seema Mustafa (New Delhi: Speaking Tiger Books, 2020), 159–172.

8. See, for example, the two volumes of Öcalan's prison writings, Abdullah Öcalan, *Prison Writings: The Roots of Civilization*, trans. Klaus Happel (London: Pluto, 2007), and *Prison Writings II: The PKK and the Kurdish Question in the 21st Century* (London: Transmedia, 2011). For an analysis of the Kurdish movement, see Axel Rudi, "Death as Victory, Victory as Death: Violence, Martyrdom, and the Cosmology of Revolution in the Kurdish Freedom Movement" (PhD diss., University of Bergen, 2019), https://bora.uib.no/bora-xmlui/handle/1956/21161?locale-attribute=en.

9. Shams is interviewed in Isaac Chotiner, "How Iran's Hijab Protest Movement Became So Powerful," *New Yorker*, October 2, 2022, https://www.newyorker.com/news/q-and-a/fatemah-shams-how-irans-hijab-protest-movement-became-so-powerful.

10. See, for instance, Nahid Siamdoust, "Women Reclaiming Their Voices for Life and Freedom: Music and the 2022 Uprising in Iran," *Iranian Studies* 56 (2023): 577–583.

11. See, for example, Peyman Jafari, "Revolt with a Revolutionary Perspective," *Iranian Studies* 56 (2023): 569–575.

Acknowledgments

I AM INDEBTED TO THE friends, colleagues, and students whose ideas and suggestions have gone into the making of this book. First among these is Shruti Kapila, with whom I have been in conversation about ideas and arguments for years now. At Oxford I am grateful in particular to Ruth Harris, who generously read and commented on my manuscript with her customary care. Conversations with Paul Betts, Maria Misra, David Priestland, and Andy Thompson have also been invaluable in allowing me to formulate my ideas. Among my students, Zaki Rehman and Galip Dalay, especially, have been wonderful interlocutors, their research having enlivened my own sense of Islam's modern history.

I am thankful for the help and suggestions I received on specific parts of my manuscript from Neguin Yavari, Syed Akbar Hyder, Aslisho Qurboniev, and Danish Khan. Some of the book's arguments were first tried out in lectures and conferences organized by Dipesh Chakrabarty, Sanjay Subrahmanyam, and Bo Strath in Budapest; Catherine Besteman and Hugh Gusterson in Sintra; Azfar Moin and Alan Strathern in Oxford; Naveeda Khan and Veena Das at Johns Hopkins; Shruti Kapila and Richard Bourke in Cambridge; Axel Rudi in Bergen; and Munis Faruqui at Berkeley. Sadia Abbas, for her part, has been a confidante across continents, between New York, Siena, and Molyvos.

I am grateful to the anonymous reviewers of my manuscript, whose well-considered advice I found to be extraordinarily helpful.

As always, I am full of admiration for the hospitality and conversation of Rachel and Michael Dwyer in London, who have a knack for opening any subject out to the larger world. And I am deeply appreciative of Christophe Carvalho's generosity in Oxford and hospitality in Mumbai and Goa, without which I would surely have been unable to write this book. My thanks, finally, to Suzanne Schneider, who put me in touch with Yale University Press, and to my editor, Jaya Chatterjee and her team, with all of whom it has been an unalloyed pleasure to work.

I have repurposed some essays in this book and am grateful to their original publishers for permission to do so. One is "Le langage de l'universalité musulmane," *Diogène* 2, no. 226 (2009): 39–57. Another is "A Caliphate Beyond Politics: The Sovereignty of ISIS," in A. A. Moin and A. Strathern, eds., *Sacred Kingship in World History* (New York: Columbia University Press, 2022), 299–322 (copyright © 2022 by Columbia University Press) (reprinted with permission of Columbia University Press). I am also grateful to Oxford University Press India for allowing me to quote extensively from Altaf Husain Hali, *Hali's Musaddas: The Flow and Ebb of Islam*, trans. Christopher Shackle and Javed Majeed (Delhi: Oxford University Press, 1997) (reproduced with permission of © Oxford University Press India 1998).

Index

Abbasid caliphate, 146
abolitionism, 25
abstraction, 36, 83, 84, 85, 92, 97, 104, 156, 204
Abu Dhabi, 46
Adnani ash-Shami, Shaykh Abu Muhammad al-, 199, 203
adultery, 131
advice literature, 141–142
Afghani, Jamal al-Din, 22
Afghanistan: Al-Qaeda in, 187; anti-Soviet jihad in, 27, 174; and the Global War on Terror, 183; Islam in, 113, 177; Muslims in, 227; Pathans from, 58; refugees from, 113; Taliban in, 14, 28, 217
Africa: clocks in, 85; colonial, 41; France and Spain in, 18; Islam in, 16, 19; religion in, 34
African laborers, 58
agency: abstract, 36, 38; divine, 96, 128; global, 27, 29, 30; of God, 12; human, 96, 219; individual, 140, 219, 225–226; in Islam, 4, 6, 7, 9, 10, 14, 36, 42, 98, 108, 112, 128, 219; lack/loss of, 43, 53; male, 128; moral, 142; of Muhammad, 61; of Muslims, 11, 12, 13, 220, 225–226;

political, 44, 45, 219, 220; theological, 45
Ahmad, Nazir, 45, 46, 123–125, 126
Ahmadis, 67–71, 75, 164, 227, 240n22
Akhtar, Shabbir, 63–64, 87, 88–89
Al-Aqsa, 213
Algerian war of independence, 213
allegory, 91
All-India Muslim League, 143
al-Mulk, Nizam, 37
Al-Qaeda: 9/11 attacks, 208, 214; attacks in the US and Europe, 184–185; context of, 218; global context of, 209; and Hayat Tahrir al-Sham, 218; ideology of, 166–167, 172, 205; and ISIS, 184–186; militancy of, 44, 182, 194, 195, 197, 207, 209, 222; mirroring by, 169, 179, 182–190, 191, 193, 201, 205, 206; near vs. far enemy, 184; Obama and, 175–176, 179; suicide bombers, 13; terrorism by, 208
Ambedkar, Bhimrao, 227–228, 232
Ameer Ali, Syed, 30–34, 35, 37, 38–39, 41–42, 103
Amini, Mahsa, 226
anarchism, 94, 95, 98, 107
angels, 153

anticapitalism, 222
anticolonialism, 182, 222
anti-monarchism, 222
antinationalism, 24, 25
anti-Semitism, 72, 212, 213, 214, 216
antistatism, 94, 107
antiterrorism, 210
apartheid, 178, 213, 214
apocalypse, 44, 104, 105, 111, 121, 146,
    202, 203, 204
Apocalypse Now (film), 196
apostasy, 62, 112
Arab boatmen, 58
Arab Revolt, 28
Arab Spring, 14, 217, 220, 221–224,
    226, 233; and Islamism, 224–225
arabesques, 92
Arabia/Arabian Peninsula, 18, 19, 45–
    46, 47, 48. *See also* Saudi Arabia
architecture, Islamic, 38, 85, 92
Arendt, Hannah, 171–172, 200, 203
Arnold, Matthew, 7
Asad, Muhammad, 118
asceticism, 78, 130, 131
Asia: clocks in, 85; colonial, 41; Islam
    in, 19; religion in, 34
Assassin's Creed (video game), 204
atheism and atheists, 113; conversion
    to, 114–115; in the Middle East,
    116; in Saudi Arabia, 116
Austria, 18
authenticity, 196–197
Axis of Resistance, 215
Aydin, Cemil, 45

Baal, 93
Babri Masjid (Babur's Mosque), 77–78
Babri Masjid dispute, 228–229
Badiou, Alain, 187, 188
Baghdad, 45, 48
Bahadur Shah II, 90–91
Bahaism, 115
Bahrain, 222
Bangladesh, 14, 226, 227

banking, Islamic, 84
Barelvi creed, 73
Barq-e Kalisa [Lightning in the
    Cathedral] (Illahabadi), 152–153
Bayat, Asef, 250n1
Bedouin, 45
Bend in the River, A (Naipaul), 196
Bentham, Jeremy, 59, 74
Bergson, Henri, 161
Bharatiya Janata Party, 77
Bihishti Zewar [Jewellery of Paradise]
    (Hali), 126
bin Laden, Osama, 166, 169, 172, 176,
    177, 179, 184, 202, 209;
    assassination of, 207–208, 210
blasphemy, 57, 59, 62, 63, 70–80, 87,
    89–90, 100, 168
Blunt, Wilfred Scawen, 15–18, 19, 20,
    22, 23, 24, 27, 28, 29–30, 45, 46
Bodin, Jean, 96
Bollinger v. Costa Brava Wines, 70
Bolsheviks, 95, 108, 134
Bombay protests, 54–58, 62
border walls, 188
Bosnians, 211
boycotts, 74, 79, 213
brainwashing, 194
Britain: civilization and freedom in, 41;
    Indians and Pakistanis in, 62; Islam
    and, 24, 29–30; in the Middle East,
    18; Muslims in, 16, 17; reaction to
    bin Laden's death, 207; religion in,
    34; Sykes-Picot agreement, 180. *See
    also* London, England
British Empire: global expanse of, 16–
    17, 25, 43; in India, 109, 144–145;
    Islam and, 25–26, 46; Islam in, 52;
    Muslims in, 27; secularism of, 68
Brown, Wendy, 188
Buchan, John, 27–29
Buddhism, 31, 154
Bukharin, Nikolai, 200–201
Bureau, Paul, 130
Burma, 227

Bush, George W., 176, 179
Bush Administration, 179, 208

Cairo University, 172–174, 179
caliphate: Abbasid, 146; abolition of,
    97; of the Islamic State, 19, 180,
    183, 189, 202; Ottoman, 17, 18, 20,
    23, 27, 30, 47, 159; in Turkey, 46.
    See also Ottoman Empire
calligraphy, 92
capitalism: agency of, 9, 36; colonial,
    33; vs. communism, 100; and the
    ethic of production, 188; in Europe,
    132; global, 213; industrial, 54–55;
    inequality of, 69; Islam and, 11;
    materialism and, 93; and religion,
    81–86; Western, 83–84
Carlyle, Thomas, 21
caste system, 132, 133
Catalan independence movement,
    231
Catholicism, 20, 177, 200. *See also*
    Christianity
Caucasus, 18, 221
censorship, 79–80
Central Asia, 18, 113, 221
Charlie Hebdo, 73
Chechnya, 187
children, 121, 122, 123, 124–125, 131
Chile, 180
China: anti-Muslim violence in, 72;
    antiterrorism in, 210; Cultural
    Revolution, 107–108; and global
    politics, 211
Christianity: agency of, 3; in America,
    34, 179; Catholic, 20, 177, 200;
    civilization and, 156; compared to
    Islam, 83; conversion to, 44, 113,
    114; in Europe, 34, 42, 158, 173;
    imagery of, 1; in India, 54;
    irrelevance of, 165; and Islam,
    16–17, 30, 42, 60, 83, 151–153, 154,
    155, 157; and the "just war," 188;
    legal protection for, 71; loss of

political authority by, 35; medieval
    church, 165; and the Middle East,
    48; missionaries for, 67, 115, 143;
    and modern civilization, 7, 156; as
    noun, 6; and the oppression of
    women, 130; Protestant, 113, 115,
    200; secular understanding of, 7;
    and sexuality, 130, 131; shrines in,
    77–78; social structures of, 33;
    tolerance of, 80; use of "Allah" by
    Christians, 88; values of, 157;
    virtues of, 159; vocabulary of
    blasphemy, 62, 70–71; in the West,
    175
Chup ki Dad [Homage to the Silent]
    (Hali), 127
Churchill, Randolph, 15, 22
Churchill, Winston, 15, 28
Citizenship Amendment Act (CAA),
    220, 227, 229, 230
civilization, 41–42, 130–132, 134, 156–
    157; and Christianity, 156; clash of,
    203; Islam as, 22
Civilization and Its Discontents (Freud),
    131
*Clash of Civilizations and the Remaking
    of World Order, The* (Huntington),
    209
class conflict, 162, 165
climate change, 40, 44, 177
clocks and clockwork, 36, 82, 85–86
Cold War: and Arab Spring, 221; and
    the Gaza war, 216, 217; geopolitics
    of, 208, 209, 211; ideologies of, 191;
    Islam and, 27, 181, 215; and
    Islamism, 224–225; Kennedy in
    Berlin, 173; in the Middle East,
    218
colonialism: anarchism and, 94–95;
    British, 95, 144–145; European, 5,
    83, 203; in India, 95; justification of,
    42–43; opponents of, 178, 214; and
    religion, 52; settler, 213; vocabulary
    of, 212; and women, 122

colonization: European, 39, 46; of
 Hindus, 155; humanitarian claims
 of, 196; of Muslims, 146. *See also*
 decolonization
color revolutions, 221, 222, 230
communism: vs. Islam, 12, 27, 36, 92,
 93, 100, 162; Iqbal on, 26;
 repudiation of, 221; Soviet, 94, 134,
 179, 201
concealment, 91
concubinage, 195
Conrad, Joseph, 196
conservatism, Muslim, 162
conversion: to atheism, 114–115; to
 Christianity, 44, 113, 114; to
 Hinduism, 114; in India, 114; to
 Islam, 20–21, 55, 62, 91, 117–118,
 127, 146, 152, 165, 174; within
 Islam, 115; of Napoleon, 20–21, 174
coronavirus pandemic, 230
cosmetic surgery, 119, 138
counterinsurgency, 216
courtesans, 135
Crusades, 146, 147
Cultural Revolution, 107–108
culture wars, 208
Cursetjee, Byramjee, 56

Dabiq (online magazine), 202
Darwin, Charles, 165
decadence, 39, 47, 48, 123, 154, 156,
 157, 200, 206
Decline of the West (Spengler), 156
decolonization, 10, 13, 164, 196, 213.
 See also colonization
defamation, 57, 59, 60, 63, 64. *See also*
 blasphemy
Deif, Mohammed, 215
Deism, 85
Delhi, 45
democracy: and the British Empire, 25,
 26; as idol, 92; in India, 24, 25;
 liberal, 203; Muslim, 106;
 opposition to, 224

Denmark, 74–75, 78–79
desecration, 76–81
determinism, biological, 134
Dhaka, 116
divestment, 213
divine law, 191. *See also* Islamic law
Doha, 46, 215
"Dover Beach" (Arnold), 7
dress codes, 118–120, 121, 136, 163,
 187, 220, 221, 230
Dubai, 46
Dutch Empire, 16, 17

East India Company, 34, 147
Eastern Europe, 18, 178, 217, 221
education: for men, 127; for women,
 123, 126–127
Egypt: Arab Spring, 222, 223; bloggers'
 response to Arab protests, 225–226;
 Cairo, 45, 48, 172, 177–178, 179,
 223; Islam in, 13, 48, 177; Muslim
 Brotherhood, 217, 224, 225;
 Napoleon in, 20, 174; Ottomans in,
 23; Tahrir Square protests, 223;
 women in, 122
End of History and the Last Man, The
 (Fukuyama), 208
Engels, Friedrich, 95, 96
Enlightenment, 36, 130, 162
Ennahda, 217, 224
environmental degradation, 169
environmentalists, 170
epicureanism, 165
eunuchs, 135
Europe: Al-Qaeda attacks on, 184–185;
 refugee crisis, 113; self-interest of,
 165
European Union, 231
ex-Muslims, 114–115, 116

Facebook, 72
Faiz, Faiz Ahmed, 232
fanaticism, 55–56, 84, 195, 200
Fanon, Frantz, 216

fatwa, 65
feminism, 119
First World War, 18, 174, 180
Flow and Ebb of Islam, The (Hali), 2–3,
    147
Foley, Jim, 183
fornication, 131
Forster, E. M., 144
France: civilization and freedom in, 41;
    in North Africa, 18; religion in, 20;
    Sykes-Picot agreement, 180
free speech, 56, 73, 79, 80
freedom of conscience, 79
Freemasons, 116
French Revolution, 84, 200
Freud, Sigmund, 131
Fukuyama, Francis, 208
fundamentalism, 13. *See also* Islamism
Future of Islam, The (Blunt), 15–18

Gandhi, Mohandas "Mahatma," 24, 94,
    95, 96, 98, 107, 132, 144, 159, 178,
    182, 198, 227, 228, 232
Gandhinamah [The Epic of Gandhi]
    (Illahabadi), 159
Gaza war, 211–218
gender dysmorphia, 135
gender hierarchy, 135
gender identity, 135
gender inequality, 125
gender reassignment surgery, 140
gender relations, 130–132, 135, 140–
    145, 220
gender roles, 121, 132–133
gender segregation, 134
Genet, Jean, 188, 192–193
Geneva, 48
genocide, 71, 72, 169, 211, 212, 213,
    214, 215
geopolitics, 48, 49, 209, 210–211
Germany: guilt in, 170; Islam and, 28;
    Kennedy's Berlin speech, 173;
    Muslim refugees in, 113
Gezi Park protests, 14

Ghalib, 151
ghazal, 3
Ghulam Ahmad, Mirza, 67–71
Gibbon, Edward, 21
Gladstone, William, 57
global consciousness, 43–44
Global War on Terror, 74, 183, 206–
    207, 209–210, 211, 212, 214, 216,
    217
global warming, 40, 177
globalization: of ISIS, 195; of Islam, 11,
    23, 41, 61, 98, 149; of Islamic
    mobilization, 222; of Muhammad,
    66–67; and sovereignty, 188, 231;
    understanding of, 7
Gobineau, Comte de, 156
Goethe, Johann Wolfgang von, 197
Goldsmith, Jemima, 72
Great Mosque (Mecca), 82
Green Movement, 14, 220, 221, 225,
    226, 231–232
Greenmantle (Buchan), 27–29
guilt, metaphysical, 171

Habsburg Empire, 16
Hadith al-Ruh [The Spirit's Converse]
    (Iqbal), 159
halal, 84
Hali, 2–3, 7, 8, 147–148, 153, 157, 161–
    162
Hali, Altaf Hussain, 126, 127
Hamas, 212, 214, 215, 216, 217
Hamidullah, Muhammad, 236n11
Hanuman Garhi temple, 78
Haq, Zia ul, 88
Hasan bin Ali, 110
Hayat Tahrir al-Sham, 218
Hazratbal incident, 228
Heart of Darkness (Conrad), 196
hedonism, 130
Hegel, Georg Friedrich, 3, 38, 84, 162,
    165
Henri IV, 20
heresy, 32, 47

heretics, 81, 199
hermaphrodites, 136–138, 139
Hezbollah, 214, 217
Hidden Imam, 101, 102, 104, 105, 106, 108, 110. *See also* Imams (Shia)
hijra community, 136
Hinduism: and the caste system, 133; conversion to, 114; imagery of, 1; in India, 77–78, 114; and Islam, 33–34, 95, 151; and the law, 154; and religious controversy, 54; virtues of, 159
Hindus: attacks on, 229; colonization of, 155; in India, 58; interactions with Muslims, 141–144
Hobbes, Thomas, 36, 96
Hodgson, Marshall, 4, 5, 7
Holocaust, 71, 72, 73, 76, 213, 215
homosexuality, 135, 138–139
Houthis, 214
hukm, 65
human rights, 71, 197
humanitarianism, 25, 43, 167, 212, 214–215, 217
Huntington, Samuel, 209
Hussein, Saddam, 216
hypocrisy, 197–201, 214

Ibn Saud family, 47
iconoclasm, 80, 81, 84, 91–92, 112
identity: American, 117; atheist, 116; biopolitical, 12; collective, 21, 158; cultural, 229; female, 91, 120; gendered, 120, 121, 134, 139; Jewish, 117; Malay, 88; of militants, 183; Muslim/Islamic, 20, 25, 32, 33, 43, 66, 84, 88, 114–115, 120, 142; national, 220, 231; personal, 116; profane, 113; religious, 25, 33, 59, 229; sectarian, 180; sexual, 138; virtual, 191, 195
identity politics, 230
ideologies: of Al-Qaeda, 166–167, 172, 205; Islam as, 5–6, 93, 134; Islamic, 162; rejection of, 201

idolatry, 12, 26, 82, 91–93, 97, 101, 108–109, 111, 112, 219–220
idols, 12, 89, 90–93, 112, 121, 122, 151, 160
Illahabadi, Akbar, 18, 125–126, 144, 151–152, 159
Imams (Shia), 105, 107, 108, 110, 148, 189–190. *See also* Hidden Imam
immigrants: in India, 227; Muslim, 10, 78, 79
imperialism: age of, 8, 156; British, 25, 26; European, 13, 15, 16, 18, 26, 27, 45, 146, 219; in Iran, 231; Western, 130
incest, 131
India: anti-Muslim violence in, 72; antiterrorism in, 210; Babri Masjid dispute, 228–229; Bombay protests, 54–58, 62; under Britain, 34, 45, 109; caste system, 132, 133; Citizenship Amendment Act (CAA), 220, 227, 229, 230; coalition governments in, 229; colonial, 33, 57, 95, 132, 141; Delhi, 227; desecration in, 77–78; film industry in, 207; Hinduism in, 33; insults to Muhammad in, 54–67; Islam in, 16, 18, 24–25, 30, 33, 46, 88, 91; Kashmir insurgency, 228; Muslim protests in, 14; Muslims in, 149–150, 214, 220, 227–229, 230, 232; National Register of Citizens (NRC), 227; popular protests in, 226–230; protests by Muslims, 232; religious conversion in, 114; as secular country, 34, 77; Shaheen Bagh, 227; social reform in, 95; sovereignty in, 94, 95–96, 182; terrorism in, 228, 229; women in, 122, 226–227
Indian National Congress, 95, 143–144, 238–239n35
Indian Penal Code, 59
Indian Rebellion, 147–148

indigenous peoples, 213
indoctrination, 194
Indonesia, 177, 178
infidels, 44, 89, 90, 91, 111, 121, 122, 127, 142, 148, 150–157, 160, 169, 196
instrumentality, 21
insurgency, 229
International Court of Justice, 212
International Criminal Court, 212
intersex individuals, 135–138
Iqbal, Muhammad: on the Ahmadis, 75, 164; and Ameer Ali, 30; antinationalism of, 25–27; criticism of sovereignty, 93–94; criticism of the Ahmadis, 75; on human liberty, 68–69; influences on, 24; on Islam, 25–26, 157–159, 161–163, 164; "Islam as a Moral and Political Idea," 25–26; *Javid Nama* (Book of Immortality), 93; *Jawab-e Shikwa* (The Complaint's Answer), 160–161; letter to Nehru, 161; on nationalism, 163; poetry of, 215; "Political Thought in Islam," 26–27; *Shikwa* (Complaint), 159–160
Iran: autonomy of, 48, 49; constitution of, 101; and the Gaza war, 214, 216; Green Movement, 14, 220, 221, 225, 226, 231–232; Hussein's war against, 216; vs. ISIS, 190; as Islamic republic, 101, 103, 217; Khomeini's authority in, 65–66; and the Kurds, 230–231; minister of culture, 75; protests in, 231–232; refugees from, 113; religion in, 115; sovereignty in, 101, 102, 103–112, 107, 189; Tehran, 102, 215; transgender individuals in, 138–139; United States in, 176; women in, 14, 226–227. *See also* Islamic Republic (Iran); Persia
Iranian people, 110–111

Iranian Revolution, 10, 14, 110, 119, 189
Iran-Iraq War, 138
Iraq: American occupation of, 187; border with Syria, 180, 181; and the Gaza war, 216; and the Global War on Terror, 183; Islam in, 177; Shia militias of, 214; Sunnis in, 184; US invasion of, 48, 176, 194; wars in, 48
Ireland, 71
Irving, Washington, 57
Isfahan, 45
ISIS (Islamic State in Syria): and Al-Qaeda, 184–186; and the caliphate, 19, 180, 183, 189, 202; capital of, 196; coins minted by, 189; context of, 218; globalization of, 195; and Hayat Tahrir al-Sham, 218; hypocrisy of, 198–201; vs. Iran, 189–190; members of, 187–190, 192–193; militancy of, 194, 195, 197, 218; propaganda of, 191, 195, 203, 204, 206; recruiting by, 222; secret structures of, 190–193; supporters of, 194; Turkish support for, 218; violence of, 13, 116, 180–181
Islam: as abstract system, 92, 99, 105, 106, 108, 111; in Afghanistan, 113, 177; in Africa, 16, 19; agency of, 7–8, 108–109, 128, 148, 174, 176, 226, 233; and the Arab Spring, 233; in Asia, 19; autonomy of, 49; and Britain, 24, 28, 29–30, 46, 52; cartography of, 220; and Christianity, 16–17, 30, 42, 60, 83, 151–153, 154, 155, 157; as civilization, 22; claim to "Allah," 88–89; commodification of, 84; compared to a woman, 106; compared to communism, 100; conversion to, 20, 55, 62, 91, 117–118, 127, 146, 152, 165, 174; conversions within, 115; decline of,

Islam (*continued*)
  19, 155–156, 157, 160; demography
  of, 220; depoliticization of, 19–20;
  domestication of, 121–127, 129–
  130, 140; as enemy of science, 22;
  and Europe, 84; fetishization of, 82,
  84, 88, 119; founding of, 50–51, 81,
  161, 163; future of, 18–19, 28;
  gender relations in, 130–132;
  geography of, 45–49; and Germany,
  28; global, 14, 16, 17, 19, 21–22, 23,
  35–36, 39–41; global mission of,
  217; globalization of, 11, 23, 41, 61,
  98, 149; God in, 12, 32, 36, 87–88;
  historical understanding of, 4–11;
  as ideology, 5–6, 93, 134; in India,
  16, 18, 24–25, 30, 33, 46, 88,
  91; as inheritance, 149;
  instrumentalization of, 24; in
  Malaysia, 87–88, 89; missionaries
  for, 67; modern, 41, 53; as moral
  force, 19; in Muslim texts, 4; as
  nontheological, 31–32; in the
  Ottoman Empire, 46; in Pakistan,
  87–88, 89; poetic portrayals of, 106;
  and politics, 23, 39, 174, 220;
  postimperial mission of, 158;
  principles of, 37; puritanical forms
  of, 47; in the Qur'an, 4, 32; radical,
  177, 195; repudiation of, 113; Salafi,
  92, 119, 185, 225; in Saudi Arabia,
  47–49; Shia, 78, 101, 104, 105, 106,
  115, 148, 164, 184, 189, 190, 191,
  199, 214, 227; shrines, 78;
  stereotypes of, 28; Sufi, 128, 131,
  161, 164, 196; Sunni, 78, 101, 115,
  180, 184, 189, 190, 199; symbols of,
  85; in Syria, 113; as system of
  governance (*nizam*), 37; and the
  telescoping of time, 109–110;
  terrorism associated with, 167, 170,
  172, 174; theology of, 36, 67–71;
  universality of, 41–42, 150, 153–
  154, 157, 158–159, 161, 162–163,
    164, 169; use of term, 1–4, 31–32,
    50; violence associated with, 13,
    113, 166–167; virtues of, 159; and
    the West, 12–13, 16–17, 19–20, 24,
    27, 28–29, 41; women and, 91. *See
    also* Ahmadis; Wahhabis
Islamic Courts Union, 217
Islamic Emirate (Afghanistan), 217
Islamic jurisprudence, 186
Islamic law, 17, 30, 71, 84, 104, 198,
    204, 228, 229; in Iran, 102–103; and
    ISIS, 191; in Pakistan, 96–97
Islamic Republic (Iran), 101, 103, 129,
    189, 217, 220, 232; Pahlavi-era, 129.
    See also Iran
Islamic Republic of Pakistan. *See*
    Pakistan
Islamic republics: Iran, 101, 103, 129,
    189, 217, 220, 232; Pakistan, 99, 106
Islamic Revolution, 101, 108
Islamic State (ISIS). *See* ISIS (Islamic
    State in Syria)
Islamism: and the Arab Spring protests,
    224–225; and authority, 108; and
    the Cold War, 217, 224–225; in
    Egypt, 222; fading of, 217–218; and
    Hamas, 215; and militancy, 13, 14,
    166–172; Pan–, 20, 23, 24, 36;
    repudiation of, 225; and sexuality,
    136, 141; and social order, 189; and
    sovereignty, 191; and theology, 99;
    in Tunisia, 217, 222; women and,
    117, 119, 121, 129–130. *See also*
    fundamentalism; Maududi, Abdul
    Ala
Islamophobia, 72, 210–211, 225
Israel: borders of, 188, 213; Hamas's
    attack on, 211, 212, 214, 215,
    216
Istanbul, 45, 47
Italian Mafia, 188

Jamaat-e Islami (Islamic Society), 94,
    117, 136, 164

Jameelah, Maryam, 117–120
Jaspers, Karl, 170–171, 172
Javid Nama (Book of Immortality), 93
Jawab-e Shikwa [The Complaint's
    Answer] (Iqbal), 160–161
Jeddah, 46
Jerusalem, 82
Jesus, 31, 50, 170
jihad, 148, 150, 174, 187, 197, 206;
    anti-British, 174; anti-Soviet, 27,
    174
Jones, Terry, 78
Judaism: compared to Islam, 83;
    conversion to Islam, 117; and the
    Holocaust, 71, 72, 73, 76, 213, 215;
    and Islam, 83, 152, 154; and the
    right of return, 213; shrines, 77;
    Zionist church, 88. *See also* anti–
    Semitism
Junaid, Muhammad, 136

Kaaba, 81, 82, 85, 90–91, 151
Kapila, Shruti, 142
Kennedy, John F., 173, 177
Kenya, 176
Khamenei, Ali, 102–103
Khan, Arsalan, 127
Khan, Imran, 71–74, 74
Khan, Syed Ahmed, 130, 143–144, 148,
    150, 153, 154, 161, 166
Khilafat-o Mulukiyyat [Caliphate and
    Monarchy] (Maududi), 97
Khomeini, Ayatollah, 64–66, 101, 102–
    103, 104, 105, 106–107, 108, 110–
    111; on gender reassignment
    surgery, 137–138; *Vilayat-e Faqih*
    (Guardianship of the Jurist), 101,
    104, 106
khwajasira community, 136
King, Martin Luther, Jr., 178
Kipling, Rudyard, 196
Kulthum, Umm, 159
Kurds, 230–231
Kuwait City, 46

Lament for the Fall of Seville (al-Rundi),
    148
Latiff, Abdool, 58
Lawrence, T. E., 28
League of Nations, 43
Lebanon, 216, 217
Lenin, Vladimir, 95, 96, 100
libel, 57, 59, 60, 63. *See also* blasphemy
liberalism, 13, 56, 162, 225
Lollywood, 207
London, England: play about
    Muhammad, 60; protests about
    Satanic Verses, 63–64

Macaulay (Lord), 59, 74, 75
Madd-o Jazr-e Islam [The Ebb and
    Flow of Islam] (Hali), 2, 162
Mafia, 188
Mahdi, 105
Majalisunissa [Gatherings of Women]
    (Hali), 126
Makkah Clock Royal Tower, 85
Malaysia, 16, 87–88, 89
Mali, 183
Mamluks, 20
Man Who Would Be King, The (Kipling),
    196
Manama, 46
Mandela, Nelson, 178
Mao Zedong, 108
Marcus, Margaret, 117. *See also*
    Jameelah, Maryam
marriage, 131
martyrdom, 13, 44, 56, 64, 65, 169, 170,
    172, 179, 192, 197, 209, 214
Marx, Karl, 165
Marxism, 26, 95, 224
Masjid al-Qiblatayn (Mosque of the
    Two Directions), 82
materialism: abstract, 93; atheistic, 163
Maududi, Abul Ala: on anarchism, 94–
    95; criticism of, 118; on gender,
    141; on idolatry, 12, 105–106, 108;
    as Islamist, 100, 181; and Jamaat–e

Maududi, Abul Ala (*continued*)
Islam, 94, 117, 136, 164; moralism
of, 165–166; on nationalism, 94,
98–99, 100; *Parda*, 130–132; on
sovereignty, 95–98, 101–102, 107;
speech in Karachi, 164–165; on
women's biology, 132–135
Mecca, 16, 17, 25, 45, 47, 48, 73, 81, 90;
capitalism in, 85–86; as marketplace,
82–83; refashioning of, 81–83
Medina, 47, 48, 82–83, 86, 112
menstruation, 132–133
Merleau-Ponty, Maurice, 200
Mexico, 188
Middle East: Arab Spring protests,
221–225, 226; atheism in, 116;
Britain in, 18; and the United
States, 216–217; and the West, 20
militancy: of Al-Qaeda, 44, 182, 194,
195, 197, 207, 209, 222; of ISIS,
194, 195, 197, 218; and appearances,
193–194; Islamic, 13–14, 166–167,
179, 182, 183, 185, 202, 220, 224
Mir Taqi Mir, 1–2, 3
miracles, 153, 161
Mir-Hosseini, Ziba, 129
mirroring, 48, 80, 85, 103, 109, 222; in
Al-Qaeda, 169, 179, 182–190, 191,
193, 201, 205, 206; for princes, 142,
147
miscegenation, 167
misogyny, 132
modernism: in art, 92; Islamic, 13, 148
modernity: and civilization, 42; of
Islam, 162
Mohammed, Khalid Sheikh, 198
Mohammedanism, 15–16, 20, 23, 31,
50. *See also* Islam
monarchy, 12, 90, 92, 105, 109
Mongols, 146, 152
Montesquieu, 38
Morocco, 109, 177, 222
mosques, 45; destruction of, 77–78
Muckba, Mahomed Ibrahim, 56

Mughal Empire, 1, 9, 135
Muhammad (Prophet): authority of,
20, 102–103, 105, 108; biographical
and devotional works about, 51–61;
biography of, 86; birthplace of, 46;
companions of, 81, 189; false
followers of, 200; family of, 148; as
final messenger of God, 160;
followers of, 13; globalization of,
66–67; and God, 53; grave of, 86;
green mantle of, 27–28;
humanization of, 50–52; insults to,
11–12, 53, 53–67, 74–76, 78–79, 87,
88–89, 222; in Islam, 81, 109; as
lawgiver, 89–90; legacy (trusts) of,
105, 107; London play about, 60;
loyalty to, 160–161; as miracle
worker, 52; modern biographies of,
21; in the Qur'an, 39–40;
relationship to all Muslims, 104;
relics of, 86; revelations of, 154; role
of, 9, 11, 31–32, 51, 53, 63, 89–90,
127, 219; sites associated with, 81–
82; stereotypes of, 21
Muhammad Ali, 23
Muhammadan Anglo-Oriental College
(Aligarh), 149
musaddas, 3
Muscat, 46
Muslim Brotherhood, 217, 224, 225
Muslim community (*ummah*), 21, 41,
44–45, 147–151, 155–157, 159, 162,
166, 209, 219
Muslim League, 95, 96
Muslims: in Afghanistan, 227; agency
of, 219–220; and Al-Qaeda, 184; in
the British Empire, 25–26, 27, 66;
colonization of, 146; conversion to
Christianity, 44, 113, 114; dress and
comportment of, 83–84; in the
Dutch Empire, 16, 17; in Europe,
83; ex-, 114–115, 116; expulsion
from Spain and Sicily, 146;
friendship with British, 144–145;

and the Gaza war, 211; ideal, 12–13, 36, 127–132, 140; as immigrants, 10; in India, 149–150, 214, 220, 227–229, 230, 232; interactions with Hindus, 95, 141–144; interactions with non-Muslims, 141–145, 221; Iranian, 110–111; marginalization of, 10; militants, 166–173, 198, 206; modern vs. traditional, 99; mystics, 152; as pilgrims, 16; protesting insults to the Prophet, 54–67, 74–76; radicalization of, 72, 191, 194–195; religious freedom for, 24; response to desecration, 76–81; responsibilities of, 112; in Southeast Asia, 49; stereotypes of, 174; in the time of Muhammad, 110; traditions of, 129; victimization of, 115; violence against, 72; and the West, 83, 151–153, 172–173, 203; women, 12, 51, 83–84, 117–120, 140, 145
Myanmar, 214
myths, 110–111

Naipaul, V. S., 196
Najmabadi, Afsaneh, 138, 139, 140
Nakba, 213
Napoleon (Bonaparte), 20–21, 23, 174
Napoleonic Wars, 24
National Register of Citizens (NRC), 227
nationalism, 12, 92, 93, 220; Arab, 224; European, 163; Hindu, 77, 78, 228, 229, 232–233; Indian, 94, 143, 163, 228; in Iran, 231; Israeli, 213; Kashmiri, 232; Kurdish, 231; Palestinian, 213; and the past, 163
Nazis, 170
Nehru, Jawaharlal, 161, 238–239n35
neoconservatism, 179, 208
neoliberalism, 13, 189, 225
Neoplatonism, 105
neotraditionalism, 14
Netherlands (Dutch Empire), 16, 17

new social movements, 181–182
Nigeria, 183
nihilism, 182
nizam, 37
noncooperation movement, 159
nonviolent resistance, 159, 178–179
Nordic countries, 78, 80
Norway, 80
nuclear catastrophe, 40, 43, 44, 177
nuclear proliferation, 177
Numani, Shibli, 149

Obama, Barack, 172–178, 179, 208
Öcalan, Abdullah, 230–231
Occupy movement, 230
Ockley, Simon, 55
oil embargo, 74
Oman, 109
Omar (Mullah), 28
On Revolution (Arendt), 200
OPEC, 74
Organization of Islamic Cooperation, 36
orientalism, 23, 28
Ottoman Empire, 1, 9, 16, 17, 18, 20, 23, 27, 28, 30, 45, 47, 94, 112, 135, 146, 159, 180, 194. *See also* caliphate

pacifists, 170
paganism, 12
Pakistan: Ahmadis in, 67, 69–70; atheists in, 116; and China, 72; constitution of, 99–100; independence of, 164; and Iqbal, 24; Islam in, 87–88, 89, 177, 183, 184, 189, 232; as Islamic republic, 99, 106; killing of bin Laden in, 207; Missionary Society, 127–128; Muslim protests in, 75; Muslims in, 72–73, 227; prime ministers of, 45; sovereignty in, 98–100; wars in, 228; women in, 226
Palestine and Palestinians, 211–215
Pan-Arabism, 224

pandemics, 177
Pan-Islamism, 20, 23, 24, 36
Parda [Veiling] (Maududi), 130–132
Parsis, 44, 57–58
Passage to India, A (Forster), 144
Pathans, 58
patriarchy, 90, 120
Paul (Saint), 114
Persia, 30. *See also* Iran
pilgrimages, 46, 73, 81–82, 90–91, 92, 229
plastic surgery, 119, 138
poetry: by al-Rundi, 148; *Barq-e Kalisa* (Lightning in the Cathedral), 152–153; blasphemy in, 89–91; courtly, 143; epic, 2–3, 147; *Gandhinamah* (The Epic of Gandhi), 159; by Ghalib, 151; *ghazal* (lyric), 151; *Hadith al-Ruh* (The Spirit's Converse), 159; by Hali, 2–3, 147–149, 150–151, 153, 154–156, 157, 161–162; by Illahabadi, 18, 125–126, 144, 151–153, 159; by Iqbal, 24, 157–158, 159–161, 160–161, 215; *Jawab-e Shikwa* (The Complaint's Answer), 160–161; by Khomeini, 105–106, 111; *Lament for the Fall of Seville*, 148; lyric (*ghazal*), 3, 142; *Madd-o Jazr-e Islam* (The Ebb and Flow of Islam), 2–3, 147, 162; *marsiya* (elegy), 148, 149; by Mir of Delhi, 1–2; by Numani, 149–150; Persian, 152; *Qawmi Musaddas* (Community Epic), 149–150; and the seduction of the West, 151–153; *shahr-ashob* (lament), 147–149, 149, 150; *Shikwa* (Complaint), 159–160; women in, 122; by Zafar, 90–91, 112
politics: absolutist, 21; clientelist, 229; decentralized, 224; democratic, 220; global, 27, 177, 206, 208, 211, 212, 216, 218; and idolatry, 12; indigenist, 214; interest-driven, 175, 179; international, 174; and Islam, 23, 39, 174, 220; media-informed, 224; Muslim, 19, 181; nationalist, 220; of Palestine, 214; postcolonial, 52; regional, 218; and religion, 9–11, 175, 220; secular, 220; self-interest of, 163
polytheism, 168
populism, 26
Prague Spring, 221
private property, 26
propaganda: anti-Islamic, 225; of ISIS, 191, 195, 203, 204, 206; terrorist, 181
property ownership, 26, 77
Protestant Reformation, 200
Protestantism, 113, 115, 200
proxy wars, 216, 217

Qawmi Musaddas [Community Epic] (Numani), 149–150
Qur'an: description of Muhammad, 39–40; destruction/defacement of, 78–80; divine authorship of, 51; "God" in, 8–9; hypocrites in, 200; insults to, 87; and the laws of Pakistan, 99; reading of, 115; Syed Ahmed Khan's commentary, 153–154; translation of, 236n11; use of "Islam" in, 4, 32; verses from, 85; women's education about, 126. See also *Satanic Verses* (Rushdie)
Qutb, Sayyid, 12, 180

race, 156–157, 158
racism, 93, 167
radicalization, 72, 191, 194–195
Reagan, Ronald, 27, 174
realism, political, 176
realpolitik, 175, 179
Reconquista, 147, 200
reform movements, 123
refugee crisis, 113
refugees, Palestinian, 213
Rehman, Zaki, 240n22

religion: in America, 34–35; and capitalism, 81–86; and colonialism, 52; colonized, 33–34; naturalization of, 154; of Obama, 179; and politics, 9–11, 175, 220

religious community, 156–157. *See also* Muslim community (*ummah*)

religious extremism, 177

religious fanaticism, 195, 200

religious freedom, 24, 68, 71

Renan, Ernest, 22

Renowned Prophets and Nations, 57–58

restitution, 214

Rohingya, 211

Romanov Empire, 16

Rome, 48, 82

Roy, Olivier, 140, 164, 195

Rundi, Abu al-Baqa al-, 148

Rushdie, Salman, 54, 62–66, 70–71, 75, 87

Russia, 216; antiterrorism in, 210; in Eastern Europe, 18; and the Ukraine war, 210–211. *See also* Soviet Union

Russian Revolution, 27

Russo-Turkish War, 148

Ryan, Maeve, 25

sacrifice, 169, 170, 175, 179, 182, 200, 206, 215. *See also* martyrdom

sacrilege, 70. *See also* blasphemy

Sadat, Anwar al-, 166

Safavid Empire, 1, 9, 135

sahaba, 189

Salafism, 92, 119, 185, 225

Salvatore, Armando, 225

Samarkand, 45

same-sex relations, 135, 139

sanctions, 74, 213

Sartre, Jean-Paul, 188, 192, 193

Satanic Verses (Rushdie), 54, 62–66; book about, 75

Saudi Arabia: atheists in, 116; changes to Mecca, 81–83, 85–86; creation of,

47–48; Islam in, 48–49, 66; secularism in, 13–14; war against Yemen, 216; women from, 83. *See also* Arabia/Arabian Peninsula; Mecca; Medina

Schmitt, Carl, 25, 99, 103, 104, 107, 108

Scott, J. Barton, 57

Scottish independence movement, 231

Second World War, 170

sectarianism, 7, 67, 180, 184, 189–190, 204

secularism: and the Ahmadis, 69; of the British Empire, 60, 68; crisis of, 10; in India, 77, 220; return to, 228; in Saudi Arabia, 13–14; tolerance of, 79, 236n9; in the United States, 35

secularists, 116

segregation, 178

self-interest, 165

sex-change operations, 136, 137–138

sexuality: heteronormative, 135; homosexuality, 135, 138–139; men-women relationships, 140–145; same-sex relations, 135, 139; third sex, 135–137; transgender individuals, 136–139, 140; Western ideas of, 136; of women, 130–131

Shah, Chandni, 136

Shahbano case, 228

Shaheen Bagh, 227

shame of being human, 171–172

Shams, Fatemeh, 232

Sharar, Abdul Halim, 245n11

sharia law, 104, 138, 198, 206. *See also* Islamic law

Sharif, Nawaz, 71

Shikwa [Complaint] (Iqbal), 159–160

Shklar, Judith, 197

Sicily, 146

Sidis, 58

Sincerity and Authenticity (Trilling), 196

Sinwar, Yahya, 215

slavery and slaves, 122, 158, 178, 195; sexual, 206

Smith, Wilfred Cantwell, 32, 235n3, 236n9

social engineering, 179

socialism, 116, 224

Soltan, Neda Agha, 226

Somalia, 217

Sorel, Georges, 110–111

Sorrows of Young Werther, The (Goethe), 197

South Africa, 213

Southeast Asia, 49, 178

sovereignty: and Al-Qaeda, 182, 183, 186, 193, 199, 205; in *Assassin's Creed*, 204; British, 34; of the caliphate, 94, 97; capitalist, 189; of communism, 93; divine, 12, 52, 53, 65, 96–99, 101, 111, 112, 189, 193, 205, 220; feudal forms of, 188; fragmentation of, 182, 188, 189; global, 236n14; globalization and, 188, 231; human desire for, 97; as idol, 93, 98; illegitimate, 201; of imperialism, 182; Indian, 94, 96, 182; indirect, 186; Iqbal's criticism of, 93–94; in Iran, 101, 102, 103–112, 107, 189; of ISIS, 187, 188, 189, 190–193, 201, 202, 204, 205, 206; juridical, 17; limitation of, 100; in the modern state, 10, 188; of Muhammad, 53, 65, 76; of the Muslim community, 141–142; Muslims, 17, 52, 53, 219; native, 52; in Pakistan, 98–100; political, 52, 91; as political theology, 104; popular, 80, 236n14; precapitalist, 188; prophetic, 53; and religion, 93; renunciation of, 96, 99, 100; in Saudi Arabia, 48; of the shah, 101; socialization of, 141, 142; Soviet, 201; of the state, 66, 94, 96–99, 181, 182, 201; traditional forms of, 231;

and tyranny, 93; in the West, 109; of women, 12

Soviet Union: in Afghanistan, 174; in Berlin, 173; Bukharin's example, 200–201; collapse of, 13, 208, 209, 210; communism in, 134, 179; establishment of, 10, 27, 94; and the Third World, 181. *See also* Russia

Spain, 146, 151, 173, 207

Spirit of Islam, The (Ameer Ali), 30–34, 35, 37, 38–39

Sri Lanka, 227

Stalin, Joseph, 200

suicide bombers, 13, 166, 182, 186–187, 197, 202, 205, 215

sultanate, 20

supernatural beings, 153

Sykes-Picot agreement, 180

Syria: Arab Spring, 223; border with Iraq, 180–181; and the Gaza war, 216; Islam in, 113; Sunnis in, 184; wars and invasions, 48. *See also* ISIS (Islamic State in Syria)

Tablighi Jamaat, 127–128

Tahrir Square protests, 223

Taliban, 14, 28, 217

Tamasha-ye Ibrat [Cautionary Spectacle] (Numani), 149

Tantawi, Sayyid, 137–138

taqiyya, 190, 199

Tareen, SherAli, 51–53, 91, 141–142

Tawbat un-Nasuh [Nasuh's Repentance] (Numani), 123–125

Tehreek-e Labbaik Pakistan, 73

Temple Mount, 213

terrorism: 9/11 attacks, 198, 208, 209, 214; of Al-Qaeda, 202; associated with ISIS, 196; associated with Islam, 167, 170, 172, 174; in Dhaka, 116; global, 207; global alliance against, 206–207, 210; in India, 228, 229; in the Middle East, 212, 214;

propaganda of, 181. *See also* Global
   War on Terror
Thanvi, Ashraf Ali, 126, 127
theory of time, 161
third sex, 135–137
Third World, 181, 231
Tocqueville, Alexis de, 34–35
Tolstoy, Leo, 94
torture, 176, 183, 188, 210
tourism, religious, 82
transcendence, 40–41, 44, 52–53, 76,
   89, 113, 191, 193, 201, 202, 204–205
transgender people, 136–139
Trilling, Lionel, 196, 197
Trump, Donald, 218
Tunisia: Arab Spring, 222, 226;
   dictatorship in, 13; Ennahda, 217,
   224
Turkey: and the Arab Spring, 225; Gezi
   Park protests, 14; Islam in, 18, 46,
   48, 49; support for Hayat Tahrir al-
   Sham, 218. *See also* Ottoman
   Empire
Turkish republic, 202. *See also* Turkey
Turks, 152
tyranny, 93, 95, 96, 105, 106

Uganda, 45
Ukraine war, 210–211, 212, 216
ummah, 21, 41, 44–45, 147–151, 155–
   157, 159, 162, 166, 209, 219
United Arab Emirates, 83
United Nations, 43, 212, 216
United States: Al-Qaeda attacks on,
   184–185; assassination of bin
   Laden, 207–208, 210; border with
   Mexico, 188; and the Gaza war, 216;
   and the Global War on Terror, 74,
   103, 206–207, 209–210, 211, 212,
   214, 216, 217; and the Middle East,
   216–217; and militant Islam, 172–
   173; and the Muslim World, 174–
   177; in Saudi Arabia, 48; Trump
   presidency, 218

universality, 41–42, 150, 153–154, 157,
   158–159, 161, 162–163, 164, 169
utilitarianism, 59, 74, 165

Victoria (Queen), 34
Vietnam War, 213
Vilayat-e Faqih [Guardianship of the
   Jurist] (Khomeini), 101, 104, 106
violence: against activists, 230; and Al-
   Qaeda, 185–187; anti-Muslim, 72,
   229; associated with Islam, 13, 113,
   166–167; *Charlie Hebdo* massacre,
   73; against Hindus, 229; against
   idols, 91; of ISIS, 180–181, 189,
   195–196, 201–202; justification of,
   167, 172, 215; and martyrdom, 44;
   Obama's denouncement of, 178; for
   offenses against the Prophet, 67–68,
   75–76; by police, 226, 227; protests
   by Muslims, 54–61, 65, 80–81;
   terrorist, 116. *See also* suicide
   bombers; terrorism

Wahhab, Muhammad ibn Abd al-, 92
Wahhabis, 82, 92, 112, 185; Indian, 47
Wars of Religion, 20
Warsaw Pact, 211
waterboarding, 183
Weiss, Leopold, 118
West Bank, 213, 215, 216
Wilhelm II (Kaiser; Germany), 174
women: and the Arab protests, 226–
   233; in Bangladesh, 226; biological
   attributes of, 132–140; in colonized
   societies, 122; commodification of,
   119; education of, 123, 126–127;
   equality of, 231; fetishization of,
   119; as ideal Muslims, 127–132,
   140; in India, 122, 226–227;
   individuality of, 140; in Iran, 14,
   226–227; and Islam, 91; Islam
   compared to, 106; and Islamism,
   117, 119, 121, 129–130;
   Islamization of, 123–125; Maryam

women (*continued*)
    Jameelah, 117–120; Muslim, 12, 51,
    83–84, 117–120, 140, 145;
    objectification of, 119; oppression
    of, 130; in Pakistan, 226; on
    pilgrimage, 90–91; as protestors,
    226–227, 230, 231; relationships
    with men, 140–145; restrictions
    on, 121; role of, 127, 132–133;
    in Saudi Arabia, 83; seclusion of,
    127, 131, 134; sexual urges of,
    130–131; status of, 125–126; in
    Turkey, 122
women's movement, 232

X, Malcolm, 216
xenophobia, 231

Yemen, 214, 216

Zafar, 90–91, 112
Zaheeruddin v. State, 70
Zarqawi, Abu Musab al-, 187
Zawahiri, Ayman al-, 166–169, 184
Zionism, 88, 213, 216, 217
Zoroaster, 55
Zoroastrianism, 1, 54, 151, 152, 154
Zuckerberg, Mark, 72
Zvi, Sabbatai, 118